HEROES, LOVERS,

and Others

The Story of Latinos in Hollywood

CLARA E. RODRÍGUEZ

OXFORD
UNIVERSITY PRESS
2008

OXFORD
UNIVERSITY PRESS

Oxford University Press, Inc., publishes works that further
Oxford University's objective of excellence
in research, scholarship, and education.

Oxford   New York
Auckland   Cape Town   Dar es Salaam   Hong Kong   Karachi
Kuala Lumpur   Madrid   Melbourne   Mexico City   Nairobi
New Delhi   Shanghai   Taipei   Toronto

With offices in
Argentina   Austria   Brazil   Chile   Czech Republic   France   Greece
Guatemala   Hungary   Italy   Japan   Poland   Portugal   Singapore
South Korea   Switzerland   Thailand   Turkey   Ukraine   Vietnam

Copyright © 2004 by Smithsonian Institution

First published by Smithsonian Books, 2004

First issued as an Oxford University Press paperback, 2008

Oxford is a registered trademark of Oxford University Press
198 Madison Avenue, New York, NY 10016

www.oup.com

Library of Congress Cataloging-in-Publication Data
Rodríguez, Clara E., 1944–
    Heroes, lovers, and others : the story of Latinos in Hollywood / by Clara E. Rodríguez.
        p.   cm.
    Includes bibliographical references and index.
    ISBN 978-0-19-533513-2 (pbk.)
    1. Hispanic American motion picture actors and actresses—Biography.   2. Hispanic
Americans in the motion picture industry—Biography.   3. Hispanic Americans in
motion pictures.   4. Latin Americans in motion pictures.   I. Title.
    PN1995.9.H47 R63   2007
    791.43089'68073—dc22   2007034898
    [B]

Photo credits: page 8, 9, courtesy Smithsonian Institution, National Museum of
American History, Archives Center, Baden Collection; 11, 14, 13, 16, 18, 20, 21, 45, 67,
courtesy Smithsonian Institution Libraries; 33, 50, 55, 60, 63, 67, 76, 77, 84, 86, 87, 89, 92,
96, 113, 115, 117, 120, 123, 132, 136, 183, courtesy The Museum of Modern Art Film Stills
Archive; 36, courtesy of the Academy of Motion Picture Arts and Sciences; 39, courtesy
Billy Rose Theatre Collection, The New York Public Library for the Performing Arts,
Astor, Lenox, and Tilden Foundations; 126, 139, 169, 201, 207, 209, 215, 218, 222, 225, 229,
231, 232, 234, 235, 238, 241, courtesy Photofest; 129, courtesy Mrs. Paul Jarrico; 141, 143,
courtesy the Felipe N. Torres Papers, Centro de Estudios Puertorriqueños, Hunter
College, City University of New York; 171, 175, 202, 210, courtesy the Academy of
Motion Picture Arts and Sciences; 173, courtesy Cheech Marin; 177, courtesy Hector
Elizondo; 203, Teitelbaum Artists Group; 205, courtesy Antonio Banderas.

Printed in the United States of America
on acid-free paper

Contents

Preface

Some film stars have been shooting stars—they shine and die out. Others grow and continue to flicker in the sky—they become eternal legends. Still others were legends in their time but have since been forgotten. The history of Latino film stars is filled with such stories.

One purpose of this book is to uncover the buried history of Latino film stars in Hollywood films. Another is to represent and reflect what the Smithsonian Institution has called "the changing American kaleidoscope" ("Latino Oversight Committee, Smithsonian Announce Results of Study," press release, October 15, 1997, 1). In this respect, the book seeks to build a new awareness of Latino culture and history as part of the full range of diversity in the United States. I seek to give voice to those whom history has too often ignored. I see my book as contributing to a shared vision in which the remarkable range of human experience is understood through the histories of all groups—in particular, those whose histories have not received sufficient attention in the past.

The history of Latinos in film is a complex one, showing change over time as well as constants. The book is organized chronologically and thematically. The first chapter is a descriptive chapter that examines the earliest period of Latin film history. It establishes an important point of departure to which subsequent periods refer. The remaining chapters examine the primary stars and films in each of the five major eras of Latino film history. Chapter 2 focuses on the stars in the earliest periods of film, from 1910 to the 1930s. Chapter 3 examines the period surrounding World War II. The next three chapters examine, respectively, the cold war era, the modern era, and the postmodern era. This chronological focus on the films and film stars in each era explores how both the public personas and the film roles of Latino stars were influenced by the temper of the times and how the stars personally navigated their own sense of identity in these times.

A Few Words of Clarification

Many of the names of the actors discussed in this book have accents in their native language. For example, the names of Lupe Vélez and Dolores Del Río are both accented in Spanish. During their careers, however, these accents were generally ignored in English-language materials or on theater marquees. In later periods, accents and other diacritical marks were rarely used. More recently, film stars have begun to use accents. However, their use has not been (and is not) consistent. Therefore, with all due respect to those who prefer to retain accents in their names—and this includes myself—I have omitted most accents in this text.

Many terms are used today to denote those of Spanish-speaking heritage—Hispanic, Spanish, Latino, Spanish American, Latino American, and American Latino—and many arguments have been advanced for the use of particular terms. In this book I tend to use the words "Latino" and "Hispanic" somewhat interchangeably. Notwithstanding, I use the word "Latin" as well, because that was the term most in vogue in the early part of film history. It is still used by many in the media today, as in "a new Latin actress" or "Latin music." I also use "Chicano" to refer to people of Mexican origin who have been born or raised in the United States. The term came into vogue during the late 1960s and early 1970s, and it reflects a political consciousness borne of the Chicano student movement. Although it is often a generational marker for many who came of age during those decades, the terms "Chicano" and "Chicana" have also been embraced by elders and children who share in the political ideals of the movement. In the past, the term was associated with those who identified themselves as nationalists and rejected accommodation strategies, but today it is much more about social justice and political and community empowerment (Vicki Ruiz, personal correspondence, September 30, 2003).

This book does not intend to be encyclopedic; rather, it presents an overview within a historical context. Consequently, many talented Latinos, both actors and those behind the cameras, are missing. I refer the reader to the selected readings listed at the end of this book, particularly two excellent and comprehensive works: Luis Reyes and Peter Rubie's 1994 *Hispanics in Hollywood: An Encyclopedia of Film and Television*, as well as their revised 2000 edition, *Hispanics in Hollywood: A Celebration of 100 Years in Film and Television;* and Gary D. Keller's *Biographical Handbook of Hispanics and United States Film* (1997).

Finally, great pains have been taken to ensure the accuracy of the material in this volume. However, a number of difficulties are inherent in research in this area—or, for that matter, in any area in which media images are often carefully constructed and protected. The age of actors (particularly in the earlier periods) may have been altered by the actors themselves or by their studios because of the concern with preserving youthful public images. Film dates may vary at times because they can refer to the date of completion, or first screening, or general release, or release in a new market. When there has been conflicting information on titles and release dates, I have followed the Internet Movie Database (www.imdb.com), the most popular source for this type of information. (For a fuller discussion of such issues in the realm of Latinos and film, see pages vii–ix in the introduction to the Keller volume cited above).

The Latino Kettle

This book focuses on Latinos as one group because this has been the dominant way they have been viewed by U.S. motion picture audiences, as Latins, Latinos, Hispanics, or just "Spanish," with occasional distinctions made by national origin. However, the Latino population is actually made up of a variety of groups that differ not only in terms of national histories, particular cultural cuisine, and the relations between their homeland and the United States, for example, but also in terms of general class status within the United States. Some of these differences are the result of particular migration histories. For example, the Cuban community's socioeconomic profile was skewed upward as a result of the early post-Castro migration of the 1960s, which brought political refugees who were generally skilled and from the upper-income classes in Cuba. In contrast, the labor migrations of Mexicans and Puerto Ricans after World War II contributed more members to the working class.

The perceived differences between the groups in this country are not necessarily reflective of their countries of origin. The higher status and stronger Republican bent of Cubans in the United States contrasts sharply with the political orientation and level of economic development in Cuba today. The differences are a function of who left, and why. As Celia Cruz, the late and great Cuban salsa singer, often said, "We [Latinos] are all brothers in a different country." We are all Latinos in the United States. However, even though many may identify in this way, most Latinos also hold on to their national-origin identities as Puerto Rican, Mexican, and so on. How large is each of the groups in the United States?

According to the U.S. census, Mexicans comprised the majority of all Latinos (58.5 percent, or 20.6 million) in 2000. The
3.4 million Puerto Ricans were the second-largest group, con-
stituting 9.6 percent of all Latinos in the United States. If the
3.8 million Puerto Ricans residing in Puerto Rico are included,
this percentage more than doubles (to 20.4 percent). Cubans
were the next-largest single national-origin group, with 3.5
percent, followed by Dominicans, with 2.2 percent. The
Central American countries collectively accounted for 4.8 percent of the total Latino pie, with Salvadorans (at 1.9 percent)
and Guatemalans (at 1.1 percent) being the two largest groups
among them. South Americans constituted another 3.8 percent of the total U.S. Latino population, with Colombians (at
1.3 percent) the largest group. All the other countries in
Central and South America constituted less than 1 percent
each of the total Latino population.

One of the most interesting results of the 2000 census
is the large proportion of people who said they were Hispanic
or Latino but did not give a national origin (17.3 percent).
Some of these may have parents from more than one country, others may be fourth- or fifth-generation "Latino
Americans" who no longer identify with any particular Latin
American country. It is this group that has shown the greatest growth over time. It may be that, with more time residing in the United States, common experiences, intermarriage, and the tendency to see all Latinos as the same, there
is increasing use of pan-Latino terms and greater bonding
among all groups.

At present, however, there is still a very diverse Latino
kettle in the United States. Because of history and migration,
it is more Mexican- and Central American–flavored in the
West and the Southwest, more Caribbean-flavored in the
Northeast and the South, and a mixture of both in the
Midwest. Yet the Latino communities in all of these regions
are undergoing tremendous change, and the Latino populations are becoming more heterogeneous in each region. For
example, the area in Miami that is known worldwide as Little

Havana is no longer predominantly Cuban; rather, Nicaraguans, Colombians, and other Latinos now constitute the majority. There are more Puerto Ricans in Florida than in New Jersey or San Juan, and they now constitute the second-largest Latino group in Florida, after Cubans. New York City now has substantial and growing Dominican, Colombian, Ecuadoran, and Mexican populations. The same is true of Los Angeles and other large cities as well as many suburban areas.

My Hopes for This Book

This book attempts to present the Latino past in motion pictures, a past that has been both glorious and problematic—but above all fascinating. It is my hope that readers will come to know many of these forgotten stars and that they will also feel a new connection to some of those with whom they may have been familiar, that they may now see them in a different light or in a different context. Perhaps having seen, through text and photos, the parade of Latino film stars from the beginning of the century to the present the reader will be able to add a strong shot of retrospective realism to the glitz and glamour of Hollywood.

It is also my hope that this book, standing as it does at the intersection of the film literature and the race and ethnicity literature, will help to fill a void in both. Film critics and researchers alike give scant voice to the presence of Latinos. Two major examples of this are the films *Salt of the Earth* and *High Noon*—both of which are classic movies that are standard components of most film studies programs. *Salt of the Earth* is often reviewed in film courses because it so exemplifies the excesses of the McCarthy era. Yet the fact that its cast is primarily Latino and that the plot is based on a real-life strike among Hispano miners in the Southwest is—at best—discussed as an incidental or tangential aspect of the film. Often, the Latino component is ignored entirely. Similarly, *High Noon* is presented in film courses because it exemplifies so well the focus on the individual in Western film and the struggle between individual heroism and group apathy in American culture. Yet attention is seldom paid to the Mexican American character played by Katy Jurado, who reflects a generally neglected part of the story of the West: the two-hundred-year history of Spanish colonial America before Anglo settlement.

The increasing numbers of Latinos in all parts of the United States has prompted a growing national awareness of the Latino presence in the United States and its antiquity, cultural richness, and expanding influence. It is my hope that this book will draw additional attention to the rich history of Latinos in the United States and to the buried Latino legacies that are part of the heritage of all the peoples of the United States, not just Latinos. It is also my hope that the book will underscore the transnational dimension of the history of Latinos in the United States, a history that has involved a continual, and often casual, crossing of hemispheric borders.

I believe that a heightened awareness of past and contemporary practices in the media can influence future policies and customs. Unfortunately, recent extensive research on the treatment of Latinos in the media continues to find that they are either invisible or relegated to minimal roles in film, print, and television. It is my hope that this book will pose questions and challenge readers to look more closely at their world and its media depictions of Latinos, as well as other groups, each of whom have had their own unique history.

The history of film is a microcosmic history of twentieth-century America, reflecting some of our best and worst moments as a nation. Scholars are just beginning to examine the influence of popular culture and mass media (in particular, film) on national identity. This book will, I hope, contribute to that reexamination. Just as it is important to look at the history of film and its role in popular culture, it is important to encourage an awareness of the history of Latinos in film as an important part of this. It is my hope that the book leads others to reexamine conventional and accepted ways of viewing our national past and to explore the stars covered here as well as others not covered. Finally, it is my hope that the book will lead people to ask deeper questions about the unique experiences of Latinos in film and popular culture.

Acknowledgments

Projects such as this, which seek to uncover what has been covered, forgotten, or manipulated for media purposes, take a huge amount of time, perseverance, and checking and rechecking. They could not be done without the assistance and support of many people along the way. I would like to acknowledge just a few who have eased the journey at particularly crucial points. The list is long and filled with wonderful people who have lightened the load immeasurably. Among those whose names are still with me are my hardworking research assistants, Katia Amaya, Arianny Nunez, Ana Orozco, Lena Rodríguez, Minerva Rodríguez Andujar, Gelvin L. Stevenson, and, in particular, Lara Pérez-Longobardo, who was involved almost from the beginning to the end; all of those in the photo posses, that is, Marta Ceballos, Marisa Ceballos, Robert Carrillo, Myra Peters-Quintero, Jessica Rodríguez, José A. Stevenson Rodríguez, Gelvina Rodríguez Stevenson, and, especially, Jimmy Rodríguez, photographer extraordinaire. The members of my initial student advisory group, Mona Butsuhara, Helen C. Hernández, Sandy Montelongo, Judazky Perez, Tino Perez, Elys Vasquez, and Valerie Yaremenko, all provided useful avenues to explore.

In addition to the anonymous reviewers and those whose work has been cited in the volume, I would like to thank the following colleagues who provided invaluable comments at critical points in the journey: Al Greco, Michael Latham, Felix Matos-Rodríguez, Barbara Mundy, John Nieto-Phillips, Fath Ruffins, Chris Schmidt-Nowara, and Kirsten Swinth. I would also like to thank the staffs of the Library of Congress, the Museum of Modern Art, the New York Public Library for the Performing Arts, and the University of Southern California, in particular, Ned Comstock and Dace Taube; Caroline Sisneros, of the American Film Institute; Lauren Buisson, of the University of California at Los Angeles Special Collections Stills; Faye Thompson, Barbara Hall, and Sandra Archer, of the Margaret Herrick Library of the Academy of Motion Picture Arts and Sciences; Kristine Krueger, of the National Film Information Service; and the wonderful folks at the Smithsonian Institution Press, in particular, Scott Mahler, Emily Sollie, Robert Poarch, and Katherine Kimball. Finally, I would like to thank Fordham University for providing me with a Faculty Research Fellowship so that I could finish this work, as well as the National Museum of American History, Archives Center, for assisting me during my time there.

HEROES, LOVERS,

and Others

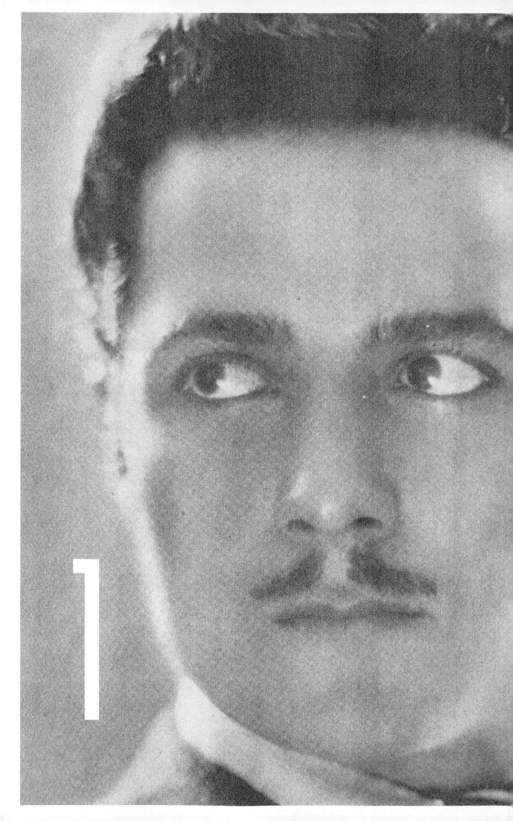

Hollywood and the Times

From its beginnings, Hollywood film has served as a mirror and recorder of the times. During World War II, for example, Japanese characters tended to be portrayed as demonic enemies; in the 1980s they were being presented as friendly, conservative businessmen. A simple and implicit narrative on race and ethnicity in classic Hollywood film holds that stereotypes have circulated easily and repeatedly from film to film; that ethnics and minorities have been most noticeable by their absence; that they have rarely been cast as protagonists, generally appearing as villains or dramatic foils or merely as local color or comic relief. Hollywood's relationship to each ethnic and minority group has been far more complex and nuanced, however, than this simple narrative suggests (López 1991). Each group has had its own complex history, and each group's portrayal has fluctuated with changes in consumer culture, economic prosperity,

1

domestic and international politics, migration patterns, and the vicissitudes of power in Hollywood. Common themes flow through each of these unique group experiences, however. Issues of race, color, class, ethnicity, and gender, as well as the social currents of the times have affected the public images and private working lives of racial-ethnic film actors in all groups.

In the case of Latinos, stereotypes such as the Latin lover and his female counterpart, the Latina spitfire, have persisted throughout all eras in film. Yet unique elements have distinguished the projection of *Latinidad*, or Hispanicity, in each era. The portrayals and employment of Latino actors in Hollywood film have had a most diverse history. The early period was very likely the most generous of times for Latinos in film; many Latinos appeared in these early films, and they appealed to a wide audience. The climate warmed in the forties, when the screen image of Latinos improved, though it remained limited. The most barren of times occurred during the cold war era. The sixties and seventies were the worst of times, in terms of the quality of Latino characterizations, and the eighties represented the greatest contrast in the treatment of Latinos. The present is—relatively speaking, at least—the best of times for Latinos in film. Many more Latino characters and actors now appear in Hollywood film, though still far too few, and there are several well-known, high-profile Latino stars.

Academic and Journalistic Amnesia in Hollywood

When Hollywood films are discussed in print, a certain journalistic and academic amnesia sets in about the role of Latinos in the history of Hollywood. This has affected the way people think of both film history and the place of Latinos in that history: "What? Latinos in film? What history?" A close examination of the early history of Hollywood through the lens of the popular press of the time yields a number of surprises. A substantial number of important early Latino stars, for example, performed with distinctly discernible Spanish surnames: Myrtle Gonzalez, Beatriz Michelena, Antonio Moreno, Ramon Novarro, Dolores Del Rio, Raquel Torres, and Lupe Velez. This is in stark contrast to subsequent periods—the fifties and early sixties, for example, when the only Latino actor seen on the big screen was the occasional Latin lover, who generally did not end up winning the leading lady. There were Latino characters in films like *West Side Story* (1961) and other gang movies, but they were generally played by non-Latino actors. Often, the Latino characters in westerns were the bad guys, the nameless "banditos," or the cantina girls who had little time or substantial presence on the screen. Moreover, the characters were usually morally or esthetically limited—on the "other side," the side where few viewers wanted to be.

Television brought in Desi Arnaz (as Ricky Ricardo) and guest appearances by Carmen Miranda, as well as *The Cisco Kid* and *Zorro* series, but they were the exceptions. Although these positive characters spoke to Latinos and the rest of America, they did not speak *about* Latinos in the United States. Nor did television, film, or English-language publications generally note their relationship to a larger Spanish-speaking or Portuguese-speaking American public. Despite the presence of these "exceptional Latins," it was clear to most concerned that a Spanish surname was not an advantage—either on screen or in society. Many people tried to obscure their Spanish surnames through pronunciation ("Die as" for Díaz) or changing their names (Rodríguez to Rogers, Rivera to Rivers). In addition, most Hollywood stars hid their ethnic origins. Ethnicity was seldom talked about on television or in most movie magazines. Rather, nonethnic star names were considered more "harmonious" than ethnic names—more in "harmony," that is, with white-bread, Anglo-Saxon expectations and sounds—except, of course, for those who, like Gina Lollabrigida and Brigitte Bardot, had temporarily landed in Hollywood from another county. No, leading Hollywood stars had names like Elizabeth Taylor, John Wayne, and Grace Kelly.

It is thus surprising to discover, in examining a variety of lesser-known sources—early news clippings and books, contemporary sources on the early Hollywood period, Internet sites on silent-film stars, and popular fan magazines of the time—that in the earliest period of film, there were a considerable number of important Latino stars. The most popular fan magazine of the time, *Photoplay*, is a good barometer of the tastes of the audiences and the movie fans. Although its subscription base may have been very middle class, its actual readership was far broader. Its circulation was six times that of all the other fan magazines combined. It was also an influential player in Hollywood. Established in 1912, by the early twenties *Photoplay* had become the "queen of the fan magazines" (Fuller 1996, 150). Its influence in Hollywood was so great that Rudolf Valentino, the first and foremost Latin lover, wrote to the editor, thanking *Photoplay* for "discovering and creating" him. "You made theater managers know me," he noted, "and you caused film magazines and newspapers to be conscious of me. I am more grateful than you will ever know" (Valentino 1923, 34). Whether true or not—many people take credit for having made Valentino a star—his remarks testify to the influence and power that *Photoplay* wielded at the time in Hollywood.

In *Photoplay* issues from 1921 to 1934, numerous photos and articles feature "Latin stars" (the term used at the time), who were seen as major marquee idols. They performed alongside those who are today considered Hollywood legends, and they sometimes had top billing. They advertised popular products like Coca-Cola and Lucky Strike cigarettes. They were regularly celebrated as the ideal in beauty and physique. Perhaps most surprising, their Latin-ness was often foregrounded; moreover, consonant with the maxim that imitation is the highest form of flattery, some non-Latino stars sought to be more "Latin." They changed their names, to sound more Spanish. The men sported mustaches, and women were photographed in Spanish dress. In 1928, for example, Joan Crawford was described as "more Spanish than the Spaniards themselves" in a caption that accompanied a large photo of her in lace mantilla and a high Spanish shawl (photo caption, *Photoplay*, June 1928, 19). These were the images projected at the time; they would change dramatically in later years.

Alongside the Legends

Early Latino stars appeared with legends of the silver screen—Greta Garbo, Clara Bow, Douglas Fairbanks, Gary Cooper, and Mae West—with equal or sometimes higher billing. Furthermore, and in contrast to subsequent periods, they appeared as leads in major movies, playing diverse character roles in a variety of social positions. The well-known classic silent film *It* (1927) is a good example.

Antonio Moreno, an immigrant from Spain, began his film career in 1912. He starred in the movie *It* as the romantic lead, opposite the famous silent-screen legend, Clara Bow. Moreno was cast as neither a Latin lover nor a criminal; rather, he played Cyrus T. Waltham, a department store magnate, who has inherited the largest department store in the world. Clara Bow is Betty Lou Spence, the working-class store clerk, who falls for her boss. While working in his store, Betty Lou comes to Waltham's attention because she has that indefinable "It" quality—what would later be called sex appeal. Waltham invites her to one of his social clubs for dinner. Hastily, and with the aid of her sister (who, by the way, is an unmarried mother and, therefore, serves as the skeleton in the closet), she assembles a makeshift dress from a pair of curtains. At the club, she is seen attempting (not altogether successfully) to camouflage, or at least bridge, the social distance between herself and the other women there, who eye her as both a competitor for the attentions of this most desirable bachelor and of an "inferior" class.

After some "appropriate" (for the time) romantic play between Mr. Waltham and the "It" girl, Betty Lou invites her boss to a less stuffy outing—to Coney Island. Here, in a tumbling ride that tosses them together in hearty laughter and sheer, joyous abandonment, both characters give up any pretense of social decorum; they see themselves, and each other, for who they really are—two human beings who, despite class differences, are meant for each other. *It* is a Cinderella story of its time. (Also telling of the time, everyone in the movie—even the extras at Coney Island—is white.)

It was a blockbuster in its time, and it left its imprint on Hollywood, particularly on its speech: For years, "the 'It' girl" or "the 'It' guy" was used to describe the actor with the greatest Hollywood buzz at the moment. Film literature contains many other references to this early film and to Clara Bow's role in the film, but seldom is any reference made to Antonio Moreno, who was at the time a leading marquee idol. He had a long career in film, and though he played many Latin lovers he also played other roles and was cast in a variety of social positions.

Early Marquee Idols

Another contrast between this early period and the years that followed was the extent to which Latino actors were recognized as important stars in their day. The best evidence of this is the extraordinary amount of media attention they received. In *Photoplay,* numerous stories, photos, ads, and full-page color portrait photos featured Latin stars, along with references to them as "matinee idols" and "famous stars." They also graced the covers of many magazines. Lupe Velez, for example, appeared on the cover of no fewer than nineteen national and international magazines. To place this in context, imagine the significance of a full-page color or cover photo of a star in an issue of *People* magazine or in international magazines today. Like other major stars of the day, the private lives of these Latin stars were projected as lavish, glamorous, and rich. Ramon Novarro's extravagant lifestyle seemed to be particularly underscored. Latin stars of the day were box-office draws and were relatively well paid for their work in film. In addition to the coverage they received in the popular press, they had a great many fans. Fox Studios regularly picked up a daily load of fan letters for Dolores Del Rio from all over the world. Until recently, few Latin stars enjoyed that kind of media attention.

Advertisements

Latin stars appeared regularly in film industry advertisements. One recurring ad that ran for a number of years pictured the major MGM stars of 1929: Ramon Novarro, Greta Garbo, Lon Chaney, William Hanes, Buster Keaton, Norma Shearer, Marion Davies, and John Gilbert. A 1931 ad for the "New De Luxe Edition of the Stars of the *Photoplay*" included photos of three Latinos—Don Alvarado, Raquel Torres, and Ramon Novarro—among the twelve stars pictured. There were also full-page ads for films headlined by Latin stars: Ramon Novarro, for example, in *The Student Prince* (1928), with Norma Shearer. Again, think of the contemporary equivalents and the significance of the few stars who get full-page ads for their films. Which stars and movies receive the greatest amount of advertising? Generally, those that bring in the biggest box-office receipts.

Given the scarcity until recently of Latinos as commercial spokespeople, it is surprising to see the use of Latin stars to sell a variety of popular products, including shoes, clothes, cigarettes, face creams, hats, Coca-Cola, and household linens. From a Hollywood perspective, these ads served a dual purpose, advertising both the stars endorsing the products and their upcoming films. Two of the most interesting and somewhat amusing ads, from our present-day perspective, touted cigarettes. In the November 16, 1931, *Playbill*, Lupe Velez endorsed Lucky Strike cigarettes; the ad notes that Miss Velez was not paid for her statement, implying a "sincere" endorsement—ostensibly unrelated to the mention of her new film in the ad. In the February 13, 1938, issue of *Vogue*, Dolores Del Rio echoes similar sentiments, telling readers how gentle Luckies are on her throat. Interestingly, although the ad features Del Rio, its tag line brags that "with men who know tobacco best, it's Luckies—2 to 1." The superior credibility of men (at least with respect to cigarettes) is mentioned twice in this ad.

Best in Beauty and Physique

Hollywood has always been about beautiful faces and beautiful bodies. Present-day Latina stars frequently make the top-ten lists ranking the most beautiful, the sexiest, and so on. This is a relatively recent phenomenon, however. Consequently, it is surprising to see the extent to which Latin stars in this early period were singled out as the most beautiful, the most handsome, or those with the best bodies. In 1931 *Photoplay* named Dolores Del Rio the actress with the best figure in Hollywood—beating out such well-known stars as Greta Garbo, Carole Lombard, Joan Crawford, Clara Bow, Bebe Daniels, and Constance Bennett Fletcher. Although this was clearly far from a scientific survey (indeed, it was very likely a publicity stunt), from a more contemporary perspective the awarding of the title to a Spanish-surnamed actress was remarkable. The selection of Del Rio, according to the article, established the superiority of the roundly turned, warmly curved figure—which, it was noted, was also the figure of some of her contenders, though they received only honorable mention ("Who Has the Best Figure in Hollywood?" 1931, 34–36, 86–87).

Each year, the Western Association of Motion Picture Advertisers (WAMPA) picked thirteen promising young starlets to be "WAMPA babies." Selection as a WAMPA baby signaled a bright future in the studio system. In 1926 the association chose Dolores Del Rio, along with Joan Crawford, Mary Astor, Fay Wray, and Janet Gaynor. Lupe Velez was similarly honored two years later. In keeping with the racist standards of the times, all the WAMPA babies were white women. The only exception to this tradition was Toshia

Latino stars were often used to advertise products. Here, Latina superstar Dolores Del Rio appears in a 1938 *Vogue* magazine ad for Lucky Strikes.

Mori, an Asian American. Mori was selected in 1932 as a last-minute replacement for Lillian Miles, who failed to show up at the award ceremony (she was apparently getting married).

The significance of Latin stars—particularly women—

continued for some time. As late as 1932, *Photoplay* highlighted Lupe Velez and Dolores Del Rio in a story about "famous faces" dining at the noted Brown Derby restaurant in Hollywood ("All the Stars Dine Here" 1932, 73–74). During the shift to talkies, the Latinas fared better than many of the Latinos. The advent of talking film favored actors whose voices or accents were deemed attractive to theatergoers. Dolores Del Rio's voice was thought to be sufficiently demure and sophisticated and to have a slightly international accent, and so she continued to play a wide variety of roles, although she played more Latin characters during the talkies era. Lupe Velez was also able to make a successful transition to sound movies in the thirties because her voice was husky and cartoon-like—a clear asset in the comedic roles she would subsequently come to play. The hands of some of these early Latin stars were immortalized in the sidewalk at Grauman's Chinese Theater in Hollywood along with other major stars in Hollywood at the time.

Latin-ness Foregrounded

The foregrounding of "Latin-ness" and Spanish or Latino origins was in keeping with a general early trend in *Photoplay* in which the origins—sometimes fabricated—of all stars were made clear. For example, *Photoplay* reported that Claudette Colbert's real name was Chauchoin and that she had been born in Paris (photo caption, *Photoplay*, January 1931, 25). Short biographies, in small print, often accompanied full-page photos of stars, giving other information such as birth date, height, weight, hair and eye color, name of spouse, and ancestral details. In the bios of "Latin" stars, even those who did not have Spanish surnames or who had changed their names to English-sounding names, their Latin American origins were accentuated. Coverage of Gilbert Roland, for example, left no doubt that he was born in Mexico.

Barry Norton (1905–56) was first introduced in a 1928 issue of *Photoplay* in a full-page photo, without reference to

The 1928 caption to this full-page photo in the largest fan magazine of the day, *Photoplay*, notes that silent-screen actor Barry Norton was born Alfredo Biraben, in Argentina.

his Latin American origins. A few months later, however, a more extensive feature article in the same magazine reported that he had been born in Buenos Aires and that his given name was Alfredo Biraben. A cute baby picture of him and a (not-so-cute) picture of his parents in Argentina were included in the article ("Doug's Office Boy Makes Good" 1929, 63, 96–97). Norton's native Argentine and upper-class origins were important features of his public image during his early years in film. (At the time, upper-class Latin American backgrounds were often underscored, and sometimes created, for many of the Latin stars.) Norton was a leading man in the silent era and appeared often in the magazine and in many Hollywood-produced English- and Spanish-language movies. However, with the advent of talkies his career declined.

Anita Page (1910–) was born Anita Pomares in New York City. Her father's family had come from El Salvador. Better known in the thirties than Barry Norton, she is also better remembered today as an important star of the silent and early talkies era—although few recall her as a Latin star. In 1929 she reportedly received more than ten thousand fan letters a week—a figure surpassed only by the reigning queen of silent film, Greta Garbo. More than one hundred fan letters came from Benito Mussolini, the Italian dictator, who wrote obsessively and several times asked for her hand in marriage. Anita Page also had a starring role in the second film ever to win an Oscar (*The Broadway Melody*, 1929). Her photo appeared often in *Photoplay*, and the magazine's coverage of her reflected an openness—albeit short lived—with regard to her Latin American origins.

Having begun in Hollywood in 1925 playing uncredited parts, Page showed up as one of three new starlets in a 1928 MGM film, *Our Dancing Daughters*. (The other two "daughters" in the film were Joan Crawford, as the redhead, and Dorothy Sebastian, as the brunette. Anita was the blonde.) A later 1928 full-page photo of her alone indicated she had just graduated from Washington Irving High School in New York and had been discovered by an arts patron (photo caption,

The 1929 caption to this photo in *Photoplay* states that "Anita Page was born Anita Pomares and she is a blond, blue-eyed Latin." She received more than ten thousand fan letters a week in 1929, second only to the reigning queen of silent film, Greta Garbo.

Photoplay, November 1928, 22). The following year, Anita appeared in a tulle-skirted flower-bedecked ballerina-type dress; the caption describes her as a "a blond, blue-eyed Latin" with "a dash of Spanish ancestry." Interestingly, despite what appears to be bobbed hair in the photo, she is also described as a new type that is superseding the boyish flapper (photo caption, *Photoplay*, August 1929, 20).

By the following year, 1930, Page's Latin American origins were foregrounded in a feature article by "Wild Mark" Busby (also known as "Don Juan"). The author jokingly describes his date with Anita, during which they were chaperoned by her family—Papa Pomares, Mrs. Pomares, and their six-year-old son, Moreno—suggesting that she came from a very strict Latin home. An accompanying illustration shows Anita playing the piano in her parents' home ("Dating Anita" 1930, 65–66, 101). The article emphasizes the extent to which Anita Page was bound by the Latin American and Spanish custom of the *chaperona*. Two more references to her later that year continue to call attention to the Latin affiliation, one noting her real name and mentioning the "Pomares tribe," the other clarifying that her father was "Spanish-French, hence the name Pomares" ("Fresh from the Camera" 1930, 19; photo caption, *Photoplay*, April 1930, 19).

After *The Broadway Melody*, in which Anita starred, won an Academy Award, references to her Latin origins disappeared. In this film, Anita played Queenie Mahoney (definitely not a Latin character), half of a singing-dancing sister act that is trying to make it on Broadway. Her character has to confront separation from her sister when she falls in love and opts for the married-with-children-and-suburban-home life over the on-the-road Broadway career. Today, though many remember her as a leading lady of Hollywood silent films, few recall her Latin connection. She retired from film in 1937, after marrying a naval officer who later taught at the University of San Diego. She raised two daughters and returned to the screen late in life and only for occasional guest appearances.

A More Latin-Sounding Name

Although it has been common practice for stars to change their names from ethnic to less ethnic, what was particularly unusual during this early period was the trend toward changing names to sound *more* Latin. Latin actors, in particular, who were born with Anglo-sounding names took on other names for their film careers to accentuate their Latin or Spanish backgrounds. The shift was openly addressed—indeed, featured—in the press at the time. For example, in 1928 *Photoplay* notes that Raquel Torres's real name was Marie Osterman and describes her as "half Mexican and half German"; the caption adds, "You can't beat that for an interesting combination" (photo caption, *Photoplay*, October 1928, 62).

In fact, Raquel Torres was born either Wilhelmina von Osterman or Paula Marie Osterman in Hermosillo, Mexico. (There are two obituaries, each giving a different birth name [Raquel Torres obituary, *Variety*, August 19, 1987; Raquel Torres obituary, *New York Times*, August 13, 1987, both in Torres clippings file]). Her father was a German mining engineer in Mexico, and her mother was apparently Mexican—although in 1933 the *New York Times* refers to her as "Spanish" (photo caption, *New York Times*, April 30, 1933, Torres clippings file). Raquel was sent to a convent school in Mexico at an early age and learned to speak both German and Spanish before she acquired English. Her mother died while Raquel was very young, and the family moved to the United States, where Raquel completed her education in a convent school in Los Angeles. Interestingly, though she came to the United States at a young age and spent most of her time here, she was commonly referred to as a "Mexican actress." Perhaps this was the other side of Latin recognition: Latinness was indelible, and one never lost it.

How much of Torres's name change was determined by her "Latin looks" and how much it reflected an attempt (hers or perhaps her studio's) to capitalize on the craze for all things

Raquel Torres, born Marie (or Wilhelmina) Osterman, starred in *White Shadows* (1928), MGM's first feature film to include fully synchronized dialogue, music, and effects. Torres is shown here in a full-page 1928 photo from *Photoplay*, the "queen of fan magazines."

Latin is not clear. It was probably a combination of both. Raquel reportedly changed her name three times "before it sounded Spanish enough to suit the movie powers that be."

According to one news report, despite her Teutonic surname, she had inherited the Latin coloring and disposition of her mother—olive complexion, black eyes, thick curly dark hair, and fiery personality—and so when opportunity knocked at her door in the form of a moving picture contract to play Spanish roles, she realized that "Billie Osterman" would never do. Adopting her mother's maiden name, she became first Hilda Torres and then, seeking a stronger connotation of "sunny Spain," Raquel Torres. Raquel made only a few films in Hollywood, where she is best remembered for having starred (at the age of nineteen) in *White Shadows* (1928), MGM's first feature film with fully synchronized dialogue, music, and effects. Torres died at the age of seventy-eight in Malibu, California, of a heart attack, having made about ten films from 1928 to 1934 ("Film Star Changed Name Three Times," *ERS*, October 21, 1931, Torres clippings file).

The case of Don Alvarado (1905–67) is similar. Born Joe Page in Amijo, New Mexico, he first appeared in *Photoplay* in 1928 with a mustache and a decidedly Latin lover quality to him. The caption to the photo further accentuates his Latin look: "As plain Joe Page, he came to Hollywood to teach dancing. The movies re-christened him Don Alvarado, as more fitting his type and his Latin ancestry. Now he is one of the most fatal of the recent discoveries" (photo caption, *Photoplay*, April 1928, 21). A few months later, in 1929, another large full-page photo of him appeared in the same magazine, but this time his mustache is gone, he is wearing a tweed jacket, and his given name is not mentioned. He could easily be Joe Page, ethnicity unknown. The caption does note his Latin ancestry, which was in "great demand" (photo caption, *Photoplay*, January 1929, 20).

Alvarado was described by one *Photoplay* reporter as "the handsomest man I have ever met" (Madeline Glass, "Spanish—with English Reserve," *Photoplay*, June 1929, Alvarado clippings file), but he did not have a major career in film. He broke into Hollywood as an extra in 1924, and toward the end of the decade he played the leading man in a few films.

Beginning as an extra in 1924, Don Alvarado, whose birth name was Joe Page, became a leading man toward the end of the decade. He is shown here in a full-page 1928 photo from *Photoplay*.

In 1937 he became an assistant director at Warner Brothers studio. He died of cancer in 1967, having spent the last nine years of his life on a ranch that he managed in Arizona. How much was his career affected by typecasting of Latins at the time? It would seem that, as he saw it, quite a bit. He was frequently referred to as Valentino's successor, and he felt that the comparison had negatively influenced his career.

That concern notwithstanding, he apparently had, or developed, a strong awareness of his own history as a Hispano in New Mexico. In an article entitled "Home Town," he notes that he came from an old ranching family in Amijo, just outside of Albuquerque, New Mexico. The land had been given to his mother's family by a royal grant, and they had lived there for three hundred years. His father was from England, a doctor who made his rounds on horseback from ranch to ranch. As a child, Alvarado had "raised his eyes from his [history] book and stared out the window and reflected, 'Why, there is a cathedral in Santa Fe and a government House built before the Mayflower ever set sail'" ("Home Town," as told by Don Alvarado to Dorothy Calhoun, ca. 1929, Alvarado clippings file).

Perhaps the most dramatic example of this emphasis on "Latin-ness" is the story of Ricardo Cortez, who was born Jacob Krantz in Vienna. At the age of three, Krantz immigrated with his family to New York City. In 1922 Jesse Lasky, the head of Paramount Studios, spotted him because of his "dark good looks." Lasky's secretary picked the name Ricardo Cortez, when it was decided the young actor needed a Latin name. The publicity on Cortez implies that he was somewhat ambivalent about being seen as another Latin lover. But he stuck with his new name and went on to make an astounding ninety pictures from 1924 to 1958—all under the name Ricardo Cortez. He also achieved a considerable degree of prominence during the early era: He was, for example, the only star billed above Garbo in her first American film, *The Torrent* (1926). He played numerous leading roles in films like *Argentine Love* (1924), *The Spaniard* (also

The caption to this 1926 *Photoplay* photo notes Ricardo Cortez's preference *not* to be seen as a "burn 'em up Latin Lover." He was born Jacob Krantz, in Austria, and immigrated with his family to New York City at a young age. He made ninety films between 1924 and 1958—all as Ricardo Cortez.

known as *Spanish Love*) (1925), and *The Sorrows of Satan* (1926). His acting career waned with the coming of sound. Undaunted, he moved into the directing role and continued to be involved in films—as Ricardo Cortez—until 1958. He died in New York City in 1977. Interestingly, his brother, Stanley Krantz, also took the surname Cortez and had a long career behind the camera in Hollywood, winning the American Society of Cinematographers' lifetime achievement award for cinematography in 1990.

Who Is a Latin?

In the early years of the twentieth century, the common term in the media press was not "Latino" or "Hispanic" but "Latin." Italians, Portuguese-speaking peoples, and Spaniards were also considered Latin—in addition to those from the Spanish-speaking Americas. Indeed, the original Latin lover, Rudolf Valentino, was from Italy. Jimmy Durante, who later had his own highly successful comedy show on television, was profiled in a 1932 issue of *Photoplay* as "the new Latin bonfire from the lower East Side" ("Hollywood's New Lover" 1932, 31). In his television show, Durante rarely (if ever) mentioned what he had described in this article as his "Eye-talian lure." Because of his enigmatic sign-off at the end of each show— "Goodnight, Mrs. Calabash, wherever you are"—many viewers obliquely assumed that he was Irish or Jewish or of no particular ethnicity. The term "Spanish" was also used in the media press, and by the stars themselves, to refer to anyone of Spanish origin—whether from Spain or Latin America. The terms "Indian" and "Mexican" were also used interchangeably on occasion.

Today, the term "Latin" is still loosely used, as in "Latin music" or "Latin star." However, it usually does not include Italians—although some academics use the term to refer to those who speak or originate from peoples who speak languages derived from Latin. In the media today, the term tends to include only those who have origins in Latin America or, as in the case of Penelope Cruz and Antonio Banderas, Spain. Today "Latino" and "Hispanic" have been added to the list. There are strong debates in some ethnic studies arenas as to whether those from Spain, Brazil, or Portugal should be included in the term "Latino"; and not all U.S. residents from these countries identify with any of these terms. Others debate whether the term "Hispanic" has any legitimacy among Latinos, and still others reject any generic term, preferring to identify themselves by their country of origin— Cuban, Salvadoran, and the like. While these debates rage, it appears that the media world has settled on excluding Italians and Portuguese-speaking peoples from the term "Latin" and referring to them by their countries of origin. The terms "Latin," "Latino," "Hispanic," and simply "ethnic" are all used for those who have Spanish or Latin American origins.

The Contexts of the Times

The prominence of these early Latin stars is all the more significant in the context of the times. The Roaring Twenties was a time of economic boom and speculative excess in many sectors of the economy. This was also the time of the Harlem Renaissance, jazz, the flapper, and the Charleston. Marketing and advertising—or what is generally called consumption marketing—expanded tremendously, particularly in areas like women's fashions and cosmetics. On the other end of this decade, however, was the Great Depression.

African Americans had begun their migratory trek from the South to the industrial cities of the Northeast and the Midwest; and substantial black communities, like the one in Harlem, had developed outside of the South. Mexicans had also intensified their northward migration, in response to the industrial revolution in the United States and to political pressures in Mexico. Both of these migrations had, by the 1920s, begun to fill in for the immigrants from Asia and eastern Europe who were no longer arriving in great numbers. New legislation in 1882 and 1917, restricting Asian immigration, and then in 1921 and 1924, restricting all immigration, had blunted the immigrant labor supply. World War I and the Bolshevik Revolution of 1917 kept European immigrants at home. As is usually the case, wars played an important role in the mobility of people.

The Mexican Revolution (1910–20) intensified the movement of Mexicans northward. Indeed, the screen idol Ramon Novarro and his family left Mexico because of the disruptions caused by Pancho Villa's troops. "The Spanish-speaking population in the United States soared between 1910 and 1930, as over one million Mexicanos migrated northward. Pushed by economic and political chaos generated by the Mexican Revolution and lured by jobs in U.S. agribusiness and industry, they settled into existing barrios and forged new communities both in the Southwest and in the Midwest, in small towns and cities" (Ruiz 1993, 109). Indeed, the Mexican immigration to the United States was so substantial that a formal census category called "Mexican" was added to the racial categories in the 1930 census. (Although this category was deleted in 1940, the population of Spanish origin continued to be counted in other ways.) More Puerto Ricans and Cubans had also begun to arrive as a result of the 1898 Spanish-American War. The 1917 passage of the Jones Act, which made Puerto Ricans citizens, their participation in World War I, and the migration of some as agricultural laborers (who subsequently stayed) also added numbers to the Puerto Rican *colonias* established in New York and elsewhere before World War II.

African Americans and Mexican Americans lived in communities that tended to be highly segregated and had high poverty levels. Restrictive U.S. covenants and segregated schools served to keep Mexican Americans separated from other Americans. In Los Angeles, of which Hollywood was a part, these measures increased dramatically between 1920 and 1950. Many restaurants, theaters, and public swimming pools discriminated against their Spanish-surnamed clientele, and "White trade only" signs were not uncommon. A

1933 study by the University of California found that Mexicans in southern California were among the most impoverished groups in the United States, and apparently little generational change with regard to poverty status occurred at the time (cited in Ruiz 1993, 112).

After the Depression set in, hundreds of thousands of Mexicans were sent back to Mexico in a government program called repatriation. Between 1931 and 1934—when both Dolores Del Rio and Lupe Velez were being sighted as "famous faces" in Hollywood restaurants—the U.S. government deported or repatriated five hundred thousand Mexican people, an astonishing one-third of the Mexican population in the United States. Many were U.S. citizens, and Mexicans were the only immigrants targeted for removal. It seems that at the beginning of the twenties Mexican workers were needed to replace the immigrant labor that had been cut off while the economy was expanding. After the 1929 depression, when jobs became scarce and the economy was contracting, they were seen as excess.

Given this context, how was it possible for so many Latins to achieve stardom during this period? One factor was surely industrial expansion and international competition, which created a need to develop new markets. Featuring foreign or "ethnic" actors in Hollywood movies broadened the appeal of those movies to international markets. It also contributed to developing markets in the United States among the African American, Asian American, and Mexican American audiences, all of which had grown substantially in number. Moreover, although Americans like Gloria Swanson and Clara Bow dominated the screen in the early twenties, two "foreign" women also claimed star status: Greta Garbo and Marlene Dietrich. Being "foreign" was clearly not a barrier to success; it may even have been an asset in the case of Latins. There was also already a somewhat established history of Latin stars and matinee idols—including Myrtle Gonzalez, Beatriz Michelena, and Antonio Moreno —that helped to pave the way for those who arrived later.

This was also an era of greater liberality. World War I was now over, and the United States had reached global ascendancy. Jazz and the flapper were part and parcel of a general shift away from the Victorian era to greater liberality. The movement for expansion of women's rights was strong between 1920 and 1924, suffrage having been secured in 1920. Because of the war, a greater number of women had been in the labor force and had tasted independence. The working woman sought a new media image, and the expansion of marketing and the increased production of women's products (including face powders, rouge, and lipsticks) facilitated this shift. The restrictive Hays Code of 1934 had yet to be implemented; movies were regulated by the more liberal Motion Picture Association of America. Finally, the Great Depression was still on a distant horizon. Interestingly, *Photoplay*'s references to stars' "Latin-ness" declined after the Depression. Until then, however, this general openness allowed foreigners and Latins a more integral place in the film scene at the time.

Latins were also in favor because of the "Latin lover" craze that was in fashion and was most strongly personified by Rudolph Valentino. Valentino's premature death in 1926 (from a perforated ulcer and blood poisoning) at the height of his career helped to fuel continued interest in the Latin lover phenomenon. Indeed, as the stories of Don Alvarado and Ricardo Cortez indicate, many stars were promoted as successors to Valentino. The craze also extended to women. While honeymooning with his wife in Mexico, Edwin Carewe, a well-known Hollywood director at the time, was looking for "a female Valentino." He met Dolores Del Rio and convinced her to come to Hollywood, where she quickly became a major success. The story of the discovery of Lupe Velez has a similar "searching for Valentino" motif. The broader view of what constituted a Latin very likely expanded the appeal of such stars to larger audiences and helped to facilitate their remarkable success.

The enormous popularity of all things Mexican between 1920 and 1935 also contributed to the possibilities for Latin stardom. In the United States, liberals and leftists admired the Mexican Revolution, and there was a fashionable interest in "authentic" peoples and cultures. Both the United States and Mexico were now at more settled points. The long period of revolutionary turmoil in Mexico was over, and both countries were experiencing a burgeoning cultural nationalism. Mexico and other Latin America countries sought to ban films that presented their countries in a negative light. This spirit of cultural nationalism and new beginnings was respected by the media industry, which attempted to alter its depictions—dropping, for example, its use of the word "greaser." Moreover, despite U.S. repatriation of Mexican workers, cultural migrants (painters, composers, and actors) continued to head north. In the United States there was enthusiasm over both Mexico's preconquest heritage and the work of contemporary artists and muralists such as Diego Rivera and José Clemente Orozco. The production of books on Mexico increased greatly. Astute diplomacy furthered relations between the two countries and made each more open to cultural exchange.

In the movies, this vogue of all things Mexican was understood and defined by Hollywood as all things Mexican, Spanish, and Latin—with few distinctions made among them. In the Hollywood media, lace mantillas, Spanish combs, ruffled lace dresses, dark sultry looks, pulled-back hair with "Spanish" side curls, toreador themes and clothes, and flamenco poses were prevalent, as were references to "Spanish" architecture, furniture, personages, places, and customs (bullfights, in particular). Spanish shawls were popular, though the shawl phenomena also incorporated intricately embroidered shawls from other countries, particularly those in the East. However awkwardly defined or understood, the popularity of "all things Latin" encouraged the adoption and promotion of the "Latin look."

Within this context, Latin stars were, in some cases, reference points. In 1933 *Photoplay* identified Fay Wray as having been born in Canada and showed her with a Spanish black lace mantilla—looking very much like a Spanish señorita. The accompanying caption describes Wray as "a DOLOROUS senorita, minus the verve and vivacity we connect with the true tropical type." The capitalization of the word "dolorous" suggests a comparison with Dolores Del Rio. "This is the way Fay Wray looks in her latest role," the caption continues, "opposite Gary Cooper in 'The Texan.' Perhaps Big Gary has changed his type and likes them a bit sad and romantic-like" (photo caption, *Photoplay*, July 1930, 24). This is an indirect reference to another major Latin star of the time, Lupe Velez, and to her very public romance with Cooper. (This relationship was fodder for the entertainment media, as were her relationships with other leading stars of the day.)

Other factors contributed to the relative abundance of successful Latin actors at the time. Accents were, of course, not a problem in silent film. Some have argued that because of the high contrast in black-and-white films, shades of color were less significant, and so olive or tanned skin appeared whiter. It has also been argued that the early filmmakers were mostly European immigrants, who were not yet hardened by American racial and ethnic prejudice. Consequently, Latin actors of the time faced less discrimination than would those of a later era. In the earliest period, acting in film was seen to be closely tied to vaudeville, nickelodeons, and mass popular entertainment appealing to the lower classes, who were often immigrant and urban, and was therefore seen as a less-than-respectable profession. These early origins may have tainted the industry in its early period, but they established a tradition of openness toward all who wished to enter.

Finally, before 1911 the film industry was centered on the East Coast. Some cite its shift to Hollywood, California, as providing the proximity and access for many, particularly Mexicans and Mexican Americans, to enter the film world. This was, indeed, the case with Ramon Novarro, who worked as an extra in Hollywood films for five years before getting his big break. Anthony Quinn's Mexican father also worked on Hollywood sets at this time as a technician and cameraman. It was, in part, his father's association with the Latin actors of the day that sparked Quinn's interest and involvement in film in the thirties.

Given the highly segregated context of the times and the individual experiences of discrimination that many Latinos experienced, the success achieved by Latin film stars, especially non-English-speaking Latin film stars, is remarkable. In part, this derived from a split-level approach to casting. All of these stars conformed to European prototypes—perhaps to southern and eastern European prototypes, but clearly in the evolving fold of what it meant to be "white" (and upper class) in the United States at the time. Latinos who were dark or non-European in appearance did not generally share in this success. Indeed, they tended to play supporting roles or were part of the masses of peasants, banditos, nameless cantina girls, or extras—when they were cast at all. Consequently, the early films could present the screen favorites, matinee idols, and Latin lovers as well as the more stereotypical greasers, buffoons, and half-breed harlots.

The tendency to view the Spanish, Mexican, and other Latin American (and perhaps southern European) communities as one big "Latin" group may also have facilitated the psychological separation of such stars from their ethnicities. Thus Mexican stars, such as Dolores Del Rio and Ramon Novarro, were seen as Latin or Spanish and therefore somehow less Mexican—even though their Mexican origins were noted positively. In other words, reference to them as Latin or Spanish (and then, specifically, upper class) may have facilitated the general public's seeing them as somehow different from, or segmented from, their ethnic communities. (This tendency to elevate and segment is similar to that noted in Spike Lee's movie, *Do the Right Thing* [1989], when Mookie [played by Spike Lee] asks Vito [played by Richard Edson] why his favorite sports heroes are black, though he does not like ordinary black people.) Both Del Rio and Novarro played a wide variety of roles, including European characters from many countries, but they did not play Mexican characters during the twenties, when their careers were at their apex.

Dolores Del Rio said that she had tried to interest her producers in stories about Mexico and that she wanted to play a Mexican; but they preferred to cast her as a French or Polynesian woman. Novarro did not play a Mexican until 1949 (in *The Big Steal*), well after he had lost his status as a major star.

Despite the success of these Latin film stars and the openness with which Latin names, backgrounds, and themes were addressed, this period produced films that incorporated stereotypical depictions of Latins (in particular, Mexicans). Banditos, easy cantina girls, and fumbling Latin characters were common, as was their general dependence on Yankee leaders who were highly moral and had innate intelligence. Evil half-breeds and "good" greasers—that is, those Mexicans who turned against their own "bad" greasers or gave their lives for the Yankee protagonists—continued to appear. Moreover, many of these character types were played by non-Latinos in brownface, in keeping with other Hollywood traditions of blackface and yellowface. The tendency to allow a Yankee to marry a highbred Mexican woman persisted; however, rarely was a Mexican man shown to have a North American wife. Finally, "films of squalor"—films showing the negative sides of Latin American countries—were also made and led many Latin American countries to make official protests. Mexico went so far as to ban the films of one company in 1922; Panama followed suit in 1923, and other Latin American countries registered other forms of protest.

Nonetheless, in the midst of opposing and negative trends, these stars reigned, and they did so with their Latinness foregrounded. Clearly, just as most Hollywood stars then and today, these Latin film stars were created by the marketing geniuses of the day. Few Hollywood stars, or films for that matter, are successful without marketing. What is significant is that the marketing efforts were made, at this particular time, and that the efforts yielded success for a substantial number of Latinos in Hollywood.

The Silent and Early Talkies Era

Who were the early Latin stars? Where did they come from? How did they come to be "in pictures," and how did their careers end? The stories of the earliest Latin stars—those in films made before 1919—are clouded in obscurity. In this early period, many films did not credit actors, and few available materials provide precise and accurate information. Only recently has some interest developed in preserving the memory of the early, pre-Hollywood film pioneers; in some cases, it may be too late. Unfortunately, there is little that indicates how their "Latin-ness" or "Spanish-ness" was perceived by others or experienced by the actors themselves. A number of them had mixed heritages, and in most cases it is not known whether they favored one heritage over the other, or whether they ever considered such a choice. We know that they performed with their given Spanish surnames. They enjoyed huge popularity with the general public. They were cast as leads in the biggest movies, and they played diverse character roles in a variety of social positions. Like many other actors at the time, almost all had had careers in the theater before going into film. Although they were recognized as major stars in their day, today they are largely forgotten.

Myrtle Gonzalez

From the information uncovered thus far, Myrtle Gonzalez (1891–1918) may have been the industry's first Latina star. She began her film career at the age of twenty with a starring role in *Ghosts* (1912). By 1917 she had starred in more than forty films, only a few of which survive. A native Mexican Californian, Gonzalez was educated in a convent school in Los Angeles. Her ancestral lineage suggests some interesting examples of both historical hybridity and the fluidity of movement to and from Mexico. The 1900 Los Angeles census indicates that her father was a grocer, born in California, and that he could read, write, and speak English. It also notes that he owned his own home, that his daughter "Mertle" was eight years old and had two younger siblings, and that his wife, Lillian Cook, had been born in New York of Irish immigrant parents. According to the census taken twenty years earlier, in 1880, some of her father's grandparents had been born in Mexico, others in California. One of these grandparents, Louis Jordan, lived with Myrtle's father as he was growing up. Jordan, who was fifty-six at the time the census was taken, had been born in Mexico, as had his father before him. The grandparents with the Spanish surname, Gonzalez, had been born in California.

In her day, Myrtle was a major screen star. A 1916 studio directory describes her as five feet, five inches tall, 125 pounds, with light brown hair and hazel eyes, and notes her favorite recreations as riding, swimming, and painting. She is identified as "a leading woman" who had a career on stage with the Belasco Stock Company in Los Angeles before beginning her screen career with Vitagraph and Universal

Myrtle Gonzalez (shown here circa 1913) was one of the silent screen's best-known leading ladies; her work at Universal earned her the title of "The Virgin Lily of the Screen."

("Studio Directory," October 21, 1916, Gonzalez clippings file). Her work at Universal earned her the title of "Virgin Lily of the Screen" (Doyle 1995, 30–31). In contrast to the common casting of Latinas in the latter part of the twentieth century as languorous urban women whose major physical exertions involved casual acts of sex, many of the films in which Myrtle starred were westerns, and she often portrayed vigorous outdoor heroines.

In *End of the Rainbow* (1916), for example, she played Ruth Bennett, the daughter of a well-to-do timber tycoon in California's redwood forest. The opening shot of the film shows Ruth apathetically writing a check to her latest charity. Having allowed her to go to business college, Ruth's father now insists that she stay home like a proper (rich) young lady. Frustrated with the limitations placed on her, Ruth pays a stenographer at her father's lumber camp to trade positions with her. At the camp, she works under an assumed name and starts a library for the workers. She also battles the bad guy and exposes corruption of which her father has been unaware. While riding on horseback, she helps to save the day, but not before she herself is also saved a few times by Simpson (the love interest). Throughout the film, Myrtle's face expresses an interesting combination of strength and softness.

Despite the vitality of the characters she tended to play, Myrtle herself was in frail health, and in 1918, at the tender young age of twenty-seven, she succumbed to Spanish influenza, leaving her husband, Allen Watt, and a seven-year-old child. As a publication of the time stated, Myrtle's death deprived the public of "one of the screen's best-known leading ladies" (cited ibid., 30–31).

Beatriz Michelena

Beatriz Michelena (1890–1942) was another important silent-film star. She had the title role in her first film *(Salomy Jane)* in 1914, and within the next five years she starred in sixteen feature films. She won the acclaim of the major trade paper of the day, which placed her on its front page and referred to her as the "greatest and most beautiful artist" in motion pictures (cited in Ríos-Bustamante 1992, 22). Beatriz was born in New York City, the daughter of Fernando Michelena, a famous tenor of his day, and by 1919 she had won for herself "a distinct place on the light opera stage" and had "stepped to the screen with considerable success" (photo caption, *Motion Picture Classic*, August 1919, Robinson Locke Collection, series 2).

Beatriz's true love was opera, and she had hoped to become "a wonderful grand opera singer," but her plan to go abroad with her father to study was abandoned when war broke out in Europe. Unable to pursue her dream, she decided to accept an offer from the California Motion Picture Company to act (Roberta Courtlandt, "At Home with a Bret Harte Heroine," *Motion Picture Classic*, August 17, 1917, Michelena clippings file). Beatriz enjoyed remarkable success through her long career. Her home, near the California Motion Picture Company studio where many of her films were made, was described as "a beautiful Swiss Chalet in the hills that surround San Rafael" (ibid.). Her movies were popular not just in the United States but abroad as well, especially in Central and South America. By 1917 "she had circled the globe at least a good dozen times in as many motion pictures" (quoted in "Where in the Life of an Actress Was Two Amazing Extremes," *Photoplay Journal*, October 1917, Michelena clippings file). She also established her own production company and made several films in Santa Cruz County, California.

A review of her performance at the University of California, where she "appeared before 100,000 people" in the leading role of the Greek Theatre's production of *The Talisman*, describes her as "a much-heralded star." The review characterizes the event as testament both to Beatriz's individual talents and to a "growing consciousness of the advancing art of the motion picture profession." Indeed, the

Beatriz Michelena, a major silent-film star, graced the covers of numerous film magazines in her day. She is shown here in her first film, *Salomy Jane* (1914).

production represented the first time that a "motion picture actress has been asked to share honors with [actors of] the legitimate stage." Her versatility was also praised: She could play "the uncouth mountain girl of the West" in her movies as well as the "impassioned Egyptian maiden" of *The Talisman* on stage (ibid.).

Beatriz Michelena made no movies after 1920, although it is not clear why. Little information exists about her private life and personal motivations. She died in 1942, at the age of fifty-two, in San Francisco. She was survived by her husband, George E. Middleton, who had directed many of her pictures, and a sister, Vera Michelena, a retired operatic performer.

George Hernandez

George F. Hernandez (1863–1922) was a well-known character actor who performed often, though he had not yet achieved leading-star status in this early period. Not much is known about his childhood or family, except that he was born in 1863 in Placerville, California, just fifteen years after the signing of the Treaty of Guadalupe Hidalgo, and educated in Oakland. It is not clear how much education he received or what he studied, but he probably did not have advanced education, for if he had it would probably have been noted in the biographical materials printed about him.

Hernandez made his first movie *(The Sanitarium)* early on, in 1910—way before the beginning of Hollywood—and went on to make sixty-six movies in the next twelve years, an average of five and a half movies a year. He had also done theater work, making his debut in 1888 at the old California Theatre in San Francisco and also performing with other stock companies. In 1893 he joined the company of J. K. Emmet and "played all over the United States and Canada." He then went back to stock at the Francois Theatre in Montreal and finally "reached out for the actor's ambition, New York." Hernandez appeared at the Grand Opera House in New York, lived for a time in Honolulu, and performed for four years in Hollywood, under Belasco management (*Picture Play Weekly*, April 24, 1915, Robinson Locke Collection, envelope 685).

He was a portly man who was described in a 1917 studio directory as being five feet, five inches tall, 196 pounds, of dark complexion, with brown hair and brown eyes. At this point in his career, he had worked for a variety of production companies, including Selig, Metro, Lasky, and Universal (*Motion Picture News Studio Directory* 1917, 72). He played mainly character roles—for example, the kindly and shrewd judge or father. He was the rich father of Myrtle Gonzalez's character in the movie *End of the Rainbow;* in fact, the two were teamed together in a number of films. He did not receive a great deal of attention in the fan magazines of the day, although he is featured in a number of photo advertisements for his movies, and in 1918 the *New York Telegraph* referred to him as the "favorite triangle character actor" (photo caption, *New York Telegraph*, January 13, 1918, Robinson Locke Collection, envelope 685). "During his career he has created many parts," noted one magazine in 1915, "and had a vast variety of experience with noted stars of the stage." The writer also found him to be "very contented with the work of the silent drama" (*Picture Play Weekly*, April 24, 1915).

Hernandez was married to Anna Dodge, from River Falls, Wisconsin, who was also an actress and played similar character parts, often older, maternal types. The couple was pictured in 1917 with the caption, "A pair of Universal favorites" (photo caption, *Photoplay*, September 1917, New York Public Library for the Performing Arts). His 1923 obituary in *Variety* describes Hernandez as a "well known character man, his stage career having covered a period of 26 years" (George Hernandez obituary, *Variety*, January 12, 1923, Margaret Herrick Library). It also notes that during the previous five years he had appeared in some of the biggest feature productions made on the coast. He died in 1922, at the age of fifty-nine, at his home in Los Angeles, California, as a result of complications following surgery. Unfortunately, despite the many movies he made, little has been written about him.

Pedro de Cordoba

Pedro de Cordoba (1881–1950) was another well-known character actor about whom little has been written and who is barely remembered today. He began his career in silent film in 1915 and made an impressive 116 films during his career. In contrast to George Hernandez, who generally played non-Latin roles, Pedro de Cordoba often played wealthy aristocratic Latins and villains of all backgrounds. Before acting in film, he had performed with various theater companies, play-

Pedro de Cordoba (shown here circa 1911) had a distinguished career in classical theater before starring in his first film, Cecil B. DeMille's *Carmen,* in 1915. He made 116 films and played a variety of leading roles, including Sam in *Sam Abramovitch* (1926), a play about a Jewish immigrant's rise to wealth and affluence in New York. He was also president of the Catholic Actors Guild of America.

ing many Shakespearean roles. He made his first stage appearance early in 1902, at the Majestic Theatre in Utica, New York, as De Nantoilet in *If I Were King*. He continued to act in the theater through the early part of the 1930s.

Like Beatriz Michelena, de Cordoba originally aspired to an operatic career. He discussed his early career in a 1915 interview: "I wanted to be an opera singer. . . . But I was a bass, and I realized that the only roles I would be given would be those of old men and kings, and as I wanted to be the hero I decided to become an actor instead. I went to the American Academy of Dramatic Art, then I joined Mr. [E. H.] Southern's company and since then I have played almost every kind of part. 'Sadie Love' is my first farce experience, and I am enjoying it for the novelty. What I want to play, of course, is romantic roles" ("The Doings of Mr. Cordoba," *[New York?] Times*, December 19, 1915, De Cordoba clippings file). "If Mr. de Cordoba had been born a tenor," the reporter concludes, "the world would have been deprived of a fine actor." This story was repeated in 1937, after De Cordoba had gone on, with his "very deep, bass voice," to appear in numerous Shakespearean plays and to build a "distinguished career [in the theater] in which he played many classic roles" (G. Horace Mortimer, "Voluntary Exiles from Broadway," *New York Herald Tribune*, February 28, 1937, De Cordoba clippings file).

Pedro de Cordoba was born in New York City, "under the shadow of the Metropolitan Opera House," to a Parisian French mother and a Cuban father (from Camaguey) who worked as a "New York custom house broker" and was the "grandson of a Spaniard from Cordoba" (ibid.). A 1942 obituary for Pedro's sister, Mathilde de Cordoba, also mentions that the de Cordobas were direct descendants of "Gonzalvo de Cordoba, who aided in the expulsion of the Moors from Spain under Ferdinand and Isabella and then became the Spanish Viceroy in Italy" ("Miss deCordoba Dies; New York Portrait Etcher," *New York Herald Tribune*, July 6, 1942, De Cordoba clippings file). Pedro de Cordoba attended St. Francis Xavier School in New York and then Seton Hall

College in New Jersey. He had planned to become a violinist when he first began his university studies; he then yearned to be a singer. Given his birth date (1881), it is possible that he, or his parents, participated in the Cuban–Puerto Rican community composed of political exiles and merchants who had established themselves in New York City toward the end of the nineteenth century. De Cordoba would have been seventeen when the 1898 Spanish-American War was fought.

Although he was born and educated in the United States and played a variety of ethnic and Shakespearean roles, de Cordoba's "Spanish" ancestry was sometimes noted by the movie press, in his press materials, and by de Cordoba himself. One company that managed some of his press observed "something of the Old World about Pedro de Cordova, a dreamy, serious, inscrutability and instinctively when one sees him, in one's mind rises visions of brave toreadors in their multi colored costumes, graciously fascinating women in waving mantillas and eyes dancing, white walls with crimson flowers growing in careless profusion; cathedrals of potent meaning with incense and the black robed figures of priests; a pen sketch of the atmosphere in which Pedro would seem at home" (Chamberlain Brown's Office, "Pedro de Cordova," De Cordoba clippings file). This metaphorical and evocative description of the actor (whose name was misspelled by the anonymous publicity writer) suggests that de Cordoba's "Latin-ness" or "Spanish-ness" was part of the context in which he would be viewed by others and would view himself. The caption accompanying a 1918 photo of de Cordoba makes a similar point: "Pedro de Cordoba, though not a native son, is true to the best little traditions of Spain. Besides looking like a Zuloaga toreador, he acts. If you saw 'Barbary Sheep,' you know" (photo caption, *Photoplay*, June 1918, De Cordoba clippings file).

In his first film, *Carmen* (1915), de Cordoba played a bullfighter. His recollection of an incident that occurred during the shooting reveals a bit about his own sense of his Latinness. "In the 'Carmen' picture I was in the arena with the bull several times. I have Spanish blood in my veins—my father was Spanish and my mother French—and it was that that kept me from being afraid, I guess, for the bulls were very much alive. I had a hunch that they wouldn't hurt me. Then the third time my hunch left me and I got out as soon as I could" ("Doings of Mr. Cordoba"). The same incident is recounted somewhat differently in a 1937 report: "On the bull's third rush, he got so close to De Cordoba that [de Cordoba] lost his capa [cloak] and had to make a hasty exit. Worse than that, it was such a near catastrophe that the camera man abandoned his camera and the scene had to be reshot" (Mortimer, "Voluntary Exiles from Broadway"). No reference here to de Cordoba's "Spanish" blood or to any "hunch" that would protect him from the bulls. Whether these details were edited out of the later account or no longer seemed important to de Cordoba twenty-two years after the event is not known.

In 1935 de Cordoba moved his family to Hollywood and began to take on more "Latin" roles in films. By this time, he was already recognized as a veteran of the theater and of Hollywood. According to a 1937 account, de Cordoba's film career began in 1915, when Jesse Lasky, Walter Wanger, and Samuel Goldwyn, pioneers who had by then gone their separate ways, invited the reigning American favorite of the opera, Geraldine Farrar, to make silent pictures in Hollywood (ibid.). De Cordoba, who by 1914 had "revealed himself as the accomplished actor" in Shakespearean theater, was engaged as her leading man ("Othello Well Approved," *New York Telegraph*, January 14, 1914, De Cordoba clippings file; Mortimer, "Voluntary Exiles from Broadway").

In 1915 he was described as busily employed, with five children, and as having "just one role after another." His shift to moving pictures created a strange duality in his life similar to that experienced by Beatriz Michelena. "I found it rather amusing," he told a reporter, "jumping from pictures to Greek drama, and from Greek drama to farce. At night when I had finished acting for the movies and between scenes I would study for roles I was to play [on stage] . . . in 'Elektra' and 'Medea'" ("Doings of Mr. Cordoba"). Like many other stars of the era, in the days of his silent-film career de Cordoba acted not just in the United States but also abroad. According to one account, he went to Egypt to play in *The Desert Sheik;* in early Gaumont Pictures films he performed in France; in Nice he acted with Lionel Barrymore in *The Enemies of Women* (1923); and he also played in his "ancestral home," Cordoba, Spain (Mortimer, "Voluntary Exiles from Broadway").

De Cordoba's silent-film and stage credits were already impressive before he made his first talking picture, *The Crusades* (1935), the Cecil B. DeMille film in which he played King Philip of France. Indeed, two years earlier, he had been described as "one of Broadway's best known thespians" who had also "been cast as leading man for several of America's outstanding actresses" ("Cordoba, Pedro de," *New York Sun,* May 6, 1933, De Cordoba clippings file). During this time, he was also well known to radio listeners: he was among the first to broadcast a Shakespearean repertoire over the air and took many difficult and important foreign roles. Later that same year, he took the role of Abraham Lincoln in a radio presentation subtitled "The Man of Sorrow," which recreated a dramatic episode of Christmas Eve, 1863 ("Pedro de Cordoba on Radio," *New York Herald Tribune,* June 4, 1933, De Cordoba clippings file).

In 1922 de Cordoba assumed the role of president of the Catholic Actors Guild of America. Asked by a reporter whether he felt that his deep religious beliefs had been a handicap to his stage career, he replied characteristically, "I have been told that they are a handicap . . . but I do not know of any single instance in my experiences." Have they aided you, the reporter asked? "Assuredly," he replied. "In the first place I have never been asked to play a role that would be offensive to my beliefs. . . . My opinion is that I have done some of my best work in such parts because I believe in them." He saw nothing extraordinary in his affiliation of church with stage and screen, as other religious denominations also had actors' guilds (Mortimer, "Voluntary Exiles from Broadway"). Although by this time he had played a number of priests in films, he had also played many other characters, including the lead role in *Sam Abramovitch* (1926), a play about a Jewish immigrant's rise to wealth and affluence, from the steppes of Russia to New York. The play was performed at the famed Belasco Theatre in New York; in a review of the play he was said to have spoken the verses "rhythmically across the footlights" (J. Brooks Atkinson, "The Play," *[New York?] Times*, January 20, 1927, De Cordoba portfolio, Players Collection).

De Cordoba also took an interesting political stand. In June 1929, while a member of the Actors' Equity Council, he became the first actor in New York to refuse to appear in a talking picture, in support of an Equity ruling that sound films had to be Equity shops. De Cordoba died in his home in 1950, at the age of sixty-eight, of an apparent heart attack. He was found dead in his easy chair, a prayer book in his lap opened to the mass he was scheduled to narrate that Sunday morning on radio (Pedro de Cordoba obituary, *[New York?] Times*, September 18, 1950, De Cordoba clippings file).

De Cordoba was a most accomplished and complex man whose long career in film is hardly remembered. In some ways, he was the Jose Ferrer of his time, although he never garnered an Academy Award for his acting. The two men shared versatility in both serious theater and film and played a variety of characters with supreme skill. Both were men of serious convictions who acted upon those convictions. And neither of them ever changed his name.

Antonio Moreno

The rise of Antonio Moreno (1888–1967) straddles the second and third decades of the twentieth century. Moreno began his career in 1912 or 1913, but it was not until the twenties that he became a major star. Born in Madrid as Antonio Garrido Monteagudo Moreno, he came to New York at the age of fourteen and completed his studies at the Williston

Antonio Moreno, a leading marquee star, made more than 146 films. This is a 1923 photo of him from the top fan magazine of the time, *Photoplay*, in which articles and photos of him appeared regularly.

Seminary in Northampton, Massachusetts. While in Madrid, he had studied at the Catholic Sisters School and in public schools (*Motion Picture News Studio Directory* 1917). He was a megastar in his time. His career spanned more than forty years, during which time he made more than 146 movies, playing the lead opposite such stars as Greta Garbo (*The Temptress* [1926]), Pola Negri (*The Spanish Dancer* [1923]), Gloria Swanson (*My American Wife* [1922]), Dorothy Gish (*Madame Pompadour* [1927]), and Clara Bow *(It)*. He also directed four films: *Revolución* (1933), *Águilas frente al Sol* (Eagles across the Sun) (1932), *Santa* (1932), and *The Veiled Mystery* (1920). He died in Beverly Hills, California, in 1967, after a lengthy illness, at the ripe old age of eighty.

During the twenties, Moreno was an important and familiar figure, at the apex of his career and of Hollywood society. However, as the twenties drew to a close, he became one of the major casualites in the transition to sound movies, as is evident in the steep decline in the number of pictures he made in the 1930s. Very likely his accent, tone, and the declining box-office appeal of the Latin lover all contributed to his fall. While he was at the top of his wave of success, however, Moreno rode very high indeed, as reflected in media coverage of him in the twenties. In addition to the numerous large color photos that appeared of him, he was also the subject of a great many extensive articles. Although some of the details were clearly fabricated, the positioning, story lines, and framing of the stories clearly stamped Tony Moreno as the most celebrated celebrity of the moment. He was the "It" boy, the one everyone wanted. His was the Hollywood life starlets dreamed of and readers envied.

Moreno's house was described as "the most beautiful home in Hollywood," with "tapestried furniture, golden-hued velvet hangings and oriental rugs. . . . Walls are tinted in a soft grey-ivory and the lofty ceilings are of dark wood that is polished and inlaid." The description makes reference to his ethnicity: "Tony's bed room is Spanish in color and type. Curtains and velvet spread are of gold and scarlet, the carved furniture is gayly upholstered in tapestry, and the bed, itself, is an early century importation from the land of olives and mantillas" ("The Most Beautiful Home in Hollywood" 1924, 68–69). A 1923 article notes his investment of "several hundred thousand dollars in Mexican petroleum oil fields" ("What Rich Stars Do with Their Money" 1923, 23). This sort of media association of Latinos with extreme wealth would disappear in subsequent eras.

Antonio Moreno held an enviable social position in Hollywood. A 1926 article describes "two friendly rival hostesses, Mrs. Antonio Moreno and Mrs. Earle Williams . . . striving for the social leadership of Hollywood." The two were seen to be in a contest for "the social crown," but it was the Morenos' "hilltop palace" that was singled out. The language used is similar to that in the Hollywood media spins accompanying today's accounts of rich and famous figures of the past and present: "[The Moreno house is] designed for entertaining upon a large scale so that forty people can dine in the apple green dining room without feeling at all crowded, and two hundred people can dance in the huge drawing room with the greatest comfort. . . . Everything moves perfectly, but without any apparent effort. . . . You can wander off into the library with a book, you can stay all evening in a corner talking politics with Charlie Chaplin, you can dance in the long corridor with—or play bridge in perfect quiet in the little drawing room with—" (York 1926, 36–37, 156).

The article drops names of the many important Hollywood dignitaries a visitor could casually encounter at the Morenos' home—Charlie Chaplin, Sam Goldwyn, Norma Shearer, and others. Interestingly enough, in a *Photoplay* account appearing four years later—at about the time that sound films began to take the lead and Tony's career began to dive—Mrs. Moreno has turned her beautiful mansion into a school for girls, and she and Tony are living in a small apartment while building a modest little home. The new contenders for the social crown are Marion Davies and Mary Pickford (Albert 1930).

Despite a ten-year marriage (1923–33) and his reputation as a Latin lover, Tony Moreno was gay. He initially resisted the pressure from his studio (and possibly from his agent as well) to marry for the sake of his public image, but eventually he gave in, and Daisy Canfield Danziger was selected to play the part. "I don't suppose anyone would call Mrs. Moreno a beauty," reports one writer at the time. "But she is lovely, she is graceful, she wears the divinest clothes, the most exquisite jewels, she has the manner of a queen or a gentlewoman. She has understanding, she has intellect, she has endless tact." Moreover, as "the daughter of the first oil king of California," Daisy had ostensibly "inherited an enormous fortune" (York 1926, 37). She was deemed worthy of Antonio, in a sense his social equal, and his choice of her spoke to his ability to respect, admire, and love a genteel, or "gentle," intelligent, though plain, woman. Daisy Moreno was a woman the readers could partially identify with and hope to emulate. (She died in 1933 when her car plunged off the road.)

Moreno seems to have identified closely with Spain, his country of origin, and was bothered by being mistakenly thought to be Latin American. He told *Motion Picture* magazine in 1924, "I am not Latin American, but in the North American mind, it's all the same. North Americans don't even distinguish between a Spanish and Italian surname, if it ends in *o* or *a*" (quoted in Hadley-Garcia 1993, 29).

Ramon Novarro

Another marquee idol in this period was Ramon Novarro (1899–1968). He was born José Ramon Samaniegos in Durango, Mexico. Rumors and family lore variously describe his family as having been in Greece centuries earlier, having sailed with Cortez to Mexico, and having descended from Montezuma. What is known for certain is that his paternal grandfather was the first Mexican city councilman of El Paso, Texas, and that his father attended high school in Las Cruces, New Mexico, before earning his degree in dentistry from the University of Pennsylvania. His mother came from a family of prosperous landowners of Spanish and Aztec descent. His immediate family was large and religious. Off and on, Novarro considered entering the religious life, as three of his sisters had done. As a child, he put on plays for his family and their friends in a marionette theater he had received as a gift, but he had done no formal stage work before coming to Hollywood. Throughout his life, he retained close ties with his family; indeed, the two Spanish-language films he produced are often referred to as "family affairs" because so many members of his family were involved in their creation.

Novarro came to Los Angeles in 1915, at the age of sixteen, hoping to make music his life's work. Like Beatriz Michelena and Pedro de Cordoba, he would never lose his desire to become a concert singer; unlike them, however, he had had no stage training. His first years in Hollywood were difficult; he had to work at a variety of odd jobs to make ends meet. He appeared as an extra in more than one hundred films before he got his first credited role in 1922 (in *Mr. Barnes of New York*), under the name Ramon Samaniegos. By the time he made *The Prisoner of Zenda* later that year, with his mentor and subsequent lifelong friend, Rex Ingram, he was working as Ramon Novarro. This was an invented name; studio executives had altered the spelling of a common Spanish surname, Navarro, to make it more unique. "Samaniegos" was apparently considered too hard to pronounce, and the studio heads thought it sounded like "ham and eggs"—or, as Ramon later said when he sought to change his name officially, "salmon eggs and things like that" (cited in Ellenberger 1999, 24).

Interestingly, it took a while for the studios and fan magazines to get Novarro's story straight. His official studio biography falsely claimed that he was a Spaniard and that his father had died—though he was still very much alive. A 1922 article in *Photoplay* made clear that the star's birthplace was Mexico and that his name had been changed to Novarro. However, even this article got a few things wrong: the headline urges readers to "Get Out Your Maps! And look up 'Buango.' Never heard of it? Neither did we. But it's destined for immortality." "'Buango!' they thrill," the article gushes. "'*He* was born there'" ("Get Out Your Maps!" 1922, 77). But readers would never find "Buango" on a map; Novarro was

Ramon Novarro was a screen idol and huge box-office draw all over the world. In 1924 he was chosen by a jury of the major female stars as first on the list of "great lovers of the screen." By 1929 he had such star power that he was able to negotiate a contract that rivaled only that of Al Jolson with regard to latitude. He is shown here in *The Prisoner of Zenda* (1922), in which he played an evil nobleman.

born in Durango.

The inaccuracies of his legend, of course, did no harm to his career. Ramon Novarro was a huge box-office draw and was highly celebrated for both his good looks and his acting ability. Even the respected journalist Adela Rogers St. Johns was struck by Novarro's "lyric charm, poetical charm, plus the beauty of a Greek boy. Think of him when you read of Keats, when you read of Byron, when you read Romeo and Juliet" (cited in Ellenberger 1999, 70). By 1923 he was receiving thirteen hundred fan letters a week (cited ibid., 28). By the time his next picture, *Scaramouche*, was released later that year, he was being described as a matinee idol, and his success was said to earn him a million dollars a year. One year later, he was ranked by a jury of the leading female stars of the day—Gloria Swanson, Pola Negri, Mary Astor, Alice Terry, Barbara La Marr, Constance Talmadge, Alma Rubens, and Norma Talmadge—at the top of the list of "great lovers of the screen" ("Great Lovers of the Screens" 1924, 28–29). The major production company in Germany, UFA Studios, wanted him to play the title role in the 1926 film rendition of the Goethe poem, *Faust*, but had to make the film without him, as he decided against this offer.

His popularity extended throughout the world, and he often had to travel in disguise in Europe and elsewhere. He was mobbed by thousands of fans in Mexico, Rio de Janeiro, Uruguay, and Buenos Aires. By 1929 his star power was such that he was able to negotiate a contract that rivaled only Al Jolson's in the latitude allowed. Even as late as 1937, when he had somewhat retired from film, he was still receiving bags of fan mail each week from all over the world, demanding his return to the silver screen.

Ramon Novarro was not just a pretty face. He was involved in the purchase and development of real estate. Fluent in English, Spanish, French, and Italian, he enjoyed reading, travel, and the opera. He directed, acted in, and composed the music for the French and Spanish versions of *Call of the Flesh* (*Le Chanteur de Seville* [1930] and *La Sevillana*

[1931]). He eventually formed his own production company and wrote the screenplay for a Spanish-language film he made, *Contra la Corriente* (1936).

Nor was he typecast into a single mold. Novarro did play a number of roles as sheik and Latin lover, and he was sometimes referred to (and referred to himself) as a Latin lover. Nevertheless, in his time he was most recognized for his leading roles in other films, including the epic film *Ben-Hur* (1925), in which he played a Jewish prince, and *Scaramouche* (1923), in which he played a Frenchman during the French Revolution.

Novarro maintained close personal ties with the Latin community. The state-of-the-art theater he built in his home could accommodate sixty people in addition to an orchestra. He gave it a Spanish name, Teatro Intimo (Intimate Theater), and on his parents' thirty-fourth wedding anniversary he celebrated its opening. Invitations were sent out in Spanish. The guest list was composed of family, friends, columnists, priests, artists, musicians, and government officials, including representatives of the president of Mexico. Novarro presented a revue that day consisting of one-act plays, songs, and dances performed entirely in Spanish by younger members of the Los Angeles Latin community. The opening was a success, and over the next ten years his theater would host many such concerts. Novarro was personally friendly with other Latin actors in Hollywood at the time—including Gilbert Roland, Antonio Moreno, Lupe Velez, Anita Page, and Dolores Del Rio, who was his cousin. He also participated in benefit performances to aid the survivors of disasters in Mexico. Finally, he made two Spanish-language films, *Contra la Corriente* and *La Virgen que Forjó una Patria* (1942) (released in English in 1944 as *The Saint Who Forged a Country*)—his contribution to Mexico's film industry. The latter film was so successful in Mexico and other Latin American countries that the president of Mexico decorated Novarro, saying his performance had contributed to religious patriotism.

Like Antonio Moreno, Ramon Novarro was gay; unlike Moreno, Novarro refused to give in to studio pressures to marry. Nonetheless, he did go along with the studio policy to keep his preference for men from public view. However, when asked about marriage, he said, "That's one mistake I've never made." Aging was difficult for Novarro. "One of the things I want to tell about in my book," he said, "is how hard it is to grow old, when you've been at the top" (cited in Ellenberger 1999, 176). His book was never completed. Aging was only one of the problems Novarro encountered in his later years, however. He developed a severe problem with alcoholism and was arrested several times for driving under the influence.

Ramon Novarro met a grisly and tragic end in 1968, when he was savagely murdered at his home by two men who sought to rob him of five thousand dollars. He was found naked and bound, having received twenty-two different injuries and lacerations on his face and head; the initial N or Z had been carved on his neck. Blood dripping into his throat from his broken nose had drained into his lungs, and he had drowned in his own blood. On the bedroom mirror was written in brown stick makeup, "Us girls are better than fagits." (This was a year before the Manson gang murdered Sharon Tate.) Two brothers, Paul and Tom Ferguson, were convicted of the murder, but both were released for different reasons before their life sentences had been completed. Neither served more than nine years for the crime. Novarro's homosexuality was an undercurrent in the trial (Ellenberger 1999, 179–94).

Dolores Del Rio

Dolores Del Rio (1905–83) is referred to by present-day writers as the first Latina superstar. In her time, she was one of the top ten moneymakers in Hollywood. Her career spanned more than half a century (1925–78) and comprised starring roles in more than fifty-five films in the United States, Mexico, Argentina, and Europe. She played a variety of leading roles, from European aristocrat to "native" girl to European peasant. Press descriptions of Dolores early in her career use the words "sophisticated," "aristocratic," "refined elegance," "glam-orous," "sedate," and "ladylike"—not "hot tamale," not "sul-try," not "hot cha cha!" References to her clothes were often similar. Nonetheless, she managed to retain her "Latin-ness" in the eyes of the public: Press coverage regularly referred to her Mexican origins. For all these reasons, she enjoyed wide popularity, as the caption to a 1929 magazine photo of her indi-cates: "Photoplay's mail bags have been jammed with letters from New Orleans and Pittsburgh and Washington singing the praises of the charm and beauty of the lovely star of Evangeline" (photo caption, *Photoplay*, October 1929, 19).

The public images of most film stars are carefully culti-vated and maintained. Del Rio's image was no exception. But her star power—the combination of her looks, talent, and historical context—makes her story especially interesting. Fortunately, hers is also well documented, because more has been written on Dolores Del Rio than on any of the other early Latin stars.

Del Rio's is a captivating story. She was born Dolores de Martínez Asúnsolo y López Negrete in Durango, Mexico, the only child of a banker. Her family fled to Mexico City to escape Pancho Villa, who had seized their home and her father's bank. Her father's family came from the Basque Provinces in Spain but had been in Mexico for a number of generations; her mother's family was of mixed Spanish and Indian ancestry. In Mexico City, the young Dolores was sent to a convent school run by French nuns, and when she was seven years old she began taking lessons in Spanish dance. In 1921, at the age of fif-teen, she married Jaime del Río, a man from a more socially prominent family and eighteen years her senior. Although they divorced in 1928, soon after her career took off, Dolores later said that Jaime had been the most positive person in her life: "If I could appreciate anything, if I knew anything, I owed it to him." However, by 1928 she realized that despite the love they felt for each other, they had taken on their "own destin[ies]." She could not "suddenly cancel" her career while he pursued his still incipient writing career (cited in Gómez-Sicre 1967, 14).

Dolores Del Rio (shown here circa 1933) was one of the top ten moneymakers in Hollywood. She did not know English when she first
arrived from Mexico and had to have the director's instructions
delivered through interpreters.

While she and Jaime were married, Dolores had taken on
the social role appropriate to her class position; with her husband's encouragement, she had also performed "intimate
ballets," which she choreographed, for friends and family. It
was at one of these social occasions, in 1925, that Edwin
Carewe, the well-known Hollywood director, saw Dolores
dance and invited her to come to Hollywood to appear in his
films. (She was, in this sense, discovered, just as Rosie Perez

and others would later be discovered, while dancing.) After numerous requests from Carewe, the del Ríos finally agreed to go to Hollywood. Jaime del Río thought he might pursue a career there as a screenwriter, and both were interested in the excitement associated with the move. Still, as Dolores later recalled, her social set had a different view of the decision to go to Hollywood. It was a scandalous thing to do: A lady would not think of becoming a motion picture actress. It had never been done before. Dolores's reply to this objection was, "Very well, I will be the first" (Bodeen 1976, 283).

Like many girls at the time, Dolores loved the movies, wrote to the stars, read movie magazines, and collected photographs. Her photo collection was rich, especially in the tragic Italians. She also admired Mary Pickford, Gloria Swanson, and Norma Talmadge. In a later interview, she recalled her thoughts about the move to Hollywood: "I didn't know what would happen but I thought it would be fun to meet all the people I idolized—like Chaplin and Valentino" (Byrne 1981, 32). In the Pullman car that took her from Mexico to California, she did not for a moment imagine that she would become a leading Hollywood actress. Little did Dolores know that she would come to work for the same company and soon be the object of an equally adoring public. Nor did she anticipate that her idol, Rudolf Valentino, would be the only artist who could understand her Spanish when she was first introduced on the set. Actually, because she did not know English when she began, the director's instructions were delivered to her through interpreters. That was the amazing thing about film in the early days: Because it was silent, language was no barrier; anyone could understand the acting. It was a truly international medium, and it developed early on in different countries throughout the world.

Del Rio's transformation into a Hollywood starlet was fast, but it was not without effort. Her manager, Edwin Carewe, and Henry Wilson, a Hollywood publicist, provided a continuous supply of stories and photos presenting Dolores as glamorous, aristocratic, and highborn, with a convent education and European training in ballet and art. Although the general picture was accurate, some features were a bit stretched—she was described as having been the richest girl in Mexico, for example, whereas in fact her husband had lost much of his money because of a cotton crop failure. Nevertheless, her popularity grew. Great attention was paid in the press to her hair: "Many heads have turned at a smart Hollywood opening to gaze admiringly at the sleek, long-haired beauty of Dolores Del Rio. She always strikes a definite note in any gathering with the simplicity with which she dresses her hair. Never a wave disturbs the off-screen contour of her head. Drawn severely from her forehead, her hair is coiled simply at the nape of her neck" (Wilson 1931, 28–30). Del Rio's hairstyle was symbolic of her contrast with others of the day—as, perhaps, was her association with what was old-fashioned but sophisticated, sleek, and classic.

Within a few years of her arrival in Hollywood, Del Rio was a major hit. In 1927, one article in *Photoplay* describes her as "the present leader of the Latin invasion whose sudden success has been equaled only by the Scandinavian Greta Garbo and the American Clara Bow" (cited in Hershfield 2000, 13). Her success was phenomenal, especially given the context within which it occurred. In a short period of time she came to command a substantial salary and to exercise control in her choice of films, scripts, and camera angles.

There were also many transformations along the way. For screen purposes, the small *d* in "del Rio" was capitalized. When films were made in Spanish, another actress was hired; the studio reserved its star for the English-speaking public. (From 1930 to 1935 and then again in 1938 and 1939, Hollywood produced Spanish-language films in an attempt to retain Latin markets, which were threatened by the advent of talkies.) When Dolores first arrived in Hollywood as a young Mexican matron of twenty, the film colony found her "interesting" and "pretty in a foreign way" but "kinda dowdy" and "too sedate" (Carr 1979, 13). In the press, she was described as a feminine woman who preferred long hair and had a certain softness about her. This was in contrast to the bobbed hair, slim sheaths, and short hems of the fashionable American flapper of the time. In some respects, she represented a "traditional woman" but also a foreign and upper-class woman with impeccable morals.

Her success as a Hollywood beauty in the mid-twenties is sometimes seen as an anomaly. In the twenties and thirties, according to some observers, blondes were usually thought to photograph best, and thus they were preferred in film. Del Rio, with her olive skin and black eyes, was a rarity. On the other hand, the silent-screen era was also an era of faces: As the character Norma Desmond reminisces in the movie classic *Sunset Boulevard* (1950), "We had faces then." Dolores had one of those fabulous faces. The internationally known photographer Baron George Hoyningen-Huene ranked her second only to Garbo and, in 1934, said that though she wore less makeup than any star he had ever met, her vividness was breathtaking: "The bone structure of her head and body is magnificent. . . . Her face is so perfectly constructed that she can be photographed in any light, at any angle. Wherever the light falls, it composes beauty" (quoted ibid., 28).

If distinctive faces were indispensable in the silent-screen star system, the more uncommon the face, the more efffective it could be: Those with more exotic looks could give "a sharper flavor to the parade of startling faces." Moreover, the prevailing interest in romantic flavor led to the appreciation of human beauty and of the exotic. Established stars such as Pola Negri, Theda Bara, Nita Naldi, Barbara La Marr, and Valentino created a cinematic setting in which Dolores Del Rio could readily find a place (ibid., 11, 5–20).

Dolores's image evolved from the richly Mexican look she brought to Hollywood in the mid-twenties to a more modern style, sophisticated and glamorous. By the early thirties, she had discarded the soft-focus prettiness of the previous decade. "She . . . cut her long hair, enlarged the shape of her mouth, altered the style of her eyebrows, and emphasized her exquisite bone structure" (ibid., 13). In the film world by this time, the rosebud mouth and the pretty pastel beauty of the earlier period were gone, and in their place had come the face with planes, or the sculpted look. The camera exploited a change in style in makeup and lighting to foster a new kind of beauty, of which Del Rio was said to be a forerunner. Moreover, Dolores could wear to great advantage the latest fashions. Her skin, which was described as "silky beautiful" and of the "palest café au lait" color, and her figure, which was slim but with "aristocratic bearing," made her "a designer's dream" (ibid., 20). Indeed, at this point, she wore only high-style clothes—both on-screen and off—that suggested no particular national origin. Her wardrobe established her as "one of Hollywood's Best Dressed Women." From the start of her career in Hollywood, fan writers and the press found her "as dazzling in appearance as she was gracious in manner" (ibid., 5).

In the early thirties, when Hollywood set the fashion pace in a way that has not been repeated anywhere since, it was said that Del Rio always dressed like a star. Women all over the world copied her makeup and dress. It was during this period that Orson Welles fell in love with Del Rio—with her image on the screen, that is. As he recalled to his biographer, after seeing her in *Bird of Paradise* "I just waited till I could find her. Oh, I was *obsessed* with her for years!" Later, when they became romantically involved in the early forties, Welles felt she represented everything that was glamorous about Hollywood. She always seemed to be impeccably made up and ready to face her adoring public (Lemming 1984, 207, 265).

In keeping with her new image, Dolores altered her choice of roles. Earlier, she had played a variety of leading ladies, including some exotic leading ladies—for example, the title role in *The Loves of Carmen* (1927), a "half-breed" Native American in *Ramona* (1928), and a South Sea island princess in *Bird of Paradise* (1932). In 1933 she struck an agreement with RKO Studios giving her the power to approve her own scripts. She now refused to wear exotic clothes and sought roles that conveyed modernity and sophistication—roles that would reflect the star image that was being advanced in the press at the time and was made visually obvious by her wardrobe. Her marriage

Dolores Del Rio (shown here circa 1935) created a wardrobe that established her as one of Hollywood's best-dressed women. Known for her sophisticated, aristocratic, elegant, and glamorous Art Deco style, her makeup and dress were copied by women all over the world.

to Cedric Gibbons (1930–41) coincided with, and further facilitated, this shift in image to a more chiseled, sophisticated, and modern Del Rio. Gibbons, a well-known art director—he was founder and chair of the original Academy Awards committee and also the designer of the Oscar statuette—designed and built a house to reflect their personalities. Photographs of Dolores set against the background of this house were commonly found in news outlets of the time. "Every line, every detail, every stick of furnishing were worked out in the brain of that ace interior decorator and master of the household, Cedric Gibbons, as the perfect background for his exotic and darkly lovely wife" (cited in Rodríguez-Estrada 1997, 489, n. 25).

Despite this transformation from the Mexican shawl to the fur, Del Rio continued to feel strongly about her heritage and her desire to play Mexican roles. In her earliest introduction to Hollywood, "Spanish actress" had been appended to her name. She had had to insist for quite a while to get the adjective changed to "Mexican." She never relinquished her Mexican citizenship and said in 1929, at the height of her popularity, "Someday I would like to play a Mexican woman and show what life in Mexico really is. No one has shown the artistic side—nor the social" (quoted in Carr 1979, 32). A year later, she expressed similar sentiments regarding the roles she played on stage: "I'd love to appear in fine, emotional dramas . . . and am eager to play in stories concerning my native people, the Mexican race. It is my dearest wish to make fans realize their real beauty, their wonder, their greatness as a people. The vast majority seem to regard Mexicans as a race of bandits, or laborers, dirty, unkempt and uneducated. My ambition is to show the best that's in my nation" (quoted ibid., 42). She also displayed a clear awareness of the racialized casting that characterized Hollywood films, noting that those with light skin could play any nationality, whereas dark-skinned actors played only servants and villains. (Villains were portrayed by both light- and dark-skinned people in darker blackface or brownface.)

By the late thirties, however, fewer offers came her way,

and the parts she was offered were often conventionally exotic secondary roles that she quickly turned down. She rarely got parts that offered opportunities for character probing. As has been the case with many other film stars, her physical beauty was highlighted to the neglect of her dramatic ability. As she later recalled, "I was forced to do glamour parts and I hated it" (quoted ibid., 32). She eventually left Hollywood for Mexico, where she felt she could exercise more control over her acting career: "I wish to chose my own stories, my own director, and camera man. I can accomplish this better in Mexico" (quoted in Rodríguez-Estrada 1997, 481). Other variables undoubtedly figured in this decision. The 1934 Production Code of the Motion Picture Industry, which defined the parameters on sexuality in film, was now strongly enforced, effectively limiting the kind of part she could play. She had not captured the public as a dancer or singer—a seeming prerequisite for the new era of "good neighbors" that emerged during World War II. There were other personal variables, as well: Her father died; she divorced her husband, Cedric Gibbons, in 1940; and she broke off her wedding engagement to Orson Welles. She was also getting older and facing the age barrier that still hinders the later careers of most Hollywood stars.

Del Rio returned to Mexico in 1943, where she received top billing in Mexican movies and became known as the First Lady of Mexican theater. She also acted in international films in 1947 and 1948 and made films and television appearances in the United States from 1960 to 1977. She received numerous awards, including Mexico's equivalent to the Oscar three times and Spain's equivalent once. Interestingly, her image underwent another radical shift when she began to appear in Mexican films. Now working in an industry with a notably nationalist agenda, she became part of Mexico's political-cultural project. In many of her films, she played a similar character, the beautiful, self-sacrificing, nationalistic, indigenous woman—a sharp contrast to the roles she had played in Hollywood.

At the age of seventy-six, reflecting on her career, Del Rio

After an exceptional career in Hollywood, Dolores Del Rio returned to Mexico, where she became known as "the First Lady of Mexican theater." She is shown here in *María Candelaria* (1946).

said she had left Hollywood because for nearly a decade she had been cast only in glamour roles.

> The Hollywood producers forgot I was an actress. . . . At first I was thrilled—a chance to wear lovely clothes—I even cut my hair to become modern. . . . But by 1940 I knew I couldn't build a satisfying career on glamour, so I came home. My father had died, and I felt a need for my country, my people. . . .
>
> I didn't want to be a star anymore, I wanted to be an actress and with all of those gowns they put on me, all of those millions of feathers, I couldn't be. I chose instead the chance to be a pioneer in the movie industry of my county, an exciting new challenge. (Quoted in O'Connor 1981, 69.)

She later recalled, "When I returned to Mexico, I joined with people eager to create the Mexican cinema. . . . We were full of dreams and had no money whatsoever, but we were able to achieve something [to] open markets for our films all over the world." She also reflected on the personal costs of her career: "I gave 50 years to my career, it was number one, two and three in my life, the thing I lived for. Everything I did was with my career in mind. I was very honest with my career, but there was a lot of personal sacrifice. . . . There were tears and pain" (Byrne 1981, 32).

Nevertheless, Dolores seemed to be at peace in her senior years. She started a nursery in 1975 for the children of working actresses, which was open twenty-four hours a day—the first of its kind (Froio 1975, 10). Here children from two weeks to six years of age were cared for while their mothers were on the job acting, singing, or dancing. "We play Brahms and Bach to them, teach them English, folklorico dancing—all the arts. I put in lots of hard work there, but they are happy hours. And I love playing with the children." Social work, she said, brought her "great happiness" (quoted in O'Connor 1981, 71).

In her mid-seventies, this woman whose "ageless beauty" had been so extolled over the years advised younger women, "Do not be afraid of age! . . . Those are wonderful years. Use them! At a certain age, look in the mirror and say, 'I am old, and I'm going to make the very best of it.' What age? You'll know, everyone gets old at a different age. You're bound to have neglected many parts of yourself during years of home-making, acting, striving to become head of the office. Find them! Fill yourself with them" (quoted ibid.).

Dolores Del Rio died in 1983 of liver failure in Newport Beach, California. It is unfortunate that so few of her Mexican and European films—which allowed her to show her true talent and development as a serious artist—have had any national showings outside of those countries. Like Katharine Hepburn, she is remembered as an actress who brought dignity and beauty to both the leading and character parts she played and one who portrayed women of all social classes with ease.

Lupe Velez

Like Del Rio, Lupe Velez began her career in the silent-film era and was similarly "discovered" in Mexico, though here the similarities ended. The two women came from different backgrounds, had different Hollywood experiences, and evolved quite contrasting public personas. Yet physically they were not all that dissimilar, and because they were both from Mexico and in Hollywood at the same time, comparison is hard to avoid.

Lupe Velez (1908–44) was born María Guadalupe Vélez de Villalobos in San Luis Potosí, Mexico. Her mother had been an opera singer. Her father, an officer in the military, thought that his spirited and rambunctious daughter needed more structure, and so, at the age of thirteen, she was sent to study at a convent school in San Antonio, Texas. Lupe later summed up this period of her life in characteristically straightforward talk: "Studied English. Liked to dance. Guess I wasn't much of a success as a student" (Parish 1974, 592). Her father died in a military skirmish two years later, and Lupe returned home to help support her mother and younger siblings. She worked as a sales girl, and after investing thirty-seven cents a session for dancing lessons, she became a featured dancer in a local musical revue. It was here that the aging matinee idol Richard Bennett caught her act, in 1925, and invited her to come to Hollywood to audition for his new production, *The Dove*.

When Velez first attempted to leave Mexico for Hollywood, she was refused admittance to the United States because she was under age; the same thing had happened to Ramon Novarro when he first tried to cross the border. "All the way back to Mexico City I cried," she later recalled, "but I'd show them. I *would* get to Hollywood some way." She appealed to Mexico's president, to the ministers, "to everybody in Mexico City. After a lot of letter writing between Mexico City and Washington and what you call 'red tape' they said I could cross the border." When she arrived in

Hollywood, however, she encountered further difficulties: Her money was stolen on the train "by a nice man who held her hand," and she was rejected for the part because she was too inexperienced in acting and looked too young for the part (opposite a fifty-three-year-old actor) (cited ibid., 593).

She did manage to get a job in the Los Angeles Music Box Revue; her performance so impressed the producer Hal Roach that he signed her to a contract in 1926. She then appeared as an extra in comedy shorts before getting her first starring role as a "mountain girl," at the age of seventeen, opposite Douglas Fairbanks Sr. in *The Gaucho* (1927). The film was well received by both the public and critics. When asked about her reaction to this "overnight success" and "sensational splash," Lupe replied, "Was I happy when *The Gaucho* opened and the public was nice to Lupe? Not happy—delirious!" (quoted ibid., 595). It is hard to say how much command Lupe had over the English language at this point, though it is clear that her accent and broken English were purposely accentuated, both onstage and off, by the press and by Lupe herself, as a "viable gimmick" (ibid.).

Soon after the release of *The Gaucho*, Lupe was selected as a WAMPA baby and made her second major film, *Stand and Deliver* (1928), in which she played a Greek peasant girl, for the Cecil B. DeMille division of Pathé Pictures. Her next film, *The Lady of the Pavements* (1929), was directed by D. W. Griffith and would be remembered for its image of the Smoking Dog Café. Here, Lupe, as the café's chanteuse, sings for the first time a number of now-classic Irving Berlin songs. She then appeared in *A Wolf Song* (1929), playing Lola Salazar, an upper-class señorita in 1840s Taos, New Mexico. She appeared opposite Gary Cooper, who played a Kentucky farm boy torn between his love for Lola (Lupe) and the lure of the hunt, the mountains, and the open range. In the end, Cooper's character returns to Lola, who succeeds in domesticating him into a settled, married, family man. Lupe made her first all-talking picture *(Tiger Rose)* in 1929 and began to take leading roles in the Spanish versions of English-language

Lupe Velez, who during her career appeared on the cover of more than nineteen national and international magazines, began her career in the silent era. She headlined eight movies as Carmelita Woods, a Mexican spitfire who possessed great charm and comedic talent. She is shown here in a 1928 photo.

films produced by Universal Studios in Hollywood during this time. She went on to star in films by Carl Laemmle and Cecil B. DeMille and in the sound version of *Resurrección* (1931)—a film that had been one of Del Rio's major commercial successes during the silent era. As the industry switched to sound production, however, Lupe became increasingly confined to fiery supporting roles, although these characters were sometimes of different ethnicities.

Lupe's public image came to parallel the tempestuousness of the characters she played, as can be seen in a number of full-page color photos of her that appeared in popular magazines. A 1928 fan-magazine photo shows her in soft light, dressed in muted colors; her hair is pulled back, her shoulders are covered, and her expression is somewhat ambiguously posed between serious and vampish—perhaps determined. She is described as "witty" and "generous," without reference to her ethnicity, and the magazine wishes her luck (photo caption, *Photoplay*, October 1928, 21). Elsewhere, she is described as "the Hot Baby of Hollywood" (*Photoplay*, February 1929, 141). Other photos suggest the future "Mexican spitfire": In another 1928 photo she is suggestively bare shouldered and heavily made up, with tousled short hair; her come-hither smile resonates with the caption, "just a Mexican wild kitten." A wild kitten, perhaps, but a friendly one as well: She is described as having "so much ease and spontaneity that it's hard to believe she is a novice before the camera" (photo caption, *Photoplay*, February 1928, 21).

In a photo published a few months later, her pose is even more sexually enticing, a fur coat casually draped over the upper part of her body insinuating nudity. The caption describes her as "Mexico's IT girl" (photo caption, *Photoplay*, April 1928, 62). A photo of Lupe the following year harks back to the early roles she played, as a traditionally dressed but fun-loving señorita who draws the attention of many men (photo caption, *Photoplay*, January 1929, 75). Another again evokes the kittenish Mexican vamp, who, as the caption suggests, is a scene (or film) stealer. Interestingly, this caption also implicitly gives her credit for having survived the shift to talkies despite her accent (photo caption, *Photoplay*, July 1929, 20). A headline asks, "What would you call the players if you knew them that well?"; the caption to a baby picture of Lupe answers, "Her name would be 'Becka'" (Parsons 1931, 80–81).

This variety of images in promotional photos was matched by the variety of products she advertised. Lupe and her "friends in pictures" drink College Inn Tomato Juice Cocktail (*Photoplay*, December 1930, 134). She advises readers to "enrich your beauty with really natural [Princess Pat] rouge" (*Photoplay*, May 1932, 107). Lux toilet soap "keeps her skin like velvet" (*Photoplay*, May 1928, 76); and it is the "Lady Pepperell colored sheets that make Lupe Velez' bedroom express her personality" (*Photoplay*, April 1929, 80). She takes "the pause that refreshes" with Coca Cola (*Photoplay*, May 1932, 22) and says that Lucky Strike cigarettes "are certainly kind to my throat" (*Photoplay*, April 1932, inside front page). Having played a Russian peasant in *Resurrección*, she appears in a full-page ad for *Photoplay's Famous Cook Book* (which contains 150 favorite recipes of the stars) that includes Lupe's best Russian recipes. The ad, entitled "Russian Recipes via Mexico," shows Lupe in Russian costume brewing tea in a samovar (*Photoplay*, January 1931, 81).

Lupe Velez—at least as presented to the public—was a woman of contrasts: on the one hand, free, fun loving, captivating, energetic, and expansive, a woman to be emulated; and on the other, the vamp, the wildcat, the vixen. Dolores Del Rio was never referred to in the latter terms; in both her screen roles and her press image, she displayed the ladylike qualities of elegance, decorum, and reserve. Del Rio was internationally exotic; Velez was decidedly ethnic and sexualized. Lupe was the engaging girl who could be quickly fired to anger and could unleash her pent-up emotions in a barrage of physical assaults on her male target (O'Neil 2000). In her later films, she displayed an aggressive, unrefined personality that permitted yelling and physical contact, behavior not generally displayed by the Anglo women characters in her films—unless, of course, Lupe's antics drove them to such extremes. These contrasting images of Lupe would become solidified in her later Mexican Spitfire movie series. In the second film of this series, Elizabeth, the Anglo female character, even refers to her as the "little Mexican wildcat." At the same time, she also retains in these movies the comical, fun-loving, sympathetic, and spunky qualities that endeared her to audiences. Lupe's Mexican-ness is also further underscored in the series by her heavy accent and grammatically flawed English.

Like Dolores Del Rio, Lupe shifted to a more modern image toward the end of the decade. However, the course of her transformation was portrayed quite differently in the media. The free-spirited Velez was seen to have attempted, but not quite accomplished, the shift; moreover, the alteration was seen to show that she was getting merely smarter, not tamer. A reporter wrote in 1929, "Outwardly, Lupe has changed. She curbs her tongue with people she doesn't know. To interviewers she talks in a dignified manner of her home, which she really loves, her dogs and her work. She dresses better. Gone are the little short pleated skirts and blouses cut almost to her waist. In her wardrobe hang gowns that any Park Avenue lady would be delighted to own. In them, of course, Lupe does not look like a Park Avenue lady, merely because she is too striking a type" (cited in Rodríguez-Estrada 1997, 482). One wonders what the reporter meant by "too striking a type," for clearly there were many "ladies" at the time who were quite striking—Eleanor Roosevelt, for example. Was the implication that Lupe was too ethnic, sexual, defiant, or open about her affairs? Or was she just not tame enough?

Whatever the case may be, adding to her public image as the Mexican hot tamale were the sparks ignited by her numerous romantic liaisons with well-known Hollywood stars. In the early thirties she was romantically involved (and often publicly linked) with Gary Cooper, Ronald Coleman, Gilbert Roland, John Gilbert, Arturo de Cordova, and Ricardo Cortez. One of her more serious long-term relationships was with Gary Cooper. When he brought Lupe home to meet his family,

Cooper's mother disapproved of his plan to marry her. Lupe's statement to the press was remarkable for its time—both in its honesty concerning his family and studio policies and in expressing her desire to be free of constraints and male domination. "I turned Cooper down," she informed the press in 1931, "because his parents didn't want me to marry him, and because the studio thought it would injure his career. Now it's over, I'm glad I feel so free. I went around New York, did whatever I wanted, had a fine time. . . . I must be free. I know men too well, they are all the same, no? If you love them, they want to be boss. I will never have a boss" (cited in Parish 1979, 598).

Her turbulent marriage to Johnny Weissmuller (the Tarzan of the time) received considerable press attention. Between the marriage in 1933 and the divorce in 1939, the couple separated three times. Each time, Lupe filed for divorce on the grounds of cruelty and physical and mental violence. Each time, she rescinded these claims.

Interestingly, Lupe apparently felt that she was misrepresented in the press, that she was far less impetuous and temperamental than people had been led to believe. Few writers accepted this view, however. Regardless of who was responsible for the public image, RKO refused to renew her contract in 1934 because of the attention brought on by her public fighting with Weissmuller. During the same year, she also took her film production company to court to collect a check owed her, and in 1935 she adopted the four-year-old child of her eldest sister. She then went abroad to make films, including one in Mexico, where more than ten thousand ecstatic fans greeted her return in 1938, after an eleven-year absence.

In 1939, following her divorce from Weissmuller, Velez began her Mexican Spitfire series. Although many see these films as B movies, the series was significant in a number of respects. The films were of sufficient interest to the public that eight were made in total. Indeed, Lupe's name and minimal presence in these pictures were sufficient to produce a tidy box-office profit. "RKO Studios had 'solid statistics' to demonstrate the success of her movies and this is why they decided to extend Velez's contract and make additional movies in the Mexican Spitfire series" (ibid., 619). The series was also seen to benefit from and contribute to the U.S. government's new Good Neighbor policy. The films were unique in their early treatment of mixed marriage and in the humor they poked at the prejudices surrounding mixed marriage, and they showed Lupe's comedic skills to good advantage. Finally, they were remarkable for being a series of films about a Latina character, Carmelita Woods, each of which was headlined by a Latina star. Few other Hollywood series can claim similar longevity—particularly with a female character—and even fewer in U.S. Latino film history.

In 1944 Lupe returned to Mexico (as had Dolores Del Rio before her) to make the film *Nana*. Once filming was over, she made plans for a new play in New York. On November 11, 1944, she announced her engagement to Harald Ramond, a relatively unknown twenty-seven-year-old French actor. Two weeks later, the gossip columnist Louella Parsons reported that the engagement was off. On December 13, 1944, after the Hollywood premiere of *Nana*, she told a friend, "I am weary with the whole world. People think that I like to fight. I have to fight for everything. I'm so tired of it all. Ever since I was a baby I've been fighting. I've never met a man with whom I didn't have to fight to exist" (cited ibid., 623).

Later that evening, Lupe Velez took a fatal overdose of sleeping pills. Unwed and five months pregnant, she left notes to Harald Ramond, the father of her child, and to Beulah Kinder, her confidant-housekeeper, explaining that she could not bring a child into this world burdened with shame. (She also suggested she would not want to harm the child, though just what she meant is not clear.)

For some, Lupe's death revealed personal limitations not often brought to light in her public life—in contrast to her independent, freedom-loving, devil-may-care attitude. Having become pregnant without benefit of marriage, her internalized Roman Catholic heritage may have made the option of abortion difficult even to consider. The prospect of living with the social stigma of unwed motherhood might have been equally unthinkable. Others guessed that she had just tired of it all; she felt that she and her child were not wanted by Ramond, and she just did not want to continue fighting.

The stars of silent films and the early talkies led fascinating lives, and they reached heights of fame and fortune that would be unconceivable in subsequent eras. There were other important Latin stars during this period, as well—Leo Carrillo, Gilbert Roland, Conchita Montenegro, Raquel Torres, Mona Rico, Donald Reed, Mona Maris, and Barry Norton, among others. The stars included foreign imports, homegrown Latins, and what would today be called transnationals. In the earliest period they tended to be of the homegrown variety—Myrtle Gonzalez, Beatriz Michelena, and Pedro de Cordoba, for example. Soon thereafter, foreigners arrived—Antonio Moreno (from Spain), Dolores Del Rio, (from Mexico), and Mona Maris (from Argentina), to name a few. Latin actors who had been born in the United States continued to appear—Leo Carrillo, Julian Rivero, and Charlie Chaplin's wife, Lita Grey (from California); Anita Page (from New York), and Don Alvarado (from New Mexico). Gilbert Roland, born in Juárez, Mexico, but raised in El Paso, Texas, is perhaps a good example of the transnational category. This curious combination of foreign, domestic, and transnational stars would continue to mark the Latin experience in subsequent decades in Hollywood film.

The "Good Neighbor" Era

As the Great Depression deepened in the late 1930s and as the world became increasingly involved in World War II, the stardust sprinkled on the former Latin luminaries began to fade. Talkies prevailed, and musicals increased in number. Latin lovers were less in evidence, supplanted by new leading men—rugged individualists whose leading ladies did not often stray far from the nonethnic "all-American" look of the time. With the exception of Lupe Velez, who came increasingly to play a stock Latina character, all of the stars discussed in the previous chapter experienced a downward turn in their Hollywood careers during the 1940s. In general, the top stars in Hollywood were not a diverse lot; nor did they reflect the nation's actual ethnic or racial makeup at the time. Rather, an antiethnic image of America came to prevail, and many have concluded that "movie classics preached an assimilationist, often sexist and racist, philosophy" (Friedman 1991, 2).

Rita Hayworth: Invisible Latins

Accordingly, it is not surprising to see that in this period some actors found it prudent, or beneficial, to relegate to the shadows their Hispanicity or Latinidad. The story of Rita Hayworth (1918–87) best personifies this compromise. Born in New York City as Margarita Carmen Cansino, Rita was the daughter of Eduardo Cansino, a Spanish flamenco dancer, who had immigrated to New York. There, in 1917, he married Rita's mother, Volga Hayworth, a showgirl of Irish and English extraction. From a very young age, Rita was trained to follow in the family's dancing tradition, and a Fox Studios head first saw her on stage when she was fifteen years old.

She made her English-language film debut at the age of sixteen, in *Dante's Inferno* (1935), and before launching her career as Rita Hayworth she made a number of other mainly B pictures under the Cansino name, playing many Mexican señoritas. Indeed, she had appeared earlier in a Spanish-lan-

The actress Margarita Cansino (pictured here circa 1935) would become Rita Hayworth.

Rita Hayworth, shown here in 1946 in *Gilda*, became known during this time as the "Love Goddess" and an "ethereal all-American girl."

guage short. It was the studio head of Columbia Pictures who anglicized her name and approved painful electrolysis treatments to draw back her hairline and thereby broaden her forehead. Having lost weight and dyed her hair red, Rita went on to become the "Love Goddess" and an "ethereal all-American girl" (Reyes and Rubie 1994, 418). It is a reflection of the times that her first major screen success was in a film called *The Strawberry Blond* (1941). She later acknowledged the significance of her altered image: "After I changed my name, the quality of roles offered to me improved greatly" (cited in Hadley-Garcia 1993, 58). She enjoyed immense popularity during the war era and was often cited as the favorite

GI pinup girl during the forties. Curiously, it was after the war and after her biggest film success in *Gilda* (1946) that her career began to decline. She died of Alzheimer's disease in 1987 at the age of sixty-eight.

The shift to more ethnically homogenous white Anglo-Saxon images was not just a "Latin" phenomenon. Many ethnicities became invisible or were remade during this era: The Jewish Danny Kaye, for instance, changed his name and dyed his hair blond, and he was generally not seen by the public as Jewish. There were scores of other examples. Moreover, there have probably always been Latinos (as well as others) who obscured or denied their ethnic origins; but it was in the "good-neighbor" era that this became a clear and successful strategy for Latino success. Other Latinos, such as Anthony Quinn and Raquel Welch, would follow the same route and become, in subsequent eras, principal actors whose Latinness would no longer be visible to the public. Later, as the century came to a close, another shift in identity presentation occurred. As it became more acceptable (and profitable) to be Latino, and as Latino parts became more available, formerly "invisible Latinos" would come to publicly embrace their hitherto hidden ethnic identities.

Latin American–Themed Films

From the mid-thirties until the end of the decade, several important Latin American–themed films were made. In general, however, Latinos were not cast in the lead roles. For example, in *Viva Villa* (1934) Wallace Beery played Pancho Villa; in *Hi Gaucho* (1935) there were no Latin actors; and in *Juarez* (1939), Paul Muni (in brownface) played Benito Juárez. Although *Juarez* was about a Mexican hero, some felt that the film's heavy-handed reliance on comparisons with Abe Lincoln reinforced the Latin American dependency on the United States that had first been articulated in the Monroe Doctrine. Throughout the film, Muni sports a Lincolnesque beard, and he walks, talks, and dresses like Lincoln—with top hat and long black overcoat. One particular moment in the film is, as we would say today, over the top: With opposition forces in hot pursuit, Juárez hastily prepares to leave his headquarters, but not before pausing to stare at the framed photo of Lincoln that has been above his desk in almost every frame of the film. Slowly and carefully he removes the photo from the wall and places it under his arm; he then runs for his life. There are other not-so-subtle analogies. It is likely that Juárez may have admired Lincoln; but turning him into the Lincoln of Mexico takes away his own complex identity, which could have been more fully explored in the film. The continual reference to and comparison with the Great Emancipator also suggests that Juárez got all his ideas from Lincoln.

Happy and Musical Latins

The good-neighbor era began during the 1930s, and in the decade that followed a number of Latino actors presented a new image: the cheerful, musical Latin. Carmen Miranda, Cesar Romero, Xavier Cugat, and Desi Arnaz came to symbolize the association of Latin Americans with music and positive images. Latin music was often a staple feature of the jubilant 1940s musicals in which they performed. The characters they played were, for the most part, optimistic, and their on-screen lives were extravagant. The public images of the stars themselves were also upbeat. Films such as *They Met in Argentina* (1941), *Down Argentine Way* (1940), and even Disney's classic animated film, *The Three Caballeros* (1944), include Latin characters, themes, and settings and project Latinos and Latin American life as warm, friendly, and quite similar to the North Americans and North American life. Many of the films show affluent Latin Americans living in modern capital cities, with skyscrapers and beautiful tree-lined avenues, and sharing with Anglos concerns about love and money. As the film historian Charles Richard Jr. has noted, "Lots of Anglos were hugging and kissing lots of

Hispanics" (Richard 1993, xxxvi). On-screen Latinos also seemed to be in love with everything in the North. Many of the films projected an image of one people in two hemispheres who could share love and friendship and thus ensure inter-American security.

In retrospect, this emphasis is somewhat paradoxical, given the greater emphasis during this time on de-ethnicized "American" star images. It also was in strong contrast to earlier representations of Latin America. Despite the presence of major Latino stars in the earlier period, Latin American countries had often complained about the depiction of their countries in Hollywood film and in some cases had prohibited their showing. How was it possible that images of Latin America could be altered so radically?

Fashioning an Image: Media Control

A primary catalyst for the change was World War II, which reintroduced a need for hemispheric unity and a greater reliance on Latin America for raw materials. As large portions of the European and Asian economies closed to the United States, Latin America also assumed greater importance as a market for American goods—including Hollywood films. These economic and military concerns led to the further articulation of the United States' Good Neighbor policy toward Latin America. The push to develop an allied hemispheric strategy worked, for eventually all of the Latin American nations declared war on the Axis; Mexico and Brazil even sent combat forces to support the Allies. Moreover, with the exception of Argentina, which still showed German newsreels, all the countries of Latin America had replaced European products with North American products. Given the political thrust and economic concerns of the times, it is not surprising that many of the films produced were upbeat musicals or dramas that presented Latin America in a positive light.

But how was it possible to ensure that only films of this

type would be made? Didn't the First Amendment to the Constitution protect the creative process? Weren't Americans free to write and present their views without regard to issues of national political and economic security? What happened during this period was a most interesting example of what today would be called media control. As the United States tried to shore up its Good Neighbor policy, government and nongovernmental agencies joined forces to bar from the screen anything that might offend the sensibilities of our Latin American allies.

In 1940, following the invasion of France by the Germans, Nelson Rockefeller urged President Franklin Roosevelt to align more closely with the other countries of the Americas to create a united front against the Axis powers' threat to the hemisphere. The Rockefeller family had extensive economic interests in Latin America. President Roosevelt acted quickly and in 1940 established, by executive order, the Office of the Coordinator of Inter-American Affairs. This office was created to focus on the press, radio broadcasts, cultural exchanges, and the film industry to harmonize all official relations with Latin America, strengthen economic ties, and thwart Nazi influence throughout the region.

The president named Rockefeller to head this newly created and congressionally funded office. Rockefeller, in turn, named John Hay "Jock" Whitney, to head up the special Motion Picture Division within it. The wealthy Jock Whitney was both well known and well liked among Hollywood's aristocracy. Whitney subsequently created a nonprofit, privately controlled California corporation, which included the major heads of the movie industry, the guilds, the agents, and the specialists in all phases of motion picture operation.

The Production Code Administration (PCA), which was to play an important role in this transformation, was already in place. The PCA had been established by the movie industry in the early 1930s in response to public pressure from the Catholic Legion of Decency and other civic groups, who had railed against Hollywood scandals and provocative sexual scenes in films. The motion-picture industry, fearful of state intervention and regulation, established the PCA to self-censure its films. The code, by which all parties agreed to abide, listed a variety of prohibitions, including pointed profanity, licentious or suggestive nudity, and scenes of actual childbirth. Clause 10 of the code forbade the defamation both of foreign nationals and of the histories of their countries. During its early years the PCA had only advisory power—it could only suggest that insults be eliminated—but by 1934 it could bar an offensive film from being exhibited in the United States. The existence of a conglomerate of eight major studios—MGM, Warner Brothers, Paramount, Twentieth Century Fox, Universal, RKO, Columbia, and United Artists—from the 1930s through the 1950s made this possible. The "Hollywood majors," as the group was known, followed the code, consolidated production, distribution, and exhibition, and agreed that no film could be widely distributed in the United States without the PCA's seal of approval. The PCA would come to work closely with government and nongovernmental agencies, acting as "watchdog" to ensure that Hollywood presented only positive images of Latin America.

Jock Whitney advised Will Hays (then head of the PCA) to hire a Latin American specialist to preview films that might be offensive to Latin America. In 1941 the PCA hired Addison Durland, who had been born in 1903 to a New York banker and a Cuban journalist and raised in Cuba. The PCA both eliminated negative images and introduced positive images of Latinos and Latin America in films: A character might comment on his "most memorable memories" of Mexico or on having met "the most wonderful girl in Mexico"; a conga dance or Latin music might be introduced in a movie that had no other Latin theme. The PCA also screened for authenticity: If a film were set in Brazil, for example, local characters would speak Portuguese, not Spanish. Interestingly, Durland did not censure films that featured prominent Latin stars—Lupe Velez's Mexican Spitfire series, for example. Perhaps he assumed that, by virtue of having a Latin star, such films would have fewer offensive or problematic representations.

Although the images may have been positive, they also tended to be limited: They generally reflected the images preferred by Latin American elites, who wanted Latin America to be seen as modern, prosperous, and a largely European set of countries, with well-bred characters who spoke flawless English (with only the hint of an accent), the men well-to-do and the women respectable. Moreover, many of the Latin characters functioned as entertainers, often exotic or comical, and were subordinate to the main characters. Carmen Miranda, for example, generally played the same character in each film—a "Souse" American (her pronunciation) singer and dancer. Latin Americans were depicted as "good neighbors," with whom North Americans could sing, dance, and flirt—though they did not end up marrying them.

Despite these problems, Latinos were more in the forefront during the forties than they had been in the late thirties, when many had been relegated to the background as local color. The images of Latinos—though not necessarily their employment—improved during the war years. In addition, the studios and government paid greater attention to complaints by Latin American countries about negative depictions in Hollywood films. Indeed, during the early forties, the studios were so concerned not to offend that they went out of their way to seek the opinions of members of the diplomatic corps and visiting Latin American historians (O'Neil 2001).

Carmen Miranda: Transcontinental Chumminess

The life stories of the stars of this era are instructive because changes in their individual work lives reflect the larger changes of the times. Carmen Miranda (1909–55), who was at the top of the Hollywood game during this period and perhaps best personifies the peppy musical style associated with Latinos in 1940s Hollywood, was to fall very quickly from the summit after the era of good neighbors was over. Born María

Carmen Miranda (shown here circa 1942) was born in Portugal and raised in Brazil. She was the highest-paid actress in Hollywood.

do Carmo Miranda da Cunha in Portugal, she moved as a child to Brazil. She was already a popular singer and an accomplished actress in Brazil when the theatrical producer Lee Shubert brought her to the United States in 1939. She appeared in fourteen Hollywood films, and at the height of her career she was the highest-paid performer in the United States. Her platform shoes, sparkling smile, radiant personality, energetic and rhythmic dancing and singing—and, perhaps most memorable, her exotic headdresses—made for a signature style that has often been imitated and parodied.

Her last busy year, 1944, coincided with the end of the war. After this she made only one film a year until 1948, then fewer and fewer films in subsequent years.

By the mid-fifties she was performing only in nightclubs and occasional television appearances. It was while taping a segment for Jimmy Durante's television show that she began to suffer a heart attack, and she died the following morning. By the time of her death, at the age of forty-six, her signature style had outlived its usefulness to transcontinental chumminess. Indeed, she had become trapped within this style. In Hollywood films, she had always been cast in the same role, as Carmen Miranda. When this role was no longer of interest, or of use, few thought she could do anything else—although she had already proved her acting ability in Brazil. Today, she and her style live on and are the subject of much discussion—concerning the African element in her style, her role as a gay icon, her sweet-sour relationship with Brazil and its relevance to geopolitics, her representation of Latin American women as sensual and primitive, and her personification as the ultimate Latin American "other" in this era of "good neighbors" (López 1991).

Xavier Cugat: The Music Man

The career of Xavier Cugat (1900–90) parallels that of Carmen Miranda along many dimensions. Cugat was also an important figure in Latin musicals during the forties, and he followed a similar downward path in popularity after the period of the upbeat Latin musical ended. Born in Spain, he was raised from the age of three in Havana, Cuba. A teenage violin prodigy, he toured Europe in concert with Enrico Caruso. After moving to the United States, Cugat worked for the *Los Angeles Times,* where he demonstrated his talent as a cartoonist. He was also a gifted composer, and he worked on developing his band at night, playing in a variety of small clubs. By 1928 he and his band secured a job at Hollywood's famous Coconut Grove nightclub, where he became well

Xavier Cugat is credited with bringing Latin music into the mainstream through film. As a teenage violin prodigy, he toured Europe with Enrico Caruso; he was also a talented cartoonist. Cugat is shown here circa 1940 with his band and lead singer, Lina Romay.

known and earned the title of "Rumba King" during the thirties. He did not begin acting in film until 1936, and most of his film appearances were in the forties—when the war and the Good Neighbor policy influenced the demand for upbeat Latin musicals. (Like Carmen Miranda, Cugat always played himself—even when his character had a different name.) He made five films during the war years and another ten before the end of the decade. Like Carmen Miranda, his prominence in films had declined by the mid-fifties. After 1955 he made occasional films, many of them overseas. After surviving a stroke in 1971, he retired and lived another twenty years, dying of heart failure in Spain at the age of ninety.

Cesar Romero (shown here circa late 1940s) was prominent in films during the forties. His long career included more than 128 films and television appearances through the 1980s, including his continuing role as the Joker on the TV series, *Batman*.

Cesar Romero: The Lighthearted Latin Lover

Cesar Romero (1907–94) was also pulled into the magic of the musical Latin moment. Born Cesar Julio Romero Jr. in New York City, he was a descendant of the Cuban liberator, Jose

Martí. He went to Hollywood in the early thirties, at the age of twenty-six, starting out as a professional dancer. Although he began acting in films in the mid-thirties, his screen heyday, like Cugat's, occurred in the 1940s. An actor of wide versatility, Romero alternated American and ethnic roles in films, but in the forties his "Latin" roles were more prominent. He played the Cisco Kid in six adventure films (1940–41) and appeared in a number of musicals, such as *Week-End in Havana* (1941) and *Springtime in the Rockies* (1942), with Carmen Miranda, and starred in *Dance Hall* (1941). But it was as a light-hearted Latin lover that Romero made a name for himself, and he viewed his success in that role as preventing him from becoming a full-fledged star. Be that as it may, he made a total of 128 films during his career. Although he made fewer films in the 1950s, he went on to have a long and substantial career in television in the 1960s, including the role of the Joker in the *Batman* series, and then again in the 1980s, when, at a vibrant seventy-eight years of age, he played the love interest (a Greek billionaire) on *Falcon Crest.* He died in 1994, at the age of eighty-seven, of bronchitis and pneumonia.

Gilbert Roland: The Romantic, Swashbuckling Latin Lover

Gilbert Roland (1905–94) established himself as an actor during the silent era; he was a leading man in numerous highly regarded films—in *Camille* (1926) and *New York Nights* (1929) opposite Norma Talmadge and in *Rose of the Golden West* (1927) opposite Mary Astor. His career waned during the 1930s, however, though he did make a number of notable movies in Spanish and English for Metro. He appeared opposite Clara Bow in *Call Her Savage* (1932) and *Resurrección* and opposite Mae West in *She Done Him Wrong* (1933). During the 1940s, Roland enlisted in the U.S. Army. When he returned from service in World War II, he began the Cisco Kid series and continued to make films until the early 1980s. Known as one of Hollywood's greatest stars, his sixty-year career included a variety of leading

Gilbert Roland, born in Juárez, Mexico, established himself as a leading man during the silent era and went on to make more than a hundred films in his sixty-year career. Handsome and athletic, he played a variety of leading and supporting roles but was often cast, and is perhaps best known, as a Latin lover. He is remembered by many as one of Hollywood's greatest stars, and he played the lead in a number of the *Cisco Kid* films. Roland is shown here circa 1940.

and supporting roles in more than a hundred films. But his name was always associated with romance, action, and adventure. Roland was often described as extraordinarily handsome and athletic but also a mannerly swashbuckler.

Roland was born Luis Antonio Damasco de Alonso in Juárez, Mexico, to Spanish-born parents. His father moved the family to El Paso, Texas, when Gilbert was a child, in response to Pancho Villa's threat to the lives of all Mexicans of Spanish descent. The de Alonsos had been bullfighters for generations, and as a child Roland had worked in his father's bullring in Juárez. In the barrios of El Paso, he grew up as one of six children and in 1913 was selling newspapers in front of a hotel. By the time he was in the sixth grade, he said, he had become "the biggest movie fan in the world" (quoted in Thomas 1998, 49). He played hooky from school to watch serials at a local movie house and wrote to his favorite stars, asking for their photographs. As a teenager he hopped a freight train and made his way to Los Angeles to break into movies.

He arrived, at the age of fourteen, with two dollars and sixty cents in his pocket. He worked as an extra and at whatever jobs he could find until he was discovered while playing in a mob scene. He recounted the discovery this way: "An extra girl who was very beautiful asked if I would get a glass of water for her. . . . Ordinarily I would have walked around the set. But this time for some reason I took a shortcut. There I was in a fine costume all alone on the set, which was brilliantly lighted. When I reached the other side a man [an agent] said, 'What is your name?'" (quoted in Reyes and Rubie 2000, 552). Soon after this encounter he signed a contract for the second lead in *The Plastic Age* (1925). He chose his screen name by combining the names of two of his favorite actors, John Gilbert and Ruth Roland.

Although he played a fairly wide variety of roles, Roland was often cast, and is best remembered, as a Latin lover. Yet he distinguished between the tough Latin lover that some expected him to be and what he considered his own more sentimental personality. In his pocket he carried a picture not of one of his various flames, or leading ladies, but of a gray-haired schoolteacher who had taught him to speak English in El Paso. He apparently wrote to her throughout his career and visited her nearly every holiday season. The gold ring he always wore was given to him by his mother. "My screen image never bothers me," he once said, "[but] I have never tried to contradict it either" (quoted ibid., 553). Nevertheless, he did fight the industry's tendency to stereotype Mexicans and Mexican Americans as clowns, and he insisted on frequent script changes to alter these depictions. He was also known to drive across the border with a carload of toys and hand them out to the children he met. He died of prostate cancer in Beverly Hills at the age of eighty-eight.

Desi Arnaz: The Conga Man

Desi Arnaz (1917–86) moved from forties musicals into a television career. However, he turned to television much sooner than Cesar Romero had. Born Desiderio Alberto Arnaz y de Acha III in Santiago, Cuba, where his father had been mayor, his family fled to Miami, Florida, after the 1933 Batista revolution. In Florida, Desi had to take a number of odd jobs, including cleaning canary cages, to make ends meet. In his autobiography, he describes what life was like when he and his father were living in an otherwise uninhabited warehouse: "I would get 'home' from a date and find my dad, who had been the king of my hometown for ten years, a good-looking, still young, wonderful guy, going around with a fucking baseball bat trying to kill the rats before we could safely go to bed. We lived there for quite a while and made it sort of a game to see which one of us could come up with an idea to fix it up better and get rid of the rats" (Arnaz 1976, 37). Always interested in music, he formed a band, was hired by Cugat, and went on to launch the conga craze in the United States. Almost all of the films he made in the forties were musicals, except for *Bataan* (1943), which was a war drama.

Desi Arnaz began appearing in films in the 1940s, but he was also a multitalented and innovative businessman. In 1948 he and his wife, Lucille Ball, formed Desilu Productions, which created and produced their number-one hit show, *I Love Lucy* (1951–57), and other hit series, including *The Untouchables*, *Our Miss Brooks*, and *The Danny Thomas Show*. He introduced production techniques still in use today—for example, filming before a live audience and using multiple cameras at the same time. Arnaz is shown here in 1956 in *Forever Darling*.

In his autobiography Arnaz recalls being asked by the State Department if he would join a group of well-known artists and movie stars (including Clark Gable, Bing Crosby, James Cagney, Mickey Rooney, Norma Shearer, and Robert Taylor) who were being sent to Mexico to kick off President Roosevelt's Good Neighbor policy. He felt at the time that he was not in the "same class" as these stars and had been invited primarily because he spoke the language, enabling him to relay the Mexican people's reaction to the government and to the Rockefeller Foundation, which was also involved in the project. The group was greeted by mobs who followed them throughout Mexico, and they performed at half a dozen theaters each day.

Arnaz thought the policy was a wonderful idea and understood its intent to be to allow people in the United States to get "a little closer to the people" living in Latin America. However, he found that the policy was met with suspicion. Arnaz describes the Mexican reaction as follows: "What is this all of a sudden? We've been here for a hundred and fifty years, nobody paid a goddam bit of attention to us. All of a sudden they say, 'I want to be your friend.' What do they want? [To] take the rest of Mexico? They already have taken a big chunk. What is it that they want now?" (ibid., 135). He likened it to a person who has lived next door for years and yet never said so much as hello to his neighbor, then suddenly one day is sending flowers to the neighbor's wife and inviting the couple to dinner. The neighbor's reaction would have to be, "What the hell does the sonofabitch want?" (ibid., 135).

It was during his first film, *Too Many Girls* (1940), that Arnaz met and married Lucille Ball, who starred in the film. The two formed the highly profitable and innovative Desilu Productions in 1948. This company created and produced not just the *I Love Lucy* television show—which made both of them famous—but many other shows as well. The idea of casting a "Latin" as the husband of an "All-American girl" was originally opposed by the backers of the show, who were sure the public would not go for it. Undaunted, Desi and Lucy developed a comedy act, took it on a theater tour, and were a huge hit throughout the United States. Their success convinced the networks and the sponsors that America could accept the duo. *I Love Lucy* went on to be the number-one hit show for six continuous years (from 1951 through 1956) and was the first show in television history to reach an audience of 10 million viewers. The couple also acquired RKO Studios, and Desilu became the biggest production company in Hollywood. Along the way, Arnaz introduced production techniques and equipment still in use today. He was the first, for example, to film before a live audience and to use multiple cameras simultaneously. He was also responsible for producing numerous other hit shows, including *The Untouchables, Our Miss Brooks,* and *The Danny Thomas Show.*

Lupe Velez: The Mexican Spitfire

Other Latin characters were equally typical of the forties. One that seemed to be a cousin to the upbeat, musical, "good neighbor" of the forties was the Mexican spitfire. Although this character had clearly existed in earlier films, it was in the forties that the Mexican spitfire blossomed into a happy and humorous woman who was married to an Anglo-American. Lupe Velez, who was by now a redhead, like Rita Hayworth, played such a character, Carmelita Woods, in a series of comedic films. The appeal of Carmelita Woods at the time is curious, for Carmelita was in many ways stereotypical and in other ways quite radical and independent for her time. She refused to put her show business career aside; she did not want to have children; she did not promote the career of her husband, Dennis; in each film, Dennis's aunt questions Carmelita's background and implores Dennis to divorce her and marry his former fiancée, Elizabeth (played by Linda Hayes), who came from "real Plymouth Rock stock." Carmelita also lacked breeding, spoke fractured English, had emotional outbursts in Spanish, rolled her eyes a lot, and used hand and body gestures that have been described by some as stereotypical.

Carmelita was popular with the U.S. public and did not seem to offend the Latin American public, for both kept paying to see her in Lupe's films. Perhaps they identified with her and her struggle against those who tried to keep her (and them) out. Perhaps they appreciated the fact that she always won in the end, or that she was not to be fooled. Maybe they liked the honesty and directness with which she expressed herself—even if she did so in fractured English. Possibly, they liked her because she was spunky, funny, and smart, often outwitted others, and always got to keep the guy in the end. Maybe they just liked the slapstick. Whatever the reasons, the films were sufficiently popular for eight of them to have been made and another to be in the planning phase by the time of Velez's death.

Maria Montez: The Exotica

Another familiar major female character in films of the forties was the "exotica"—a sex symbol of various mysterious nationalities, often set against foreign locales where much adventure usually dominated nefarious proceedings. The exotica was often a siren of exceptional beauty, with skimpy clothes and a sultry, languid air. However, the exotica was also somehow in charge (often she was a queen of something)—although she was inevitably saved from peril by a gallant hero, with whom, it was generally implied, she lived happily ever after.

In these films, which are sometimes referred to as "sand and sandals" epics, there was much action and romance but not a lot of exceptional acting. The exotica character was not necessarily seen to be Latin or Latina, but it was Maria Montez who embodied the type in the forties. Montez's films were expensive to make and immensely popular during this period. Like the spitfire character, the exotica had clearly existed before in film, but it was in the forties that the type became most popular with the public. Perhaps the continu-

Maria Montez (shown here circa 1943) was born in the Dominican Republic and discovered by a talent scout in Manhattan in 1940. She became a top moneymaker for Universal Films during the 1940s, appearing in eighteen films, the majority of them in Technicolor. She was a favorite pinup girl of servicemen during World War II.

ing weight of the Great Depression and the war brought about a need for exotic escapist fare.

Maria Montez (1917–51) was born in Barahona, Dominican Republic, and her given name was María Africa Antonia Gracia Vidal de Santo Silas. Her father was a Spanish consul, and so she was educated in a convent school in the Canary Islands. She traveled and lived in South America, France, England, and Ireland before arriving in New York, where she worked for a while as a model. Discovered in Manhattan in 1940 by a talent scout, she became a top moneymaker for Universal Films during the 1940s. She made eighteen films, fourteen of them in Technicolor, and she was a pinup-girl favorite of servicemen during World War II. Her name became synonymous with exotic adventure epics. With the end of the war, the interest in escapist films diminished, and Maria left with her husband, the French actor Jean-Pierre Aumont, to live and make films in Europe. She appeared in a number of French, Italian, and German films before she was discovered in her bath, dead of a heart attack at the age of thirty-four.

Latinos in the United States

After the war—when the spirit-lifting music suddenly seemed to stop—the focus shifted to average Latinos living within U.S. borders. The 1945 film *A Medal for Benny* represented an important turning point in this regard. With some significant exceptions—*Bordertown* (1935), for example—Hollywood films had generally shown Latin Americans in Latin America or the well-to-do Latin American temporarily visiting the United States to shop, vacation, romance an "American," or secure a privileged education. The film *Bordertown* focused on the border area and the Latino community there. It starred Paul Muni (in brownface) as Johnny Rodriguez, who eventually goes back to his barrio—as he says in the movie, "back where I belong . . . with my own people" (cited in Noriega 1997, 93). *Bordertown* was a social-problem film and consequently was distinct from the 1945 upbeat comedy, *A Medal for Benny*. In *A Medal for Benny*, the main character is Benny Martin (Martín in Spanish), a Mexican American GI who has already died when the film opens but who has been posthumously awarded a Congressional Medal of Honor for having "killed a hundred Japs."

The Martins live in a hundred-year-old Mexican American community in Panera, California. When Mayor Smiley hears that government officials will be coming to his town to award the medal to Benny's family, he sees an opportunity to encourage tourism, raise real estate values, and sell hot dogs. The problem is that the Martins live on the wrong side of town—where all the Panera Mexicans seem to live. The mayor seeks to alter the backdrop for the public event. There are a number of comedic scenes, many of which center around this central embarrassment: that the hero lives in a barrio. The family ends up staying in their home, where they are presented with the award. The moral of the story is that "good people come from all kinds of houses," and "some mighty fine Americans have come from shacks." Despite the humorous tone and upbeat message, the film addresses some important, and still relevant, issues of citizenship and cultural and linguistic difference. Benny is a hero, a citizen who has given his life for his country. Yet he is culturally, linguistically, and economically different. His family home is initially deemed an inappropriate backdrop against which to celebrate his heroism. Why his family, along with all the Mexicans in town, are still living in this least affluent part of Panera is not given much attention.

There were other Latin stars during the prewar and war years—Anthony Quinn, Olga San Juan, Ricardo Montalban, Jose Ferrer, and Juano Hernandez, to name a few—but many of them were only beginning their careers or did not yet have major box-office appeal, name recognition, or participation in films. There were also, as in all eras, numerous—and, sadly, now nameless—Latino actors, writers, costumers, and others working both in front of and behind the scenes. It would be interesting to see whether the lives of these other less well known participants similarly reflected the times in which they lived—and how their lives might have been affected by the times. To some degree, the parallels noted in this chapter between the work lives of the major actors and the times in which they lived were facilitated by the actions of the Production Code Administration and the Office of the Coordinator of Inter-American Affairs—but not completely. Why, for example, were those who hid their ethnic or Latino origins more successful at this point? Why were comical or exotic Latinas more in demand than comical or exotic Latinos? As the country returned from war and began the work of rebuilding, it would begin to enter yet another era, one also characterized by war—in this case, the cold war. This more politically conservative period would lead to yet new arrangements for Latinos on the Hollywood film set.

The Cold War Era

Duromg the cold war era, the sizzling south-of-the-border sights and sounds chilled in a climate of inward-looking conservatism. The Eisenhower years were highlighted by the House Un-American Activities Committee hearings under Senator Joseph McCarthy. In this new national mood, the prominence of the Latin stars of the forties declined. As Ramon Novarro, a Latino star of an earlier era, later explained, "The Latin image was starker, and the music and gaiety were forgotten as the war receded. . . . There was less need not to offend former war allies. . . . I turned down many roles in which I would have played a villain or a caricature insulting to my own people" (quoted in Hadley-Garcia 1993, 137).

Olga San Juan, known during the forties as "the Puerto Rican pepperpot," indirectly commented on the shift when asked why she had retired from film as early as she did (her last Hollywood picture was released in

1949): "I had a stroke but also the times were beginning to change and so I began to dedicate myself more to my family" (quoted in Miluka Rivera, "Entrevista Espectacular: Olga San Juan en la Galaxia de Hollywood," *El Nuevo Día*, October 22, 2000, 125 [author's translation]). Even Desi Arnaz admitted in his autobiography that he had left MGM to develop his own band because he wondered how many parts were going to come up for Latin leads. Stars like Cesar Romero and Maria Montez took lesser roles or went abroad to make pictures. Those who stayed, or began their careers in this era, contended with narrowing options.

The Times

What were these times like? Why did life change so drastically for Latino actors? What caused the shift to a chilly postwar climate? A principal reason was the fear of the threat of communism. By 1949 the Soviet Union had detonated its first atomic bomb, and by 1953 its first hydrogen bomb. China, another country huge in population and vast in terms of land, had also adopted the communist system of government by 1949 and would soon develop nuclear capacity. In the 1950s, after a period of skirmishes and a civil war, communist North Korea invaded South Korea, and the United States soon entered the fray. The worldwide decolonization process begun in 1945 also intensified in the fifties. By 1950 there were new influential political actors on the scene. India and Indonesia became independent, followed soon thereafter by other Asian and African countries. It was not always clear what system of government these new states would adhere to or to which side in the cold war these new states would align. The state of Israel was established, introducing new tensions in the Middle East—tensions as yet not clearly understood by the United States.

The Western Hemisphere saw other movements that, from the U.S. perspective, appeared to threaten hemispheric stability. After the Chilean and Guatemalan coups in 1954, and the ascension of Rafael Trujillo in the Dominican Republic in 1956, the U.S. vice president Richard Nixon went to visit Ecuador and Venezuela in 1958. In Ecuador, he was met by antagonistic and hostile crowds protesting President Dwight D. Eisenhower's support of the right-wing dictatorship. Castro came to power in Cuba in 1959; President John F. Kennedy and Premier Nikita Khrushchev came eyeball to eyeball over Russian intercontinental missiles in Cuba; and the possibility of nuclear war in the Western Hemisphere loomed large for a moment. Though war was averted, the iron curtain was definitively drawn. Prominently communist were Mao Zedong's People's Republic of China, the Union of the Soviet Socialist Republics, North Korea, and half of Berlin and Germany, as well as nascent states that had yet to ideologically commit to the United States.

After World War II, President Harry S. Truman pushed through the Marshall Plan to rebuild western Europe and stop communist advances. Eisenhower continued the cold war position vis-à-vis the Soviet Union, which had taken over many of the Eastern European countries. Truman also created the Central Intelligence Agency and, in an action that brings to mind our own recent creation of a homeland defense unit, put all military branches under the Defense Department. Schoolchildren throughout the country were taught to cover their heads and hide under their desks in the event of an air strike. Bomb shelters loaded with supplies were built or improvised—depending on the family's economic resources or political fears (or both). Pervading the times was the heavy air of McCarthyism and the House Un-American Activities Committee hearings—with its particular focus on Hollywood. The ensuing persecution and firing of individuals in all corners of the country had a silencing effect on others.

Yet the classic picture of the fifties, as projected in the photos on the front pages of the *New York Times*, for example, is of a more placid, nonconflictual existence—especially for those living in middle America. Icons of the era included hula hoops, crinolines, pink poodles, flying saucers, Smoky the Bear, folk songs in Washington Square Park, Mickey Mantle and the Yankees, Marilyn Monroe and Joe DiMaggio, James Dean, Frank Sinatra, Marilyn Monroe and Arthur Miller. Television had come to rival the movies—this medium being more in keeping with, and accessible to, suburban extensions that had yet to develop today's ubiquitous malls and cinema duplexes. Television shows reflected a similar harmony, tranquility, and sexlessness—TV's *Father Knows Best, I Love Lucy, Jackie Gleason, I Remember Mama,* and *The Red Skelton Show. Doggie in the Window* was a hit song on the popular television show, *Hit Parade.* Indeed, Elvis Presley's appearance on *The Ed Sullivan Show* was so risqué for its time that only the top part of his body was in camera view: "Elvis the Pelvis" was enough to make most viewers blush. Sex and sexuality were purged from public images: Sex was something other people did—and it tended to get them into trouble. It occurred only after marriage, and even the happily married Ricardos on *I Love Lucy* slept in separate twin beds. Within this climate of political, cultural, and sexual repression, the Latin lover and the bombshell did not represent "public values" of the time.

"High culture," on the other hand, was permeated with alienation, abstraction, and distance from life as it was being lived. The beat poets and writers, such as Jack Kerouac, Norman Mailer, and Stanley Kubrick, wrote about disaffection. On a more pedestrian level, beatnik bards imitated their style in coffeehouses, on campuses, and elsewhere. In the art world, the huge canvasses of abstract expressionism reflected a depoliticized sense of art for art's sake. Gone were the socially conscious works that had been so prominent in the 1930s, works like those of Diego Rivera and the artists of the Works Progress Administration, which sought to connect high culture, ordinary people, social responsibility, and collective action. Indeed, realism and representational art seemed to have developed a bad reputation during this period, and engagement in social and political issues had become aesthetically incorrect. Martha Graham garnered popularity with her modern, abstract form of dance in 1958. University professors strove to appear balanced and impartial and avoided questioning too hard the current political, economic, and social systems.

The 1950s were times of relative economic prosperity. The deprivations of the Depression and the war years now over, pent-up demand was unleashed as returning soldiers married, bought and furnished houses, returned to school, found jobs or opened businesses, and started families in what would become the postwar baby boom. Military spending for the cold war and the Korean War contributed to the economic expansion. This was the era in which heavy industrialization spread through the United States, particularly in the Northeast and Midwest. Life was good for many people. Workers were needed. The steel industry was expanding, highways were being extended, and suburbs flourished. The Chrysler assembly line in Pittsburgh represented the essence and strength of America. A Univac computer forecast the outcome of the 1954 presidential election—though Americans could not know that computers would still be subject to the all-too-human deciphering of "hanging chads" in the 2000 presidential elections. The double-helix structure of DNA was discovered—though Americans did not yet understand its significance. Russia launched its Sputnik, and John Glenn would soon follow the Russians into space in the first manned U.S. spacecraft.

Curiously, at the same time that art evaded reality through abstraction and television projected a seamless image of perfect marriages, children, and happy endings, other news images suggested a grittier domestic and international turbulence. In the 1948 presidential elections, Strom Thurmond, running as an independent, won four states in the South on a segregationist platform. Rosa Parks refused to give up her seat on a public bus, and the contemporary civil rights movement was born. The Supreme Court's decision in *Brown v. Board of Education* (1954) declared that separate was not equal, and the first African American students began to attend white schools in Little Rock, Arkansas, accompanied by the federal troops that Eisenhower had called in to enforce desegregation. In 1956 Martin Luther King Jr. began his campaign of passive resistance; Emmett Till was killed in 1955; the Ku Klux Klan was active, especially through the South; and in 1957 the newly built development in Levittown, New York, was accused of bias in suburban housing. Jimmy Hoffa, head of the Teamsters Union, went to jail on corruption charges, and Ethel and Julius Rosenberg were found guilty of espionage charges. Their convictions followed those of others who had been accused of spying for the communists. The Chief Justice of the Supreme Court upheld the conspiracy convictions of other U.S. communists and declared communism to be a "clear and present danger."

Although civil rights struggles intensified in the fifties, individual African Americans gained greater recognition; Marian Anderson was the first black singer to appear at New York's Metropolitan Opera House, and the names of Miles Davis, Paul Robeson, Wilt Chamberlain, and Ella Fitzgerald were well known. The times were changing. But where were Latinos?

Latinos in the 1950s

Latinos were increasing in number, particularly in central cities in the Northeast and Midwest and in the West and Southwest (where they had always composed substantial portions of the population). At the same time, the postwar policies of the federal government emphasized highway building and suburban residential development and ignored development of the inner cities. However, in the fifties the government would begin to build housing projects in central cities that would result in the further concentration of low-income Latinos, African Americans, and other poor people in dense inner-city high-rise buildings. Already established social and economic fissures in politics, neighborhoods, schools, jobs, and public social spaces (like beaches, parks, and hangouts) would deepen. Local power brokers would defend these divisions through informal and formal policies—such as restrictive covenants, mortgage and insurance redlining, and highway construction and "separate-but-equal" service delivery, transit systems, and educational policies. Along with the return of the troops from the Korean War, the heroin trade lodged decisively and corrosively in many black and Latino inner-city communities.

Latino migration to the states had picked up after 1920 and filled the labor void left by the cessation of European immigration to the United States. (Restrictive U.S. immigration laws, wars, better economic times in Europe, and the establishment of political systems that forbade emigration kept many potential European immigrants home after 1920.) During and after World War II, Latino migration again increased as the Bracero program brought additional Mexicans across the border. Established by the U.S. government in 1942 to fill the labor shortage caused by the U.S. entry into the war, the program provided for Mexican workers to come to the United States to work, mainly as agricultural laborers. As with contemporary guest-worker programs in Europe, many of these workers stayed and had American children. Thus a new generation of Mexican Americans, the children of Mexican immigrants, who came of age between 1930 and 1960, was added to the Latino population.

Puerto Ricans also migrated in substantial numbers during the post–World War II period. Puerto Ricans had been migrating to the United States in significant numbers since the late nineteenth century and had established small communities in the Northeast; but during the fifties they began to arrive in large numbers. More than fifty-two thousand Puerto Ricans landed on U.S. shores in 1952 alone. Puerto Ricans were everywhere—in Illinois, New Jersey, Connecticut, Massachusetts, and particularly in New York City. The Cuban migration would begin in earnest in the following decade, in response to the takeover by Fidel Castro. It would similarly flood the Miami area, but communities of

Cuban exiles would also emerge in other parts of the United States—New Jersey, for example.

Why did so many Puerto Ricans come during this period? After World War II, Puerto Rico began Operation Bootstrap, an economic development program to modernize the island and improve its economy. Because of the capital-intensive nature of this initiative, tens of thousands of workers were displaced from traditional pursuits and from more labor-intensive industries. They found their way to jobs in the industrial, commercial, manufacturing, and service sectors in the Northeast, especially New York, and in the Midwest. (Interestingly, Operation Bootstrap would subsequently serve as a model for developing countries throughout the world, and it would similarly spin off excess and rural populations in the 1970s and 1980s to other urban centers, including the United States.)

Improved communications and transportation systems also induced and facilitated the migration. As occurs today with respect to other countries, the development of electricity and highways in rural areas, an improved postal system, increasing communication by phone, and greater exposure to U.S. television and film brought the United States and Puerto Rico closer together. The development of affordable commercial air travel made migration from Puerto Rico to the states economically feasible. Moreover, Puerto Ricans were U.S. citizens; having served in the war, they had learned much about the states and the opportunities to be had there. Also facilitating the migration was the Puerto Rican government and the active recruitment by agricultural agents and private companies that were anxious to fill jobs, particularly in New York City's manufacturing and service sectors, and in agriculture and industries outside of New York. Finally, earlier beachhead communities (or colonias, as they were known at the time) also provided incentive, information, and support (Sánchez Korrol 1994).

Puerto Ricans and other Latinos who arrived during the fifties encountered a chilly political and cultural climate.

They were settling in large numbers in circumscribed (mainly working-class) areas—generally not the easiest way for any immigrant group to enter a new society. In addition, they were arriving after a thirty-year hiatus in immigration. New York, formerly (and presently) the immigrant capital of the world, had not seen a significant influx of immigrants in more than a generation and a half. Like immigrants before them, Puerto Ricans settled in central cities and generally took low-level jobs. However, the central cities were now in decline, having been abandoned for the suburbs by the middle classes and the upwardly mobile. Reflecting the shift to the suburbs, in 1950, for the first time, more than half of all occupied housing units were owned rather than rented. The country, especially the now assimilated offspring of earlier generations of immigrants, was not particularly receptive to cultural or linguistic difference nor to the increasing concentration of African Americans in central cities across the nation. The cold war era was a time in which homogeneity and assimilation were the national goals. It was not a good time to be different in America.

Further complicating the arrival of Puerto Ricans was the fact that they were arriving from an unincorporated territory of the United States, where there had been a long-term, extended struggle for independence dating from the nineteenth century. Members of the Puerto Rican Nationalist Party attacked Blair House, in Washington, in 1950; and a commando unit, headed by the nationalist Lolita Lebrón, fired twenty-five rounds from the gallery into the Capitol chamber of the House of Representatives in 1954, wounding five. Both acts were attempts to draw attention to Puerto Rico's colonial status; both were treated as terrorist acts by the major national media. Government agents quickly swooped down on Puerto Rican communities to ferret out more terrorists—or those connected to activities deemed suspect. Unfortunately, in the ultraconservative climate of the day, this turn of events cast a veil of suspicion over the entire Puerto Rican community. In seeming ignorance of the valuable service offered by Puerto Rican citizens and the lives sacrificed through two world wars, the Puerto Rican migration was now seen more as a problematic invasion than a continuing migration that contributed to U.S. society. The themes of invasion and difficult circumstances would be reflected in films of the day, though the history of Puerto Rico or Puerto Rican contributions would not.

Also not evident in films of the fifties was the historically vacillating welcome that the U.S. government gave the Mexican immigration. During the Depression, welfare costs rose greatly because of the great many unemployed, and five hundred thousand Mexicans and Mexican Americans were repatriated between 1929 and 1934. During World War II, the U.S. Bracero program brought Mexican workers to work in the United States, but by the 1950s, the return of soldiers from foreign combat had rendered the Bracero program unnecessary. In 1952 the U.S. government put into place Operation Wetback, the purpose of which was to repatriate workers who had come earlier and stayed and those who had subsequently waded across the Rio Grande (hence the name "wetback") to find work in the United States. As a consequence, from 1952 to 1956 close to 3 million Mexicans and Mexican Americans were deported. (In 1964 the Bracero program was expanded once again because of an agricultural labor shortage, and Mexican labor returned.) Films like *My Man and I* (1952) presented Mexicans as "alien" to mainstream life.

Options for Latinos

With a few important exceptions, many of the films that featured Latino characters during this era focused on social problems and were steeped in historical myths, machismo, or stereotypes of Latin lovers and Latina bombshells. (Indeed, strong female stars of all backgrounds were also shunted aside during this era.) The choices for Latino actors were generally limited: They could either Europeanize their images (by discarding any ethnic references) or play up the stereotypes. Consequently, in this period, the distinction between visible and invisible Latino actors became stronger, and invisibility became a more clear-cut strategy for navigating identity and careers. The absence of middle-ground positions in film reflected the intolerance for ambiguity characteristic of this era. The roles available often called for proverbial characters: victims incapable of defending themselves, vixens, alien invaders, and young punks. In essence, fewer roles were open to Latino actors, and of the few that were available many were mere clichés. Some actors also became victims of the McCarthyism that was emblematic of the times.

Latin Lovers, Bombshells, Spitfires, and Sultry Latinas

Some might wonder why being seen as a Latin lover, or a Latina bombshell, is problematic. What is so wrong with this? First, it should be made clear that in Hollywood movies at the time there was not much distinction (other than the obvious) between Latin lovers, bombshells, spitfires, and sultry Latinas; the difference was often merely a matter of degree or gender. It should also be made clear that Latin lover and Latina bombshell characterizations were in many ways desirable. They were the men and women that audiences yearned to touch, lusted after, the ones their mothers had warned them about; they made their viewers' hearts skip a beat and promised rapture and full surrender. What was wrong with being projected as sexually desirable? Don't most of us strive for this in one way or another or at one time or another?

The problem was that, in the case of Latinos, the characters were erotic and exotic, and little else. The dark, forbidden, dream lovers generally had no other role; they were not lucky in love, and they frequently preferred non-Latinos as partners. The characters were often morally inferior and ended up reinforcing the comfortable American status quo that relegated people like them to the back seat. True, the Latino characters inspired unspeakable desire and desirability, especially at this time, when non-Latin men and women were often portrayed as prim, clumsy, restrained sexual partners. In the end, however, once the escapist fantasy had subsided, it was the non-Latinos who had the good morals, sense, and intelligence and were "the real thing"—the ones to be taken seriously in marriage, as well as in other areas of life.

Ricardo Montalban and Fernando Lamas: Quintessential Latin Lovers

Ricardo Montalban (1920–) played a variety of roles during the fifties, including Native Americans in the TV series *Broken Arrow* (1956) and the film *Across the Wide Missouri* (1951) and non-Latinos in other films such as *The Saracen Blade* (1954) and *Sayonara* (1957), but he is best remembered during this period for his roles as the quintessential Latin lover. Indeed, he had the starring role in the movie *Latin Lovers* (1953). Nevertheless, as he notes in his autobiography, he opposed the stereotype of the Latin lover and questioned the concept, saying that, if it meant needing a new conquest every day, he found nothing admirable in it. Clearly, it was easy to be obsessed with the chase and to seek the thrill of change, but that did not take much imagination: "Dogs do the same thing," he observes. To his mind, the greatest Latin lover was his father, who had been faithful and respectful toward his mother for fifty-three years, had an active sex life to the end of his days, and was never bored: "Imagine the romanticism that it took to keep a love affair going all those years!" (Montalban 1980, 22). *That* was the true Latin lover.

Montalban also rejected parts that he considered racist, and he played his role as the romantic lead with what has been called "an aura of steely self-control, creating sexual tension by playing hard to get" (Thomas 1998, 68). Although during the 1940s (when he first began his career) and the

Ricardo Montalban, the "reluctant" Latin lover, was a committed reformer during the cold war and modern eras. Today, he is perhaps best known for his roles as Mr. Roarke on television's *Fantasy Island* (1978–84), as Khan in *Star Trek: The Wrath of Khan* (1982), and as the grandfather in the *Spy Kids* films (2002, 2003). Montalban is shown here circa 1950.

1950s he played mostly Latino characters, his character was not always the romantic, dramatic screen favorite—although he is most remembered this way. During the forties he appeared in musicals, as did most other Latinos, and in the fifties he took parts in crime movies, thrillers, and adventure films as well as romantic dramas. He was always respected as an actor. Born and raised in Mexico, Montalban was the youngest of five children born to a middle-class couple who had emigrated from Castile, Spain. He came to Los Angeles for his high school education, did some stage work in New York, and then returned to Mexico, where he established a successful film career, before coming to Hollywood to make films. In his long and versatile career in film he has made at least ninety-four movies. He has also had an extensive and multifaceted career in television, beginning with his first TV movie in 1955 *(Cicero)* and including a highly successful six-year run on *Fantasy Island* (1978–84) as Mr. Roarke, the non-Latino head of the island. He was also instrumental in forming Nosotros in 1969, an organization that seeks to improve opportunities for Latinos in the media.

Like Ricardo Montalban, Fernando Lamas (1915–82) made his film debut in his native country (in his case, Argentina, in 1942), and he starred in many films in the United States during the fifties, usually as the romantic lead. Also like Montalban, he disliked being typecast as a Latin lover. In contrast to Montalban, who has been called "the reluctant Romeo" and who sought in his private life to differentiate himself from the Latin lover stereotype, Lamas appeared to enjoy the image in his personal life. "I couldn't break the Latin Lover image, hard as I tried," he once reflected. "It was a great image to have off the screen, but a pain in the ass in the movies" (cited ibid., 66, 76).

Lamas had been a prize-winning boxer and swimmer and an established stage, screen, and radio star in Argentina. In contrast to his roles in the United States, he had been cast as the villain in most of the twenty-one films he made in Latin America and Europe. During his time in Hollywood, he

Fernando Lamas, the charming Latin lover, is shown here circa 1950.
His son, by film star Arlene Dahl, is the actor Lorenzo Lamas of the
TV series *Falcon Crest* and *Renegade*.

was often romantically linked with other stars, and he married two of his costars, Arlene Dahl and Esther Williams (his fourth and last wife). He described his childhood as lonely: Orphaned at the age of four, he was raised by a stern grandmother and an aunt. In the 1960s he acted in Italian films and played European roles of indefinite ethnicity. He also turned to directing: His credits include films, a variety of television series, and segments of the soap opera *Falcon Crest,* in which his son (with Arlene Dahl) Lorenzo Lamas starred. He died in 1982 of cancer.

Katy Jurado: Sultry Latina

Like Ricardo Montalban, who is most remembered as a Latin lover despite the variety of roles he played, the range of Katy Jurado's acting abilities were subsumed to her appeal as the sultry Latina. Indeed, her recent obituary begins by saying that she is most remembered for her roles as "a sultry wildcat in American films of the 1950s" (Jurado obituary, *Boston Globe,* July 6, 2002). Born María Cristina Jurado García in Guadalajara, Mexico, Katy Jurado (1924–2002) was already a highly talented and accomplished actor in Mexico before she came to Hollywood in 1951. She was nominated for an Oscar as a supporting actress for her role in the 1954 western *Broken Lance,* and she received an Ariel, Mexico's equivalent, for her role in Luis Buñuel's film *El Bruto* (1952). She made films in both Mexico and the United States, and she was also the mother of two children, a motion picture columnist for seven Mexican magazines and a few newspapers, a radio reporter, and an acknowledged bullfight critic. She indicated she had actually done some bullfighting with cows, claiming she had the scars to prove it. Discovered in 1951 while watching a bullfight in Mexico, she was immediately cast in her first Hollywood film, *Bullfighter and the Lady* (1951), in which—having not yet learned English—she spoke lines that had no meaning to her. Jurado made a total of seventy-one films during her career, and in the mid-1980s she played the mother in one of

Katy Jurado, the Mexican film star, appeared as "the other woman" (in black) with Grace Kelly (in white) and Gary Cooper (in black and white) in *High Noon* (1952).

the few Latino-themed television sitcoms, *a.k.a. Pablo*.

Like Dolores Del Rio, Katy Jurado was born to a well-to-do old family in Mexico who opposed her entry into film as beneath her social status. According to her 1955 publicity materials, six generations earlier Jurado's ancestors had owned all the land that is now Texas—and, she claimed, she had the papers to prove it. Whether or not this was true, it is noteworthy that her first role in a major Hollywood film,

High Noon (1952), would be a western, set in the southwestern United States. *High Noon* was one of the few films of the 1950s to have a substantial Latino component. A major film, and still a classic, it won four Academy Awards and is listed as thirty-third in the American Film Institute's listing of the top one hundred films of the twentieth century. Considered required viewing for film buffs and media students, a paragon of filmmaking, the movie is widely described as the quintessential western—a perfect 10. It is also interpreted by some as an allegory of the McCarthy era. In this view, the fearful and selfish townspeople who turn their backs on the main character, Kane, represent the movie industry that abandoned those who were blacklisted as communists. John Wayne called the film un-American, preferring a more heroic view of Americans. Yet others saw the film as simply a tale of human nature. Few scholars, however, have focused on the film's Latino components.

In *High Noon*, Jurado plays Helen Ramirez, a strong Latina character who has been a mistress to the two leading men. She is also the proprietor of a store and a saloon in town. Although she clearly loses her man to the blond, sedate, prim, and pacifist Amy Fowler (played by Grace Kelly), she lectures Amy on true love, morality, and the real high ground in life. She leaves town, though one does not know to where. Helen, the only significant Mexican character in the film, feels compelled to go elsewhere because the town has never accepted her. Beyond her presence, however, there is little in the narrative to suggest the earlier history of Hadleyville, New Mexico (a state that had been a part of Mexico only a hundred years earlier). The film reasserts the traditional contrast set up in Hollywood film between the virtuous, all-American girl next door and "the other woman," who is often considered less deserving by virtue of her "otherness"—her race, color, creed, class, or sexual laxity. As Leonard Maltin notes it in his 1994 biography of Jurado, her passion is "effectively contrasted with Grace Kelly's patrician reserve" (Maltin 1994, 450). Interestingly, Jurado was gen-

erally cast in Mexican films as a glamour girl or a wealthy
socialite; sometimes she also sang and danced. In American
films, however, she almost always played a sultry Mexican
beauty, Indian squaw, or suffering mother.

Rita Moreno: Spitfires and Invaders in West Side Story

Rita Moreno (1931–) was also a major star of this era, but just
as many leading men at the time were typecast as Latin lovers,
she was habitually cast as a Latin bombshell, spitfire, or sultry Latina and had to struggle against the limitations of this
typecasting. In *Untamed* (1955), for example, she was cast as
"a fiery love machine"; another writer called her a "Puerto
Rican firecracker" (cited in Suntree 1993, 55). She was born
Rosa Dolores Alverio in Humacao, Puerto Rico, but she was
raised in New York City. Moreno admits that economic neces-
sity forced her to accept many of the fourteen film roles she
played during the first eleven years of her career (Reyes and
Rubie 2000, 520). She played all these roles the same way:
"barefoot with my nostrils flaring." She was dubbed by the
press "Rita the Cheetah." Struggling against the spitfire
stereotype, she left the screen for eight years after her Oscar-
winning role as Anita in *West Side Story* (1961). The only roles
she was offered, she recalls, were "the conventional Rosita and
Pepita type roles," and, having received recognition for her
acting skill, she refused to demean her talent any longer. It was
at this point that she expanded into other performance arenas, such as theater, clubs, and television. Her struggle against
the spitfire image was ultimately successful. She was the first
Latina to win an Academy Award and is the only Latina—and
one of the few actors—to have won all four coveted entertainment awards: Oscar, Tony, Emmy, and Grammy.

The story of two love affairs between teenage New
Yorkers, *West Side Story* reflects the times in ways that most
contemporary viewers miss. It is generally seen as a high-spir-
ited musical and dance production and an engaging love story.
At the time, many residents of the West Side and areas like it

Rita Moreno is shown here as a Latin spitfire, on location for *Untamed,* in 1955. She was the first Latina to win an Academy Award and is the only Latina—and one of the few actors—to have won all four coveted entertainment awards: the Oscar, the Tony, the Emmy, and the Grammy.

in New York saw the film as a "silly" representation of the streets of New York. What self-respecting young street-wise guy would dance ballet-style in the streets of New York? Yes, the love story is profoundly moving and reflects the tragedy of bigotry. Maria's song "I Feel Pretty" resonates with the experience of being a girl; and the love songs "Maria" and "Tonight" are pure romance. The dance contests and the rumbles between the groups are dramatic exaggerations of more subtle realities of the time. Examined from a more critical, retrospective view, however, the film also conveys an "otherness" and a judgment about the "place" of Latinos. In essence, seen through the lens of today, the film conveys the message (or the view at the time) that Puerto Ricans (and perhaps more generally all Latinos) are the invaders and their place is elsewhere (Sandoval Sánchez 1997).

West Side Story first opened as a play on Broadway in 1957; its smashing success spawned the film version, released four years later. As was the norm at the time, few Latinos appeared in the film or the play. Nevertheless, the film was a mega hit, becoming the top-grossing film of 1961. It also received an impressive ten Academy Awards: best picture, best director, best cinematography, best art direction and set decoration, best sound, best score, best editing, best costumes, best supporting actor, and an honorary award for choreography given to Jerome Robbins. The film received other prestigious awards as well, including Golden Globe awards for best film (in musical and comedy), best supporting actor, and best supporting actress, and the Directors Guild of America award for best director. Indeed, no other film had ever garnered as many awards, and few have matched this record since.

The first major film (and play) to focus on Latinos in the Northeast, *West Side Story* had a significant impact on the perception of Puerto Ricans. Interestingly, the projection of Puerto Ricans in this film was not too dissimilar from that of Latinos in other films of the time. It was the same Latino cocktail: poverty, juvenile delinquency, urban landscapes, hot tempers, and knife-carrying gang members who solve their problems through violence. Indeed, but for clues to the context—references by others to nationality, culture, locale, or accent—it was (and still is) difficult for many audience members, particularly the non-Latino audience, to distinguish Chicanos from Puerto Ricans from Dominicans or any other kind of Latinos in film. Part of this difficulty arises from the film's portrayal of Puerto Ricans as immigrants. Indeed, Anita calls her Puerto Rican boyfriend an "immigrant." In point of fact, however, Puerto Ricans, although culturally and linguistically different, were technically not immigrants. They were citizens of the United States. The film contributed to the developing Latino immigrant narrative that would intensify in subsequent eras.

When the play was first written, by Arthur Laurents in 1949, its central story involved a Jewish girl and an Italian Catholic boy, but the scriptwriters who were producing the play on Broadway thought the original conflict dated. News stories of gang activity led Leonard Bernstein (who with Steven Sondheim wrote the songs) to the idea of Chicano gangs fighting "Americans." The new story line was considered too dangerous to be produced in Los Angeles, however, and so New York was chosen as the locale. Puerto Ricans, because they were concentrated in New York and had arrived in large numbers during the 1950s, fit the bill. Sondheim was originally reluctant to do the show, saying he could not write songs about Puerto Ricans because he had never been that poor.

The film enjoyed huge popularity in its time, and it has had continuing appeal as a high school and college drama production. At the same time, it also projects some disturbing binary oppositions. First, of course, is the basic confrontation over turf between white Americans and foreign Latino "others"—those with less claim to the space, those whose place is elsewhere. The newcomers are "the Sharks," the predators. They fight "the Jets," a name that symbolizes all that is modern and progressive. The Jets wear white sneakers, the Sharks black. The Puerto Ricans are uniformly dark-haired, dark-eyed, dark-skinned—Natalie Wood, play-

The Sharks face the Jets in *West Side Story* (1961).

ing the female lead, wore brownface—and the Jets tend toward fair skin. The Jets are the first to appear, in the opening scene, and they seem to be the absolute owners of the open spaces, the streets, and the basketball courts. The institutional representatives in the neighborhood, the police, tolerate the shenanigans of the Jets and ask the Sharks to leave the basketball court after the first confrontation (Sandoval Sánchez 1997).

The focus, as the title implies, is on "stories," not histories. The long history of Puerto Ricans on the West Side and in New York (since the nineteenth century) is overlooked—as is the long and rich immigrant history of the West Side. Also ignored is the long-standing political and economic relationship between the United States and Puerto Rico, which contributed to the migration of Puerto Ricans to New York and made Puerto Ricans citizens. The title implicitly distinguishes Manhattan's West Side (where, at the time, the working classes lived) and its East Side (where those who could afford silk stockings lived).

Finally, *West Side Story* personifies and establishes in the public mind a dualist image of Puerto Rican women as either madonna—the innocent, passive, virginal Maria—or as whore or spitfire—the hot-blooded, fiery, sexy Anita (Perez 1997). This duality reflects, more generally, entrenched images, for women have historically been portrayed as one-dimensional, as either good girls or bad, and as extensions of and subordinate to men. The duality also harks back to earlier images of the Latina as a "hot-blooded tamale," personified by Lupe Velez in the thirties and Carmen Miranda during the forties and fifties. The image of the virtuous "Virgin Maria" also has its antecedents among the earlier Latina leading ladies— Dolores Del Rio and Maria Montez, for example. What made subsequent Latina images different from those of women in general is that the characters were more narrowly developed and were more consistently of lower socioeconomic status and that there were so few alternative images to be had.

The film also sends colliding messages about the possibility and desirability of assimilation and acceptance. As Anita and her girlfriends sing about their dreams of American life, in the song "America," their boyfriends respond with lyrics betraying their own somewhat jaded experience. Nevertheless, Anita's last song reverses her assimilationist position, as she advises Maria to "stick to your own kind" (in "A Boy Like That" / "I Have a Love"), now advocating segregation and endogamy. The Mexican folk song "La Cucaracha" plays in the background as Anita approaches the store within Jets' territory that is the scene of the interrupted gang rape of Anita. The lovers, Tony and Maria, are transgressors in this social order. They do not have a space where they can be together. The last song in the film, "Somewhere," is about the search for just such a place, beyond this real, segregated space on the West Side, where their romance is doomed.

Elsa Cardenas: *Saved by Anglos in* Giant

In many ways, *West Side Story* paralleled the impact that *Giant* (1956)—a film of the same era and magnitude—had on the perception of Chicanos and Mexican Americans. In both films, Latinos are trespassers. Both films portray a romance between Latino and non-Latino, projected as a violation of the accepted norms. Like *West Side Story, Giant* was a box-office hit, and it was one of the few major Hollywood films to have a Latino theme. The film featured the biggest stars of the era, was tagged as a legendary epic as big as Texas, and was more than three and a half hours long. Elsa Cardenas's role, though minor, was the most important part played by any Latino in the film. A Mexican actress born in Tijuana in 1935, Cardenas appeared in her first English-language film, *The Brave One,* in early 1957. After completing the shooting of *Giant* later that year, she stayed off the American screen until 1963, when she appeared as a lady bullfighter opposite Elvis Presley in *Fun in Acapulco* (1963). She has mainly concentrated on Spanish-language film and television, making more than seventy appearances in television and film to date.

In contrast to *West Side Story,* Anglo saviors play important roles in *Giant.* Although quite prevalent during this era, the white, gringo, or Anglo savior character had been present from earliest times. Some film scholars contend that the savior was a filmic representation of the Monroe Doctrine, in which the United States recognized the independence of Latin American nations from Spain but in return claimed for itself the exclusive right to interfere in the internal affairs of countries in the Western Hemisphere. The intervention was always couched in terms of helping the Latin American countries to fend off other evils—privately understood to threaten not only the particular Latin American country but also the United States and its interests in Latin America. The filmic equivalents of the doctrine were the Anglo "good Samaritans" that appeared in many of the earlier westerns. These saviors were often Anglo cowboys who fought "bad" Mexicans in defense of "good" Mexicans—because the Mexicans could not help themselves.

Elsa Cardenas, born in Tijuana, Mexico, was one of the few Latinas to appear in a major Hollywood film during the 1950s. She is shown here as Juana Benedict in *Giant* (1956). Most recently, she has concentrated on Spanish-language film and television.

Giant portrays the life and tribulations of a Texas ranching family over two decades. Although the central plot in the film concerns change and the rivalry over status between old money, in the form of patriarch Bick Benedict (played by Rock Hudson), and new money, represented by Jett Rink (played by James Dean), there is a subplot. One of the Benedict children marries Juana, a Mexican woman played by Elsa Cardenas. Leslie Lynnton (played by Elizabeth Taylor) marries Bick Benedict; she is portrayed as an easterner, from Maryland, unburdened by racial prejudice. Early in the film Leslie makes the point (though in the form of a question) that the lands in Texas originally belonged to the Mexicans, but the movie does not address the implications. Each of the Benedict children has one child; one has dark hair and brown skin and eyes, the other is blond with fair skin and blue eyes. Contrasting close-ups of each are frequent and close the film.

The film is safe and in keeping with the times. It recognizes and bemoans the discrimination, but not much changes. The Benedicts stop at a restaurant for a bite, and Bick Benedict gets into a fight when the owners indicate they will serve everyone except the Mexicans—Juana, her child, and her father. Bick wins the fight, with little help from the Mexicans themselves. At other points in the film, Juana is stopped from entering a Benedict party by security men, and a hairdressing salon refuses to work on her hair. In each instance, the white savior, in this case her husband, intervenes on her behalf. Though Juana is introduced in the film as highly educated, she is apparently incapable of handling any of these events. Each of the interventions by the white saviors ends in strife, and the victories are only symbolic: Bick wins the fight, but the family does not eat there, nor is there any reason to think that the restaurant will now serve Mexicans.

The character Angel Obregon II is played by the young Italian American heartthrob of the day, Sal Mineo. Obregon is the son of the Benedicts' long-time service employee. Toward the end of the film, he tentatively approaches a social gathering in the Benedicts' home while dressed in military uniform. In this scene, the audience is led to expect that he will not be allowed to join the group or that there will be trouble if he does. However, to everyone's surprise—including those who are part of the gathering (and perhaps also Angel and his father)—Mrs. Benedict graciously welcomes him. She and her husband wish him well as he goes off to war—more saviors. This saves the Obregons and others any embarrassment while implicitly underscoring the social distance between the Obregons and the Benedicts.

Rosaura Revueltas: Labor Oppression in Salt of the Earth

Salt of the Earth (1954), an exceptional film of this time, had Latino protagonists, was set in a Hispano mining community in New Mexico, and used many nonprofessional Latino actors. The female lead was played by Rosaura Revueltas (1909–96), a sophisticated and talented actress who had already won two national awards for her films in Mexico. Rosaura was born in Durango, Mexico, in 1909, the daughter of an impoverished shopkeeper. Despite poverty, Rosaura's was a remarkably accomplished family. Rosaura taught herself to speak English, French, German, and Italian, and she raised her son to do the same. Her siblings included one of Mexico's greatest composers, one of the most gifted of the newer Mexican painters, and a leading novelist and screenwriter. After the film's release she was accused of being a communist, blacklisted, and deported to Mexico. She made few films after this, turning instead to dance and writing.

Salt of the Earth was exceptional for a number of other reasons. It focused on a real-life miners' strike in which the miners' wives had taken over the picket line. (Coincidentally, Revueltas's maternal grandfather had been a miner in northern Mexico.) In the film, the women (and children) are imprisoned, though they eventually triumph over the corporation's refusal to improve labor, living, and safety conditions. The film broke new ground in its treatment of sexism, racism,

Rosaura Revueltas, a sophisticated, multilingual, and talented
Mexican actress, played the female lead in Herbert Biberman's blacklisted *Salt of the Earth* (1954). Rosaura, accused of being a communist,
was also blacklisted and was subsequently deported.

and labor oppression and in having a female voice-over, that
of Revueltas, narrate the events. It was far ahead of its time in
dealing with gender inequality within Latino communities.
True to its times, however, the film's racial and ethnic dimensions are overshadowed by the political struggles it presents.
Its production and release underscores the impact and sever-

ity of cold war politics and the McCarthy hearings on Hollywood. (Parenthetically, although supportive of labor, the film in no way challenged the U.S. government.)

The film's director, Herbert Biberman, had spent six months in jail as one of the "Hollywood Ten" who had refused to answer questions posed by the House Un-American Activities Committee concerning his political affiliations. The government had no right, he contended, to know his political views or associations. According to Biberman's biography, more than two hundred writers, directors, actors, and others in the film industry were similarly blacklisted between 1947 and 1954. Biberman made the film to prove that it was possible to make a commercially successful independent film that did not use the film studios' distribution and production system and did not conform to the "Hollywood formula."

After much travail and hysteria surrounding its production, however, the film was shown in only nineteen theaters in the United States. (It was dubbed "subversive" at the time.) Biberman sued the movie industry on grounds that they had conspired to prevent his picture from reaching theaters and were, therefore, violating antitrust laws. Indeed, Howard Hughes, a major player in the film industry at the time, admitted that he and a few others owned "all the means of producing motion pictures" (cited in Biberman 1965, 131). Although Biberman fought the good fight for eight years, a New York City jury (with no African American or Latino members) found that there were insufficient grounds to prove conspiracy and violation of antitrust laws. Despite its limited showing in the United States, the film received the International Grand Prize for the year's best film, awarded by the Paris Academy of Film in 1955, and it has become a film classic.

The Exceptional Jose Ferrer

As in all the earlier decades, some talented actors in the 1950s were able to avoid the typecasting of the times, but even they were affected by the times in which they lived. Foremost among these was Jose Ferrer (1909–92). He was known as the Renaissance man of theater because of his superior abilities to act, direct, write, and produce. Born José Vicente Ferrer Otero y Cintron in Puerto Rico, he was the first Latino to win an Oscar, for best actor in *Cyrano de Bergerac* (1950). He was also the first actor to receive the U.S. National Medal of Arts (in 1985). In contrast to many of the other major Latino stars during the 1950s, he did not play the usual romantic leading man. During his extensive and diversified career in various mediums, Jose Ferrer also received three New York Drama Critics Circle Awards and five Tony Awards, plus additional Oscar nominations.

Ferrer came to live in the United States at the age of six and attended private and public schools. Considered a child prodigy at the piano, he was accepted into Princeton University at the tender age of fifteen. However, he spent a year in a Swiss school because the university felt he was too young to matriculate. He graduated from Princeton in 1933 with a degree in architecture and went on to study French literature at Columbia University, with the intention of becoming a teacher. It was at this point that the stage beckoned and he began to act on Broadway. He established the New York Center Repertory Theatre, which presented a wide variety of plays (Martínez 1974, 62). A man of extensive and distinguished abilities, he made his film debut in 1948 and went on to act in more than one hundred films, to direct eight, to make numerous notable appearances, and to play recurring roles on television. Ferrer was fluent in five languages; legend has it that at one press conference he responded to the questions from different countries in each of these languages. He was married five times, twice to Rosemary Clooney (singer and aunt of George Clooney), with whom he had five children.

Despite his many accomplishments, Ferrer also fell victim to McCarthyism. Along with Biberman and others, like Zero Mostel and Orson Welles, he refused, on principle, to take a loyalty pledge or to answer the question, "Are you

Jose Ferrer, the "Renaissance man of theater," is shown here in *I Accuse* (1958). He was the first Latino to win an Oscar, for best actor in *Cyrano de Bergerac* (1950), and also the first actor to receive the U.S. National Medal of Arts (in 1985).

now, or have you ever been, a member of the Communist party?" For his refusal, he was blacklisted. Crowds protested at the premieres of films Ferrer had made before the Senate hearings. With the aid of the famous lawyer, Abe Fortas, he was able to fight the blacklisting, but not without cost.

The impact of the political climate on Hollywood at the

time was conveyed in Desi Arnaz's autobiography. When Desi Arnaz's wife, Lucille Ball, was being investigated by the House Un-American Activities Committee, he contacted the sponsor of the couple's number-one hit show, *I Love Lucy*, to find out whether the show would be canceled. The formerly fully supportive CEO said that the difficult decision had not yet been made. As Arnaz notes in his autobiography, "In those days the climate was bad for even the smallest innuendos" (Arnaz 1976, 241). Although being a member of the Communist party was not a crime, it was impossible to get a job in Hollywood after such an admission. Often the mere allegation of party membership tarnished one's reputation and chances of being hired. Through skillful and clever handling of the media and of powerful persons in government, communications, and Hollywood, Arnaz was able to dislodge the charge against his wife (Arnaz 1976, 240–57).

The witch-hunt ended when the U.S. Senate voted seventy-eight to twenty-two to censure McCarthy for conduct unbecoming a senator. McCarthy died in 1957, alcoholic, ashamed, and with the tide of public opinion having turned against him. But his hearings had ruined the careers of many and affected the way the United States thought about political dissent. The McCarthy hearings were televised before 20 million people and went on for thirty-six days. Even Dolores Del Rio was barred during the McCarthy era from obtaining a visa to return to America to work, thereby losing out on a role in a film. (The U.S. government has since apologized.)

Although it was during this cold war era that the McCarthy hearings occurred, the concern with political correctness had much earlier roots. Almost thirteen years before the hearings began, Hollywood was given a taste of the hysteria to come, and, curiously, a number of Latinos were caught in that net. In August 1934 police raided Communist Party headquarters in Sacramento, where the names of Lupe Velez, Dolores Del Rio, and Ramon Novarro were found among the effects of Caroline Decker, the secretary of the Cannery and Agricultural Workers' Union (composed primarily of Mexican and immigrant workers). The district attorney, Neil McAllister, asked for injunctions against the stars in the event they were found guilty of being Communist sympathizers. (He also cited actor James Cagney—who responded that McAllister's actions were a bid for personal publicity at the expense of Cagney's reputation.) The reactions of the accused Latino stars are revealing of their particular personalities. Ramon Novarro was unavailable for comment. Lupe Velez responded, "Me a Communist? Ho, I don't even know what the blazes a Communist is! . . . I don't give my money to anybody. I need my own dough. What is the matter with this Sacramento man, anyway? I think maybe they should put him in the lockup tight" (cited in Ellenberger 1999, 131).

Cedric Gibbons, a well-known and respected Hollywood art director, was indignant and declared that his wife, Dolores Del Rio, was not interested in such activities. "It's too silly for words," added Dolores. "It's ridiculous. I never had anything to do with Communists. I don't even know any Communist and I've never contributed a cent to anything but worthy charities. Why doesn't this man in Sacramento find out about things before he talks so much?" (cited ibid.). Fortunately, in the early 1930s such charges were not taken as seriously as they would be during the politically charged cold war era.

Other Visible Latino Actors

There were other Latino actors who received much public attention during this period. Chita Rivera (1933–) was born in Washington, D.C., the daughter of a Puerto Rican musician who played in the U.S. Navy Band and a mixed Scots-Irish–Puerto Rican mother. She played Anita in the play version of *West Side Story* and has received numerous awards for her work. Mel Ferrer (1917–) was born in Elberon, New Jersey, the son of a Cuban-born surgeon and a Manhattan socialite. He made his screen-acting debut in 1949 in *Lost*

Boundaries, playing a black man who passes for white. He was also well known for directing and producing: He directed Claudette Colbert in *The Secret Fury* (1950) and Audrey Hepburn (to whom he was married, from 1954 to 1968) in *Green Mansions* (1959), and he produced *Wait until Dark* (1967). Most of his work has been in Europe, but during the early 1980s he took on a TV role, as Jane Wyman's lawyer in the series *Falcon Crest*.

Other Latino actors achieved more moderate popularity in U.S. films, including Susan Kohner (the daughter of the Mexican actress Lupita Tovar and the agent Paul Kohner), who was nominated for an Oscar for her role in *Imitation of Life* (1959), Joaquin Murieta, Rosenda Monteros (from Mexico), and Pedro Gonzalez Gonzalez (from San Antonio, Texas). Others had more transnational careers: Cantinflas, Sarita Montiel, Rita Macedo, Miroslava Stern, Armando Silvestre, Maria Elena Marquez, and Carmen Sevilla made films in both Mexico and the United States. Linda Cristal, who was born in Argentina but debuted in Mexican cinema in 1951, would continue her career into the next era.

More Invisible Latinos: Anthony Quinn, Raquel Welch, and Juano Hernandez

Given the climate of the times, it is not surprising that two of the biggest Latino stars in the fifties were invisible as Latinos. The career of Anthony Quinn (1915–2001), begun in 1936, reached its zenith during this period. Few at the time thought of him as a Latino actor, though he had actually entered the country as an "illegal" immigrant and traveled with his family as a migrant worker picking grapes, fruits, and lettuce; it was not until 1940, when he was well into his Hollywood career, that he became a U.S. citizen. He began life in Chihuahua, Mexico, the son of an Irish Mexican father and a Mexican mother, and he was raised in the East Los Angeles Mexican barrio, where he shined shoes and sold newspapers. He later found work as a butcher, a boxer, a

Born in Chihuahua, Mexico, Anthony Quinn was raised in the Mexican barrio of East Los Angeles. He won two Academy Awards for best supporting actor, one in 1952 for his role in *Viva Zapata*, the other in 1956 for his portrayal of Paul Gauguin in *Lust for Life*. He made more than 167 films and many notable TV guest appearances. Quinn is shown here circa 1940 with Christopher Anthony, his son by his first wife, Katherine DeMille.

street-corner preacher, and a slaughterhouse worker.

In each of his two autobiographies he acknowledges the economically difficult circumstances of his childhood and his ethnic origins. However, in his public statements, he seemed to play down his ethnic identity, saying that it made no difference as long as he was a person in the world. Nevertheless, his autobiographies present a young boy who is a character visible only to Quinn and who appears in Quinn's life to haunt and, in some cases, to taunt him.

Literary critics contend this character really represents Anthony Quinn as the young Antonio Rudolfo Oaxaca Quinn. In both biographies, Quinn seeks to make peace with the boy and to have the boy leave him alone. But in neither book is the boy *within* him (Quinn 1972 and 1995).

Few Latino actors can rival Quinn's long and illustrious career and his bigger-than-life persona. Federico Fellini once remarked of Quinn that he filled up the screen like a panorama (cited in Thomas 1998, 111). Quinn also had the remarkable ability to make viewers believe they had known his characters all their lives. He won two Academy Awards for best supporting actor, one in 1952 for his role as Emiliano Zapata's brother in *Viva Zapata* and the other in 1956 for his portrayal of Paul Gauguin in *Lust for Life*. But he is perhaps best remembered for his role in *Zorba, the Greek* (1964), for which he was also nominated for an Academy Award, and for his roles in *Lawrence of Arabia* (1962) and *Requiem for a Heavyweight* (1962). His career included an astounding 167 entries—in addition to his many notable TV guest appearances, his roles as producer, and his one directing credit in *The Buccaneer* (1958). He played a wide variety of character roles both on screen and in the theater, although early in his career he was hired mainly to play ethnic character parts, often Native Americans. He wrote a best-selling autobiography and developed his artistic talents as a sculptor and a painter. He also won a scholarship to study architecture with Frank Lloyd Wright. He fathered thirteen children and had three wives, the first of whom was Katherine DeMille, the adopted daughter of Cecil B. DeMille. He died in 2001, at the age of eighty-six, of throat cancer.

Another important performer of this period whose Latinidad was hidden from public view is Raquel Welch. Born Jo Raquel Tejada in Chicago, her father was a Bolivian-born engineer, and her mother was of English descent. Raquel began her film career toward the end of this era, in *A House Is Not a Home* (1964). But she was ubiquitous during the middle and late 1960s. She burst into movie stardom in 1966 in two science-fiction classics, *Fantastic Voyage* and *One Million Years*, B.C. By 1969, *Time* magazine referred to her as "Today's Sex Symbol" and featured her, in her bikini, on their cover (*Time*, November 28, 1969). Despite the extensive coverage she received during this period, no mention was made of her ethnic background, nor did she play a Latina until she was established in her career. Years later, at the start of the next century, Raquel Welch began to rediscover her roots and reflected on her earlier period of ethnic invisibility. When she first tried to break into Hollywood, she recalls, she was told that if she emphasized her Hispanic background, she would be typecast. "You just couldn't be too different," she notes. She agreed to have her hair dyed blond and change her last name (Welch was another name in her family), but she refused to change her first name: "[At the time, I thought,] if I can't even have the Raquel, that's really selling out completely, that's really turning my back on everything that I really am" (quoted in Mireya Navarro, "Raquel Welch Is Reinvented as a Latina," *New York Times*, June 11, 2002).

Raquel says that she never hid her ethnic background; it just never became common knowledge. Adding to the studio and marketing pressure to de-ethnicize her image, there was also her upbringing. Her father, raising his family in California, felt that in order to "make it in the American system," he had to suppress all Latino qualities. He never spoke Spanish at home, so that the children would not have an accent, and the family always lived in non-Latino neighborhoods. "In a way he didn't have a choice," Raquel has noted; everyone suffered, including her father. "There was a sense of shame on his part" amid the confusion and prejudice against Latinos prevalent at the time (quoted ibid.).

Raquel's subsequent awakening to her Latina identity may also reflect contemporary times, for in the twenty-first century Latino actors are once again "in." Notwithstanding this, her shift might also reflect the trajectory of most sex symbols, particularly as they age. Raquel Welch might agree with this, for she observed on turning sixty-one, "You can be

Raquel Welch, born Raquel Tejada in Chicago, is shown here in *One Million Years* B.C. (1966).

a legitimate sex symbol up 'til the age of 35 and then after that you just can't take that seriously. As I was coming up to 40, I was looking for breadcrumbs along the road of sex symbol-dom. And I couldn't find any that were very positive. Most of the American sex symbols have come to rather tragic endings" ("Cries and Whispers: The Week in Quotes," *Hollywood Reporter*, October 2, 2001, 18, Welch clippings file).

Despite the tremendous fame that becoming America's number-one sex symbol bestowed on her, and that many women would envy, like many other sex symbols Raquel expressed dissatisfaction, feeling imprisoned by the status. Although flattered to have been a sex symbol, she was also aware of the boundaries her fame had placed on the further development of her career. Ironically, Raquel escaped being stereotyped as a "Latin," Latina, or ethnic actor only to be pigeonholed into yet another box. However, she feels proud to have endured. She is now enjoying a rebirth in her career. Thus far, she has amassed an impressive sixty-two film credits and has had a strong and continuing role on PBS's first dramatic Latino series, *An American Family*. In addition to her movie career, she also made a triumphant Broadway debut in 1981 in the hit musical *Woman of the Year*. She has performed nationally and internationally in her own highly successful musical review, was a regular major character on television's *Central Park West*, and continues an active career in both film and television.

Some Latinos were invisible not because they denied their *Latinismo* but because they did not conform to the stereotype. Juano Hernandez (1898–1970), for example, appeared in more than thirty movies during his Hollywood career. Usually playing African American or African characters in films, he was acknowledged for his fine acting, deep, resonant voice, and dignified presence. Born in 1898 in Puerto Rico, he was orphaned and went to live with his aunt in Brazil, where he joined a group of street urchins who sang, danced, and performed acrobatics. Having run away with a carnival, he toured Latin American and the Caribbean and

Juano Hernandez, born in Puerto Rico, was admired for his fine acting, his deep, resonant voice, and his dignified presence. He is shown here circa 1950.

finally came to New Orleans in 1915. He taught himself to read and write, acquired knowledge of Shakespearean and classical works, and learned several languages. After a varied series of careers, which included professional boxing, vaudeville, circus acrobatics, radio script writing and announcing, theater work, and a stint as a baritone singer, he went to Hollywood and in 1949, at the age of fifty-one, starred in

Faulkner's *Intruder in the Dust.* Hernandez is remembered as an actor who played the roles of black men with dignity, a rare characterization in his day. In his *New York Times* obituary, he is described as "a towering mahogany-skinned man with little formal schooling but great dignity" (Hernandez obituary, *New York Times*, July 19, 1970). According to the African American historian Donald Bogle, Hernandez's early success in films paved the way for the high visibility and subsequent success of Sidney Poitier. Hernandez died in 1970 in Puerto Rico, where he had lent his eminent talents to the development of the art and media industries.

The Social-Problem Genre

The options open to Latino actors at this time were also delimited by the popularity of films dealing with social problems. Ricardo Montalban, Anthony Quinn, Rafael Campos (born in the Dominican Republic and raised in New York City), and Lalo Rios (born in Mexico and raised in East Los Angeles) all took roles in a number of films that focused on life in the barrio and the place of Latinos in American society. Many of these films—*Right Cross* (1950), *My Man and I*, *Trial* (1955), *The Ring* (1952), *The Lawless* (1950), and *Requiem for a Heavyweight*—involve inciting acts of violence—for example, an accusation of interracial rape or a crime of passion—which the narrative tries to resolve. There is usually a forbidden romance—with a blond girlfriend (generally working class or ethnic), for example—but one that often has failed by the end of the film. Frequently, Latina females assist in returning the Latino male protagonist to his community of origin. The few words of Spanish spoken in these films generally go untranslated, the language being simply a symbol for ethnicity (Noriega 1997).

In film after film during this era, teenagers (often Latinos) are depicted as juvenile delinquents. These include, in addition to *West Side Story, City across the River* (1949), *Blackboard Jungle* (1955), *Rock, Rock, Rock* (1956), *Cry Tough* (1959), and *The Young*

Savages (1961). Many of these films take a deficit approach to the Latino communities, focusing on the problematic nature of the Latino lifestyle and culture and celebrating the virtues of assimilation and the ability of U.S. institutions (the judicial system, for example) or the indefatigable white saviors to resolve problems of the—generally male—Latino protagonists. In many of these films, the Latino characters are ultimately shown to have been saved so that they can redirect their inherent violence toward "making it" under American capitalism, usually with the help of Anglo friends. By the end of the film, the main Latino character is seen as involved in more acceptable and distant areas, helping his people in the barrio or fighting for his country overseas. In the end, the character has assimilated, but the narrative does not address his general lack of economic power or political clout.

Zorro *and* The Cisco Kid

The resurgent popularity of two movie and television series increased the presence of Latino characters during this time. The main character in each series represents the Latino Robin Hood, fighting for and defending the poor. One was *Zorro*, originally written as a magazine story in 1919, set in turn-of-the-century California. Since release of the first film, *The Mark of Zorro*, in 1920 (with Douglas Fairbanks Sr. in the title role), at least seventeen versions have been made—in the United States alone. Some thirty years later, *Zorro* became a hugely popular television show, with Guy Williams in the lead role. It ran for two seasons, from 1957 to 1959, and spawned subsequent follow-ups on television. Earlier Zorro films were also rereleased in the fifties and sixties. The Zorro craze of the fifties also gave birth to one of the early joint-merchandising successes, producing a demand for Zorro lunchboxes, capes, hats, masks, and swords. The *Zorro* theme song became a best-selling record, and Zs were written by students all over America on their homework assignments. It was not until 1983, however, when Henry Darrow (a New

York–born Puerto Rican actor) played Zorro on a short-lived comedy TV series, that the role was played by a Latino.

The Cisco Kid films and television series, modeled on O. Henry's 1907 short story, *The Caballero's Way*, were similar. The character in all versions was a positive role model: He was nonviolent, he threatened nobody, he did good deeds, he never outstayed his welcome, and he had a sense of humor. Although he sometimes flirted with women, marriage never happened. The beginnings of this series predate *Zorro*. Stan Dunn was the first actor to play the Cisco Kid, in a series of one-reel films produced by a French company between 1914 and 1916. Warner Baxter followed in the 1930s, and Cesar Romero, Duncan Renaldo, and Gilbert Roland in the forties. In the 1950s the Cisco Kid reached television, and Duncan Renaldo reprised the lead role on the highly successful show from 1950 to 1954.

In the TV series, Cisco's sidekick, Pancho, was played by Leo Carrillo, a versatile character actor who began his film career in 1929 and went on to make more than one hundred films. Earlier, Carrillo had had a Broadway career, appearing in his first play, *Twin Beds*, in 1914. His family had deep historical roots in California, having been part of the original settlement by Spanish conquistadors. Carillo was a man of many talents who had worked for the engineering department of the Southern Pacific Railroad and as a cartoonist for the *San Francisco Examiner*. Like *Zorro*, *The Cisco Kid* induced a merchandising frenzy in coloring books, gun belts, and lunchboxes as well as a comic strip produced by Jose Luis Salinas. The Cisco Kid became a major pop figure alongside the other cowboys and western figures of the day, most notably, Davy Crockett.

Sympathetic Portrayals of Latinos

Despite the limited portrayals of Latinos during the cold war era, the experience of Latinos may have been better than that of other groups. Through Clause 10 of the Production Code, which required that neither foreign nationals nor the history of their countries be defamed, the Production Code Administration censored and removed the harshest of negative Latin American or Spanish stereotypes from movies in the fifties. This was not routinely done for African Americans, Asians, Arabs, or indigenous people. It was also not always done for U.S.-born Latinos. In some cases, countries like Mexico may have been consulted on the depictions of Mexican Americans. Moreover, although the code prohibited miscegenation in films, Latin Americans (particularly women, all of whom were European prototypes) married white Anglos. In contrast, marriages or "unions" of whites with blacks, Indians, or Asians in Hollywood film were rare. However, some films projected sympathy for a variety of social problems involving Latinos, including Anglo intolerance and immigration, and revolution as a positive means of ameliorating social injustice.

For Latinos in film, the 1950s was neither the best of times nor the worst. It was the era in which the seeds were planted for the violent, lower-class, criminal image that would blossom more fully in the next decade. The depiction of Latinos as poverty-stricken invaders, foreigners, "others" in need of help, or drug-addicted and criminally inclined would intensify as both white flight and the presence of Latinos in central cities increased. The relatively mild fifties stereotypes of Latin lover and Latina bombshell would become more intensely "other"—more alien, exoticized, eroticized, and violent— beginning in the sixties, intensifying in the seventies and continuing into the eighties. Then, as in other eras, Latinos in film would be framed by the times in which they lived.

5

The Era of Contestation

I n 1961 John F. Kennedy assumed the presidency. Although his administration was short (ending with his assassination in November 1963), Kennedy brought a new consciousness to the nation. The slogan for which he is most remembered—"Ask not what your country can do for you; ask what you can do for your country"—would come to symbolize an activist approach and a turning away from the earlier cold war isolationism. The cold war would not officially end, however, until much later. Kennedy's assassination propelled his vice president, Lyndon B. Johnson, into the presidency. Johnson led the country into greater involvement in Vietnam and into major new social initiatives, which would later be termed the War on Poverty. He also expanded Kennedy's Peace Corps and initiated the Alliance for Progress in Latin America, sending ordinary American citizens to assist in the modernization efforts in developing countries. Most significant for the purposes of this book, Johnson signed the historic 1965 Immigration Act, which, contrary to expectations, would bring large numbers of Asians and Latin Americans—and not the anticipated southern and eastern Europeans—to American shores. Many of these new immigrants came fleeing war, hunger, and political instability or counterinsurgency movements in their native countries.

It was also in this era that social mores were challenged and the culture of flower children and hippies reigned. The World War II baby boomers, who came of age during the late 1960s and early 1970s, reacted against the repressive, dour, conformist climate of their upbringing. Begotten during the cold war era, in homes concentrated on material prosperity and a guarded political and social correctness, they would preach peace, love, and freedom in every form and venue—free sex, drugs, health care, education, politics, work and gender roles.

The black power movement, which grew out of the civil rights activism of the fifties, would also intensify in the latter part of the sixties and through the seventies. Suburbanization continued the pursuit of the American Dream through ownership of the single-family home; by 1970 a majority of the country's population was living in suburbs. White flight, low-income high-rise housing, and urban renewal programs in central cities combined with real estate and banking practices to create a nation of suburbs that were essentially white and middle class and inner cities increasingly populated by African Americans, Latinos, non-European immigrants, and low-income or working-class whites. A metaphor used in the seventies to describe the demography of many metropolitan areas was the donut—a ring of white suburbs surrounding a dark or empty hole.

The administrations of Richard Nixon (1969–74), Gerald Ford (1974–77), and Jimmy Carter (1977–81) carried the nation into the early eighties. The United States would pull out of Vietnam and see more change in both the racial-ethnic composition of the country and in social policies. Although the War on Poverty programs would begin to be dismantled in the seventies (and eliminated by the eighties), government and foundation monies would sustain their impetus throughout the seventies. This era would also see new ethnic actors and organizations (primarily African American but also Puerto Rican, Chicano, Asian American, Native American, and even ethnic white) emerge on both local and national political stages. For many Latinos coming of age during this time, the political debate spanned radical Marxism and black militancy (mainly the Black Panthers and Malcolm X) on one side and Martin Luther King Jr. on the other. Cassius Clay, who would become Muhammad Ali, was probably somewhere in the middle. Their relevant Latino equivalents—for example, Rudy Acuña and Manuel Maldonado-Denis—would be less well known on the national scale, but they were just as clear and immovable about their political positioning on the local level and in their writings. Everyone else was a political dinosaur—obsolete in this new sixties (really the late sixties and early seventies) world.

The era that is generally referred to as the sixties was a time of seismic change. This was an era not just of the Black Panthers and the Young Lords but also of varied, heretofore unheard-of actions: Armed black militants disrupted business at Cornell University, and students took over Columbia University. There were student walkouts in high schools and mass demonstrations against the war, racism, poverty, and inequality. Community-based and religiously based outreach programs, grassroots organizing, and youth-based street programs were common. Takeovers of religious institutions, hospitals, ROTC buildings, libraries, nonprofit organizations, and university buildings by students and community groups were not unusual and often lasted until demands had been met or the protestors had been arrested. Indeed, the first Latino-oriented program on national public television (*Realidades*, 1972–75) came about as a result of community pressure. Street academies were set up in storefronts to introduce material not being taught in the schools and to counter some of what was being taught.

There was also a flowering of street culture, particularly in the visual arts, literature, and music, and many from the various diasporas began to write, paint, and compose. Theater companies were established to spread culture and ideas to inner-city neighborhoods and to the countryside, where migrant workers lived. Ethnic studies programs sprang up and multiplied quickly in universities and elsewhere. Affirmative action programs were implemented and monitored throughout the country. Many of the leading Latino organizations and institutions were born during this time, first on a local level and then, in the late seventies, on a national scale. Mexican American and the Puerto Rican legal-defense organizations, for example, were founded to challenge systemic discrimination; new museums, art institutes, colleges, and civic and social service institutions emerged. Latino filmmakers took up the camera, as others might have taken up a gun, and began through their filmmaking to expose and correct existing images of their cultures and peoples and to create alternative images, countering those being projected on the small and big screens (Jiménez 1997). Each of these new ventures was accompanied by myriad contestations between the established order and those challenging it.

Media Images and the Real World

Yet much of the local activity was out of the view of most Americans, being omitted, filtered, or just not observed by mainstream media. Most Americans did not live in these communities, and those who were making Hollywood films were even more distant from the members of these communities, rarely interacting with them beyond the service level. Sensationalist events, those involving violence or riots, for example, made the news and heightened many Americans' fear of "the others." Screen images of Latinos continued patterns established earlier, though intensified with regard to violence and sex. Puerto Ricans, in particular, were portrayed as "a loud, greasy bunch of lazy bums, welfare cases at best, addicts and criminals at worst"—to quote Marifé Hernández, a Latina newscaster speaking in 1972 (cited in Acosta-Belén et. al. 2000, 64). While words like "black power," "ethnic pride," and "community control" were restructuring the American vernacular, Hernández saw only minor changes in the portrayals of Puerto Ricans on television. From her vantage point, the images of the Puerto Rican junkie, prostitute, and criminal continued to appear and make the headlines but were no longer considered discriminatory reporting. The Puerto Ricans had become "the victims of reform journalism, crusading to expose the gory hell of Puerto Rican life in New York, expecting the shock to provide the cure" (ibid., 64–65).

According to Hernández, the real "success story" of Puerto Ricans, the "impressive story of a poorly-educated migrant community, in an alien and sometimes hostile environment"—a community that, after only twenty-five years, now stood ready to "contribute impressive people to every field of endeavor in this nation"—was left untold. She defines these men and women as those who could be judged successful according to the American standards of efficiency and professionalism but, at the same time, had not lost "the warmth, honor, love, rhythm, passion and poetry" that is their own heritage. She points to Puerto Ricans who were building theater companies, travel agencies, dance companies, printing shops, and merchant associations, leading school boards, planning boards, and political campaigns. Their ranks were growing daily "through work, study and guts"; they were not an "elite group in the making" but rather "a majority of the Puerto Rican community that is dedicated to bringing along those of its members not on board" (ibid.). However, Hernández suggests that, given the media coverage, many Puerto Ricans themselves sometimes doubted and lost sight of their success story. The accomplishments and struggles of the Mexican American and other Latino communities similarly went uncovered, and their members similarly often lost sight of their own successes.

Latino Stars: Few and Invisible

Perhaps propelled by the civil rights slogan "Black is beautiful," the seventies also signaled a flowering of diverse ethnicities on the big screen and in the living room. If black could be beautiful, why not also Italian? Jewish? And others? In a reversal of earlier assimilationist orientations, ethnicity was "in." Consequently, the 1970s saw a shift to recognizably ethnic characters no longer trying to drown their differences in the melting pot. Such ethnic characters made superstars of Barbra Streisand, Dustin Hoffman, Robert De Niro, Al Pacino, Sylvester Stallone, and others. "Blaxploitation" films flourished, and the "brown avenger" also made his debut. Because of the greater emphasis on ethnicity, Hollywood's Latino film stars were generally doing better in the seventies than they had during the lean sixties. Nonetheless, there were few major Latino stars, and those Latino images that did exist were selective.

Moreover, despite the emphasis on ethnicity in this decade, the tendency to obscure Latino origins continued. On television, for example, the Latino ethnicity of many stars was generally unknown until recently; these included Victoria Principal on *Dallas*, Lynda Carter on *Wonder Woman* (born Lynda Jean Córdoba), Catherine Bach (of German-Mexican extraction) on *The Dukes of Hazzard*, and Barbara Carrera, who for one year played a rich European on the series *Dallas*. Nor was the Latino ethnicity of popular singers of the time—Vikki Carr, Eydie Gorme, Linda Ronstadt, and Joan Baez—publicly extolled. There were not many top box-office Latino movie stars in this era. Although it has been said that the seventies produced no true superstars in any creative field, this seems to have been even more the case for Latinos. Many of the earlier Latino actors of the fifties and sixties continued to work in films, but their roles were shallower. A few new actors began to appear in the early seventies— Hector Elizondo, Cheech Marin, Raul Julia, Edward James Olmos—but their careers would not take off until the following decades. The few Latina actors emerging at this time also failed to achieve much notice.

Patterns in Film

During this period of contestation nationwide, Hollywood films continued and intensified earlier hackneyed patterns. In contrast to the ongoing challenges to the social order that were occurring in myriad arenas, from the Vietnam War protests to the battles over control of local schools, the films of this period emphasized selected picturesque or violent stereotypes rather than examining the varied experiences of Latinos. Mexican banditos made a comeback, particularly in the popular "spaghetti westerns." Cowboys who would right the wrongs came thundering back into Hollywood films, with Mexican settings and history prevalent but superficially presented. Given the concerns with poverty, white flight, the physical demise of the central cities, the greater visibility of Latinos, civil rights, the defiant assertions of racial-ethnic identity, and the generally unseen efforts afoot in Latino communities, the emphasis on urban settings and urban missionaries was not surprising. Urban banditos were common in film and were treacherous, violent transgressors of the law. Moreover, reflecting the increasing numbers and heterogeneity of the Latino population, these banditos were no longer just Mexican and Puerto Rican but also Cuban and of other, or unidentified, Latino origins. There was a more insistent projection of all Latinos—U.S. citizens as well as legal and illegal noncitizen residents—as "aliens." The ageless demand to "go back to where you came from" seemed to underlie, as subtext, many of the films of this era. Finally, the spitfires and bombshells became more libidinous. This was probably the worst of times for Latino characters and actors.

There were a number of exceptions to these patterns, however. The independent film *The Children of Sanchez* (1978), based on a book by Oscar Lewis, cast several leading Latino stars, including Anthony Quinn, Dolores Del Rio, Katy Jurado, and Lupita Ferrer, in primary roles. Although a dud by all accounts, the film focused on poverty in Mexico. The situation of Mexican farmworkers in the United States also received some attention—albeit indirectly and with a strong victimization overlay—in *Mr. Majestyk* (1974), which pitted a Slavic-Mexican Vietnam-veteran farm owner (played by Charles Bronson) and his girlfriend, Nancy Chavez (played by Linda Cristal), against Italian American mobsters over the farm owner's hiring of Mexican workers. When the mobsters machine-gun his melons, Mr. Majestyk destroys them single-handedly. Countries other than Mexico also served as backdrops.

The much-touted but poorly received *Che!* (1969), which starred Omar Sharif as Che Guevara and Jack Palance as Fidel Castro, was filmed in Puerto Rico. There was also *Cuba* (1979), though the country of the title served as little more than a setting for a love affair between a Britisher (played by Sean Connery) and a local socialite during the reign of Fulgencio Batista. Woody Allen also visited South America in his comedy *Bananas* (1971). In addition, Latino characters and actors played small or supporting parts in other types of movies; Dolores Del Rio, for example, returned to Hollywood to play the Spanish mother of a Native American in *Cheyenne Autumn* (1964). In sum, though the seventies did little for Hollywood representations of Latinos, qualitatively or quantitatively, the decade did bring ethnicity (in general) out of the closet.

The West: History and Its Representations

Latino and Latin American ethnicity was represented on the large screen in westerns and in films set in Mexico. However, these films tended to ignore Latino history and Latin American perspectives. For example, most westerns portrayed the West as barren but for a few generally "savage" Indian tribes. The heroes were "American"—English-speaking settlers seeking to tame a wild frontier. The centuries-old settled existence of earlier peoples was generally ignored, as were earlier explorations by non-Anglo groups.

Yet the settlement history of Spanish-speaking peoples in what is today the continental United States preceded that of the English by more than half a century. Spanish-speaking peoples first settled in diverse parts of the present-day United States in the sixteenth and seventeenth centuries—in South Carolina (Santa Elena, in 1560), Florida (St. Augustine, in 1565), New Mexico (Juan de Oñate's colony, in 1598), and elsewhere. These all preceded the establishment of English-speaking Jamestown in 1607 and Plymouth in 1620. Spanish-speaking missionary settlements were also established in the seventeenth and eighteenth centuries throughout the South, in Texas, and in California to convert the indigenous peoples to Catholicism.

In the early nineteenth century, however, the United States began to expand its borders, especially through the Louisiana Purchase (1803), the acquisition of Florida (1811–21), and the Gadsden Purchase (1853). This expansion came to be rationalized by the concept of Manifest Destiny, by which the United States came to see itself as "destined" to settle the lands to its west and south. An important assumption of this policy was that these lands were either unpopulated—that is, Mexicans and Native Americans were absent—or inhabited by people who were unfit to rule—or, at least, less fit to rule than the Yankees. The history of the nineteenth-century settlement of the western part of the continent was generally told in terms of how the West was won by the United States, not in terms of how it was lost by Native Americans and early Spanish settlers. As settlers claimed these lands, the cultures and proprietary rights of earlier residents were often ignored or quickly disposed of.

In the early nineteenth century, many other Central and South American countries also began their quests for independence from Spain. These struggles would come to play a part in the development of the U.S. policy of Manifest Destiny and the articulation of the Monroe Doctrine. In 1822 President James Monroe recognized the status of Mexico, Argentina, Chile, Peru, and Colombia as independent countries. Nonetheless, while recognizing that these countries were now independent of Spain, the Monroe Doctrine officially reserved for the United States intervention rights in the

Spanish American republics and declared the Western Hemisphere off limits to further European expansion and political ideology. As a result, Latin America and the Caribbean came to be viewed by the United States as quasi-dependent political states in need of protection. The U.S. views of this history would be reflected in film.

Remember the Alamo?

The numerous film depictions of the battle of the Alamo provide illuminating examples of how the history of the conquest of the West (in this case, the Southwest), like all conquests, would be written from the victor's perspective. The slogan "Remember the Alamo" is immortalized in U.S. history books and has often been cried out in films, but few Americans know how or why the actual event took place.

In 1821 Mexico achieved its independence from Spain. At this time, Mexico included present-day Utah, Nevada, California, Texas, and New Mexico and parts of Arizona and Colorado. Spanish conquistadors, missionaries, and colonizers had explored and settled these areas in the sixteenth and seventeenth centuries, mixing with, exterminating, or coexisting with the already-present indigenous peoples (and sometimes a combination of the three). According to Nicolás Kanellos (1998, chap. 3), Anglos began arriving in Texas in substantial numbers in 1798, when Moses Austin, a Yankee, obtained a grant from the Spanish government to mine in the Missouri territory. As a Spanish subject, he later applied for and was given a grant to settle families in Texas. Other Yankees began to arrive soon thereafter, so that by the end of the 1820s, twenty thousand settlers had come into Texas, and by the 1830s, the Mexican government was discouraging Anglo colonization.

By this time, however, Texas colonists, both Anglos and Mexicans (many of whom had lived in Texas for generations), were actively working to create a republic of Texas, independent of the Mexican government. These colonists won their independence from Mexico in a decisive victory over Mexico's general Antonio López de Santa Anna in April 1836. "Remember the Alamo," the colonists' battle cry, recalled their defeat at Santa Anna's hands some weeks earlier. Unfortunately, the contributions of the long-term Mexican colonists, who participated in and even led some of the independence efforts, was screened out of movies on the Alamo—and also left out of many history books.

In 1837 the U.S. government recognized Texas as an independent republic. By this time, Anglos had come to outnumber Mexicans eight to one (thirty thousand Anglo settlers, four thousand Tejanos). Eight years later, in 1845, Texas was annexed to the United States. In response, Mexico severed its ties to the United States, and skirmishes broke out in disputed territory adjacent to the Rio Grande. As a result of one such dispute, the U.S. government declared war on Mexico the following year (in 1846). The war ended two years later with the signing of the Treaty of Guadalupe Hidalgo, under which Mexico lost half of its land (the present-day states of the Southwest and the state of California). Although the treaty ostensibly guaranteed "Mexican Americans" their property, civil rights, and freedom of religion, Mexicans throughout these territories experienced a variety of abuses for decades, including expropriation of their lands, violation of property and civil rights, illegal squatting, segregation, and even lynching.

The decade of the 1960s was bracketed by two westerns with Latino themes: *The Alamo* (1960) and *Viva Max* (1970). The former film, starring, produced by, and directed by John Wayne, is a historically inaccurate but patriotic U.S. view of the event. *Viva Max* is also about the Alamo; but this film ridicules the historical event, presenting a bumbling, allegedly hilarious Mexican general retaking the Alamo. In both depictions, the Mexican view is absent. Hollywood films of this time would also convey an "otherness" in their portrayals that contributed to the view of Latinos as alien and often menacing.

Mexican Backdrops and Banditos

Despite the emphasis on westerns during this time, the films on the silver screen seldom presented the West as having been inhabited by Spanish-speaking peoples for centuries before the arrival of the cowboys. Hollywood westerns became progressively more violent, repulsive, and sexually spiced as the decade of the sixties and early seventies advanced. The perennial Mexican banditos returned, as did the Mexican backdrops (whether filmed in Mexico or elsewhere). Moreover, with some exceptions, non-Latinos generally played the Latinos, in both Latino and non-Latino settings. Some of the better-known films from this period include *Villa!* (1958), which uncharacteristically employed Latino actors—Rudolfo Hoyos Jr., a Mexican-born character actor, in the title role of Pancho Villa and Cesar Romero and Rosenda Monteros in supporting roles. In *The Magnificent Seven* (1960), seven gunmen (two of whom were Mexican) have been recruited by a Mexican village to rid themselves of marauding Mexican banditos. Pedro Armendariz Jr., the son of the Mexican screen idol of the same name, had a supporting role, as did Rodolfo Acosta, a character actor who was born near El Paso (in a then American town) and who played in westerns during this time. Marlon Brando directed and starred in *One-Eyed Jacks* (1961); also in contrast to other westerns of the time, Brando cast Pina Pellicer, a Mexican stage and screen actress, as his costar and gave supporting roles to other Latino actors, including Miriam Colon, a Puerto Rican actress, who also established the Puerto Rican Traveling Theatre in New York City, and Larry Duran, a Mexican American actor and stuntman.

The Professionals (1966)—set in 1917 Mexico though filmed in Nevada—portrayed American mercenaries participating in the Mexican Revolution. The film featured Burt Lancaster and Lee Marvin in the title roles and a few Latinos in minor roles— Maria Gomez, for example, as Chiquita. *The Return of the Seven* (1966) was a sequel to *The Magnificent Seven*. Filmed in Spain but set in Mexico, it starred Yul Brynner. In a supporting role was the legendary Mexican director Emilio (Indio) Fernandez, who had had bit parts in early Hollywood but returned to Mexico, where he played a crucial role in the formation of a uniquely nationalist Mexican cinema. Ironically, during this period in Hollywood, Fernandez was often cast as a despicable Mexican general or bandito, in films such as *The Wild Bunch* (1969) and others. *Villa Rides* (1968) was also filmed in Spain, as the producers feared the Mexican government would deny approval to shoot in Mexico. Yul Brynner was also featured in this film (this time as Villa), with Charles Bronson as his aide and a cold-blooded killer, Robert Mitchum as an American soldier of fortune, and the Spanish actor Fernando Rey in a small role. The spaghetti western *The Good, the Bad, and the Ugly* (1967) was an international hit and launched Clint Eastwood into stardom. The "Ugly" of the title was a Mexican bandit, played by Eli Wallach. Anthony Quinn played a Mexican outlaw in *Guns for San Sebastian* (1968), and Raquel Welch was a Mexican, newly widowed, former prostitute in *Bandolero* (1968).

The western thrust, with ubiquitous Mexican backdrops and ever-present banditos, continued into the early seventies with films like *Bring Me the Head of Alfredo Garcia* (1974), which set a new low for abhorrent and meaningless violence. It starred Warren Oates and costarred Emilio Fernandez and Isela Vega, a Mexican actress who had begun to make Hollywood films in the early seventies. Other films were less gory but generally adhered to easy formulas that included thrill-seeking adventures, explicit violence, and non-Latino major actors (and often characters). Films were increasingly targeted to younger audiences, and many of them were set in Mexico—*A Town Called Hell* (1971), for example, set in nineteenth-century Mexico. *Pancho Villa* (1972), a brawling spectacle in which Telly Savalas played an improbable and bald Villa, was also promoted during this time. Clint Walker, Anne Francis, and Chuck Connors also had leading roles in this film, which was shot in Spain.

Also filmed in Spain was *Valdez Is Coming* (1971), which starred Burt Lancaster (as Valdez) but also featured Hector

Elizondo as one of the banditos and Frank Silvera as a Mexican general. Silvera, a character actor who played a variety of ethnic types, is often assumed to be simply Latino. However, he was born in Jamaica, the son of a Spanish Jewish father and a Jamaican mother. For more than two decades, he worked on stage, on screen, and in television without anyone's realizing he was from Jamaica. Echoing the sentiments of many Latino actors quoted in this volume, he said in 1966: "I didn't hide [my heritage], I simply made no point of it. I agreed with my agent that I wanted to realize myself as an actor, per se, not a Negro actor. In my profession the word Negro meant death. . . . [There were no roles] unless one wanted to play servants or slaves for the rest of a career. . . . I was accepted as a Latin, [and] I let it go at that" (cited in Reyes and Rubie 2000, 567). Another spaghetti western, *Duck, You Sucker* (1972), featured Rod Steiger as a Mexican peasant who goads James Coburn, an Irish Republican Army supporter, to rob a bank with him in 1913 Mexico.

As well as being a prime (if not always an accurate or authentic) historical backdrop, Mexico appeared in Hollywood films as the place to which bandits and other culprits ran to escape the law. In *The Wrath of God* (1972), for example, an Irish terrorist (played by Robert Mitchum) is on the lam in Mexico in the 1920s. Interestingly, this was also Rita Hayworth's first screen appearance as a Mexican since her transformation from Margarita Cansino. Because of illness, it would also be her last film role. Gregory Sierra, a New York–born Latino, who became better known to the public as Detective Chamo in the television series *Barney Miller* (1975–82), also played a supporting role. In *The Revengers* (1972), the culprits also flee to Mexico, and the star, William Holden, follows them and takes the law into his own hands. In *The Deadly Trackers* (1973), a gang of incorrigibles heads to Mexico after each of its crimes.

Latin American locations were exotic and offered cheap extras. But some films that used Mexico as the setting were shot in other countries: *The Five Man Army* (1970) was filmed in Spain and Italy, but it was set in 1914 Mexico. *El Condor*

(1970) was made in Spain but set in late-nineteenth-century Mexico, with sleepy Mexican villages, violent men, women as sex objects, and no Latinos in substantial roles. *Cannon for Cordoba* (1970), a British-Spanish production, was about 1912 Mexican bandits and revolutionaries. These westerns with Mexican backdrops were popular during this time, but "backlot Mexico" has had a long and continuing tradition in film. Indeed, most Hollywood studios had a permanent standing set of a typical Mexican adobe town (Reyes and Rubie 2000, 3–4). Films made on these lots perpetuated myths such as "banana republics, sleepy villages with lazy peons basking in the sun, uncivilized half-naked Indians, violent government coups spearheaded by cruel dictators, mustachioed bandits, beautiful senoritas and the idea that one Anglo is worth ten Latinos" (ibid., 3).

Although Mexico was the backdrop of choice during this time, in subsequent eras Nicaragua, El Salvador, and Panama would be discovered, and all of Central and South America would "seem to melt into a single, amorphous South-of-the-border culture." All the land to the south would become just one giant Mexico, "a place to escape from American law, a place of corrupt anarchy, overwhelming poverty, and cheap hedonism . . . where dark-haired, copper skinned beauties will share their beds for a few pesos" but where, at the same time, a visitor can expect "to be murdered on holiday in Mexico" (ibid., 3, 4).

By the late 1970s, the western had declined in popularity. This meant there would be fewer Latino roles. Qualitatively there was little improvement in other areas.

A Contrast from the Future

Most audiences of this period enjoyed the westerns. Indeed, the problems with the depiction of Latin America and Latinos were missed by many moviegoers. It was not until the subsequent era, when alternative filmmakers and films from abroad began to enter the American consciousness, that these problems were explicitly addressed. The popular film *Like Water for Chocolate* (1992) provides another view of early and rural Mexico, and it makes several departures from the films of the earlier eras. First, it focuses not on sex, corruption, and violence but on the relation between food and emotions, a heretofore generally ignored area in film. Like many of the earlier films, *Like Water for Chocolate* is set in early Mexico, and the set has a "western" feel to it. Its characters, however, are not outlaws but the members of a Mexican family. One is a gringo who has married into the family, though there is no consternation or discussion about "interracial" trespassing. This suggests that intermarriage was not uncommon, which is not surprising, given the proximity between the U.S. and Mexican territories. That is, after all, how Anthony Quinn got his surname, and it is a theme in the biographies of the early Latin film stars (see Chapter 2 in this volume).

Another departure is that Latinos play the Mexican characters and speak in Spanish (there are English subtitles). Although sex is clearly part of the picture, the focal point is on food and the sensual gratification of food. The characters are interesting, three-dimensional, and of varied types. The backdrop is attractive and suggests the history of the moment—no sombrero-wearing villagers napping at the hitching post, no sleazy, rapacious banditos stalking innocent fair ladies; rather, the quiet but emotionally rich bustle of everyday life. It is in the performance of everyday activities, chores, and social events that we come to know the characters, their relationships to one another and their cultural habits.

In strong contrast to earlier characterizations of suffering peasant women or lounging, lusting Mexican cantina girls in westerns, *Like Water for Chocolate* treats the viewer to a melange of women performing a variety of activities and roles. In one scene, one of the daughters in this highly traditionalist and suppressed middle-class Mexican family takes an unconventional path. She rides off on a horse, with her glorious mane of unbraided sun-kissed hair trailing behind her, to accompany her soldier lover. She subsequently leads the soldiers in a battle for justice and equality. This too presents a dimension of Mexican history not often noted: that Mexican women often accompanied their men in battle and sometimes fought alongside or led them. The film explores relationships between women and between women and men. But these women are not like the suffering Maria and spitfire Anita of *West Side Story* fame, who are basically unable to change their fates or the structure within which they live. The men are "real men," not simply good guys, bad guys, or confused guys in a malevolent world. There are conflicts within the family. Patriarchy, matriarchal controls, and the heavy weight of tradition over individual interests are evident, and they are not easily or immediately resolved. There are sexual relations, but love lives within and beyond these. Time itself plays a role in determining the action and ending.

The filmmaker responsible for *Like Water for Chocolate* is Alfonso Arau (1932–), who was born in Cuba but developed professionally in Mexican cinema, where he has made more than twenty-five films. *Like Water for Chocolate* is based on a best-selling novel written by his wife, Laura Esquivel. The film received more than forty international awards. Arau has received six Arieles, the Mexican Oscar equivalent, for his other films and has become a renowned writer, producer, director, and actor in both film and theater. Interestingly, although this film was made in Spanish and was not released in the United States until 1993, Arau has been involved with U.S. films since the mid-sixties. Indeed, his feature film *Mojado Power* (1979) was set in the United States and was a satirical look at what would happen if undocumented Mexican workers asserted themselves in the United States as black power advocates had done at the time. He has continued to direct highly acclaimed U.S. films, including *A Walk in the Clouds* (1995) and his most recent work, TV's *The Magnificent Ambersons* (2002). His career, and also that of the Peruvian Luis Llosa (who has been working in the United States since 1977), illustrates what has historically been the case but is not often acknowledged: that Latin American talent has been involved in Hollywood from early on.

Aliens: Why Don't They Go Back to Where They Came From?

Another tendency in the films of the late sixties and seventies was to project Latinos as aliens, or as an "alien nation" within the United States. At the same time, the white-bread personality continued to dominate Hollywood film. Consequently, many of the former Latino leading men had to leave Hollywood for Europe to continue in lead roles. Ramon Novarro, a marquee idol of an earlier era, summarized the period as follows: "I love the United States of America, and I love being here. . . . But as an actor and as an individual, I find myself in a dual position. Like others from Latin America, I am part of an alien nation within a larger nation. . . . The fruits of our labor are prized and needed, but we are kept apart, due to our language and culture. They like our food and admire our colorful art, but do not accept us as peers. Even in Hollywood, and not even after decades of positive change in other arenas" (cited in Hadley-Garcia 1993, 183).

Closely associated with this idea of an alien nation was the idea that "they" should go back where they came from. (See, for example, the films *My Man and I* [1952], *West Side Story* [1961], and *Zoot Suit* [1982].) The concept of "alien" implies borders and the illicit crossing of borders. Thus there is also a sense of not belonging. At best, this attitude is a clear declaration of a competition for space, with the implication that "they" are invading "our" space. On another level, it may also imply that the "aliens" cannot be a part of the mainstream, dominant culture and should go back to their barrio or to "their" country, to help their own people.

This is an ancient theme. It has been sounded in many movies and has been used with many other individuals or groups considered to be outside the norm. However, its use is particularly ironic for Latinos, as it must be for Native Americans. Where are they to go, the Californios, the

Tejanos, the Hispanos of New Mexico, who have lived in these areas for generations, and stateside Puerto Ricans, who have been Spanish-speaking American citizens for more than three-quarters of a century? These groups for the most part did not come to the United States; the United States came to them. Moreover, the majority of Latinos living in the United States today were born here, so where are they to go back to? Of course, if all Americans were to go back to where their ancestors came from, there would be very few people left. With the exception of Native Americans, the United States is a nation of immigrants.

It was not until the next era that a Hollywood film would illustrate this irony. In *Born in East L.A.* (1987), the main character, Rudy Robles (played by Cheech Marin), is a third-generation Mexican American, an auto mechanic, whose adventures bring to mind Charlie Chaplin's beloved Tramp. Robles's mother calls him and awakens him with the request that he pick up a Mexican cousin at a toy factory. In his haste he leaves his wallet behind. He inadvertently walks into an INS raid at the factory and is deported along with others (who do not have "papers") back to Mexico, where they are assumed to have come from. We next see him in Tijuana, penniless and unable to understand the language or the country, for he has never traveled south of the border and is a foreigner there. He now has to find a way to enter the United States illegally.

The film provides a humorous look at a serious issue, but it also expands our view of the situation by showing the diversity of ethnicity on both sides of the border. At one point, Marin coaches OTMs ("other than Mexicans"), who are trying to enter the United States without papers, on how to pass themselves off as barrio boys, teaching them the laid-back walk and how to greet others with a "Wass sappening?" He instructs Asians to wear headbands low, so as to hide their slanted eyes. The title purposefully echoes the Bruce Springsteen song, "Born in the USA," to illustrate that one can be born in the United States and yet still be considered a foreigner.

Urban Settings and Urban Missionaries

In films of the late sixties and early seventies, there was also a particular focus on Puerto Ricans living in urban squalor. In the film *Popi* (1969), for example, a single father with two children is living in such a difficult situation that he devises a desperate plan. He will place his children in a boat and have them be picked up as Cuban refugees, so that a rich family will adopt them or they will receive the benefits being extended to Cuban refugees at the time. As the tagline of this film says, "Better to drown in the ocean than in the sewer." The movie highlights the harsh living conditions of Puerto Rican citizens and the inequities in the government's policies toward them as compared with Cuban refugees. A number of Latino actors played the film's Latino characters, including Rita Moreno in a primary role, but the main role went to Alan Arkin, who played his part well but whose accented English was not very convincing.

Another common theme in films of the day was the rescue of inner-city residents by "urban missionaries" and "urban cowboys." In some ways, this was a reincarnation of the Yankee saviors who intervened to fight against bigotry toward Latinos in the United States (such as in *Giant*). In films of this era, however, the venue and the occupations of the saviors were changed: White teachers, doctors, nuns, and priests were going into urban areas to "save" the often Latino residents. Sometimes, the urban missionary was initially rejected or assaulted before at least some of the residents "saw the light." The urban missionary theme is seen in films such as *Up the Down Staircase* (1967), which follows a rookie high school teacher learning to handle the chaos and despair in an inner-city high school. The film was set in Spanish Harlem, and some local teenagers were hired, but it failed to feature any Latinos in major roles. The tagline for the film was something like this: The first mistake the pretty young teacher made was to get off the bus. The second was to walk into Calvin Coolidge High School for the first time. The third was to fall in love with it.

Change of Habit (1969) featured Elvis Presley as a doctor and Mary Tyler Moore as an incognito nun trying to address some of the problems plaguing an inner-city Latino community—abused children, recalcitrant parents, and highly sexed teens. Again, there were no major Latino players, although Puerto Rico–born Laura Figueroa had a bit part. *The Pawnbroker* (1964), also set in Spanish Harlem, presented a Holocaust survivor working as a pawnbroker in an inner-city neighborhood. Memories of the concentration camp are juxtaposed against views of the eerie and barren world of his neighborhood. There are only a few redeeming Latino or other ghetto residents here. The pawnbroker's apprentice was played by Jaime Sanchez, a Puerto Rican actor who also played in *The Wild Bunch* and other movies during this time. In *The Possession of Joel Delaney* (1972), a seventeen-year-old Puerto Rican murderer inhabits the body of his best friend, Joel, which turns Joel into a murderer. Miriam Colon and Edmundo Rivera Alvarez had secondary roles in this film, the locale of which shifts from Spanish Harlem to other parts of New York. One reviewer in the *Hollywood Reporter* commented at the time that "the most remarkable thing about the film is that it is wildly anti–Puerto Rican" ("Shirley MacLaine Stars in 'Possession of Joel Delancy'" 1972, 3). Barrio residents are constantly referred to as "they"—as in "*They* are all believers in witchcraft."

To a large degree, these movies fit in well with President Johnson's War on Poverty and the liberal perspective of the day (Perez 1997). There was a strong push at the time to focus on poverty within urban areas, which incidentally were also the site of many urban disturbances during this time. Within this perspective, external conditions were seen to be causal factors contributing to delinquency and crime. Consequently, such factors were amenable to change by the upstanding and morally strong protagonists in the films. Nonetheless, in most of these films, Puerto Ricans, other Latinos, and African Americans appeared only as background characters. They were not actors in their own lives, they were acted upon by white characters. Moreover, even the well-intentioned films like *The Pawnbroker* projected a racial hierarchy. In addition, examples of concurrent local activism within these same communities rarely appeared in these films, nor were nationally televised events, occurring at the same time as the making of these movies, part of the backdrop. There was no suggestion of the civil rights demonstrations, struggles over low-income housing, the New York City District 1's struggle for community control of its schools, the Selma civil rights marches, voter registration drives, and urban rebellions in Watts, Chicago, San Diego, Forest Hills, and elsewhere (Perez 1997).

Urban Cowboys and Urban Banditos

In *West Side Story*, Puerto Ricans were portrayed as potentially (although somewhat problematically) assimilable. This attitude changed in the late sixties and seventies as the image hardened. Latino characters went from those who could conceivably "make it"—a struggling ghetto boxer, for example— to those who were forever trapped in their circumstances— junkies, drug dealers, and urban gangs. The presidency was held by Richard Nixon; it was the time of "winter in America," "dirty tricks," white backlash, and the quiet burial of the War on Poverty policy. *Dirty Harry* (1971) and his signature slogan, "Make my day," epitomized the contemporary hero: a lone vigilante righting what had gone wrong. Fairly despicable Latino characters appeared in urban films, often as background or minor characters. Some films focused on gangs in both Chicano settings (*Boulevard Nights* [1979], *The New Centurions* [1972]) and in New York (*The Warriors* [1979], *The Seven-Ups* [1973]). Also set in New York City was *Short Eyes* (1977), a film based on Miguel Piñero's play about a Puerto Rican child molester in prison.

At the end of this era appeared *Fort Apache, the Bronx* (1981), a film that was so offensive in its depiction of the community (Lewis 1987, 69; Perez 1997, 160) that it elicited boycotts, during its filming as well as afterward, on the part of the Latino community in the Bronx. Rachel Ticotin

Rachel Ticotin starred with Paul Newman in *Fort Apache, the Bronx* (1981).

(1958–), who was born in New York of Dominican parents and continues to act in film and television, had a supporting role in this film. *Badge 373* (1973) disparaged the Puerto Rican political movement; perhaps it is only coincidence that the film was produced at the same time that the United Nations General Assembly approved by majority vote Puerto Rico's right to independence and self-determination.

As Latinos increased in number in the United States and as the barrio became the predominant backdrop in most films featuring Latino characters, the representation of "legitimately" affluent Latinos (that is, other than drug lords) declined. Few upper-class Latino characters appeared in contemporary movies, and fewer still had attained their wealth through legal means. Urban "bandito" characters—drug lords, dope dealers, and junkies—set against inner-city backdrops prevailed, and the seeds of the violent, lower-class criminal image blossomed in the seventies, when the crime and the violence associated with them escalated. Urban cowboys often battled these urban banditos. The cowboy had moved from the wide-open spaces of the West to the dirty and dangerous streets of urban America. Promotional language in vigilante flicks such as *The Exterminator* (1980) painted a picture of heroes responding to horrendous wrongs perpetrated by the evil, threatening armies of the night that ruled these inner-city areas, outnumbering or outfoxing the police and threatening to hold everyone hostage to their rule of fear, crime, and intimidation. In *Death Wish* (1974), it is the bleeding-heart-liberal architect who sets out to avenge the murder and rape of his wife in New York City.

Latina Faces

Whereas the Latino men were increasingly drug addicts, drug dealers, or sexual predators and violators of the law, Hollywood's Latina characters continued to be sexy, but they became even more secondary—and more lustful. The world of Latinas on screen was made up of victims, vamps, and victimizers. The occasional "virgins" who appeared were generally characterless casualties—sometimes under the age of thirteen. For Latina characters, sex was a throwaway, quickly volunteered but often rejected. The Latina characters were frequently sexual adjuncts, pure background to titillate the viewers. Although some actors found ways to enhance these roles, they were limited by the script, the direction, or the editing process. Few had the power then to do as Gilbert Roland had done in the 1940s, when he insisted that a scene be written in *The Cisco Kid* (in which he had the title role) to show his character reading Shakespeare on a riverbank. As Roland said, "I wanted to be sure the *mexicano* was not portrayed as an unwashed, uneducated, savage clown" (quoted in Thomas 1998, 52).

Some new Latina faces appeared during this era. Linda Cristal (1934–), born Marta Victoria Moya Burges in Buenos Aires, Argentina, began making U.S. films in the late fifties and appeared in a number of major movies during the next two decades, including *The Alamo* and *Mr. Majestyk,* and on television, in 1967, in *High Chaparral.* Linda Christian (1924–), born in Tampico, Mexico, as Blanca Rosa Welter of Dutch and Mexican ancestry, also increased her Hollywood and international movie production during the sixties but retired soon after. Married to the movie idol Tyrone Power (from 1949 to 1956), she was well traveled and educated, having

Tagged the "coochie-coochie girl," Charo was also an internationally recognized classical guitarist.

attended universities in Mexico, Venezuela, Palestine, South Africa, Holland, and Italy. Barbara Carrera (1951–) was born in Managua, Nicaragua, and first began to appear in films in the 1970s. She made her major screen debut in *The Master Gunfighter* (1975) and continued to act in other films and television projects throughout the eighties and to the present.

The Ever-Present Charo

Also much in evidence during this period was Charo (1941–). She was born María Rosario Pilar Martínez in Murcia, Spain, and although she did not appear in many films, she was better known than other Latinas of the time because of her greater exposure on television talk shows in the 1970s. Charo had been the wife of Xavier Cugat, who was forty-eight years her senior, and the singer in his band. At least once in each of her appearances she would shake her hips and squeal "cuchi-cuchi!," earning her the nickname "coochie-coochie girl." She also repeated the earlier comical style of Carmen Miranda and Lupe Velez, with her hyper persona and her heavily accented English, often laced with humorous errors. Despite her cute, sexy, and dizzy personality, Charo was an accomplished classical guitarist, having won a scholarship when she was fourteen to study with Andrés Segovia. She was fluent in French, Italian, and Japanese, in addition to Spanish and English. This dizzy blond and accomplished musician was acutely aware of the contrast she presented, but she had no complaints: Cuchi-cuchi took her all the way to the bank.

This duality of images and Charo's awareness and ability to use this duality to her personal advantage distinguishes her from other Latina actors of the time, who seemed to have less control over, or contrast in, their public images. The term "spitfire," attributed to Lupe Velez's popular character, was often used to describe the Latina characters of this era. However, there are important differences between Velez's character and many of the Latina characters portrayed during this and subsequent eras. Lupe Velez's Mexican spitfire character, Carmelita Woods, was the main protagonist; she was clever, funny, married, and never had sex with strangers. In sharp contrast, spitfires in this era were often marginal characters who never got the guy and were often hypersexual and occasionally violent and vulgar. They were humorless, shallow, and not very bright. They generally had few lines and little relation to the plot. As the end of the century drew near, Latina characters would change again. They would retain their hypersexuality but would project greater sensuality, savvy, and sometimes great strength. At the beginning of the twenty-first century, some humor would also return.

The New Latinos: Cheech Marin, Raul Julia, and Hector Elizondo

There were, of course, exceptions to the patterns of urban banditos, cowboys, missionaries, and lascivious Latinas. One was the team of Cheech and Chong, who made six films together during this period, the first of which, *Up in Smoke* (1978), was the highest-grossing comedy of that year (West and Crowdus 1988, 34–37). These films followed the adven-

Cheech Marin is a well-known comedian and the creator, director, and star of *Born in East L.A.* (1987).

tures of the comedic duo, Thomas Chong and Richard "Cheech" Marin, who played two perpetually pot-smoking hippies. (The name Cheech is derived from the Spanish word *chicharron*, meaning deep-fried pork skin.) Marin (1946–), the Latino member of the duo, was born in Los Angeles, the son of a thirty-year veteran of the Los Angeles police department and his wife, Elza Meza, who was a secretary. He attended California State University at Northridge and received a bachelor's degree in English. Before breaking into Hollywood, he recorded several "gold" albums, one of which received the 1973 Grammy for the best comedy record. After the duo broke up in 1984, Marin went on to write, direct, and star in the critically acclaimed movie, *Born in East L.A.* He cowrote, with Tommy Chong, the screenplays for their movies, and he has also written a children's book. He has continued his acting career, playing a police officer (like his father) in the long-running TV series *Nash Bridges* and a number of supporting roles in major films.

In stark contrast to Cheech Marin is the work of Raul Julia (1948–94). Whereas Marin's work during this period played well to the hippie culture of the time, Julia's reached a broader audience. He was born Raúl Rafael Carlos Julia y Arcelay in San Juan, Puerto Rico, the son of a prosperous restaurateur. He attended private schools in Puerto Rico and graduated from the University of Puerto Rico. He considered going to law school but decided instead to do what he most enjoyed, acting. He had his first film credit in 1971 in *Been Down So Long It Looks Like Up to Me*. He also appeared in various television shows and movies during this period, including *King Lear* (1974) (as Edmund), *Othello* (1979) (as Othello), and *The Tempest* (1982), a modern version of the Shakespearean play. He went on to make more than twenty-seven films and garnered acclaim for his intense dramatic ability and his versatility—in serious theater, as well as on the musical stage, and in film. As one reviewer has noted, "One wonders if there isn't anything he can't do" (Hodenfield 1980, 188). He is particularly remembered for films such as *Romero* (1989), *The Penitent* (1988), *The Kiss of the Spider Woman* (1985), and the TV movie, *The Burning Season* (1994), for which he was posthumously awarded a Golden Globe and an Emmy. But he became best known for his role as Gomez in the popular *The Addams Family* movies.

A dedicated activist, Julia had a strong sense of being Puerto Rican and of contributing to this community; he also worked tirelessly for the Hunger Project, as well as many other causes. He died early in his career (at the age of fifty-four) of a cancer-related stroke in New York. He had a well-established career and was known particularly for the depth of his portrayals and the seriousness with which he approached his craft and chose his roles. An obituary notes that his talent was such that he was hardly ever typecast (Laurie Winer, "Raul Julia: A Talent beyond Typecasting," *Los Angeles Times*, October 25, 1994). Nevertheless, parts of his

Raul Julia was a talented and multifaceted actor who was acknowledged for his masterful portrayals in serious Shakespearean theater
as well as dramatic films and comedies. A dedicated activist who
worked tirelessly for many causes, including the Hunger Project, Julia
died early in his career, at the age of fifty-four. He is shown here in
1993 as Gomez in *Addams Family Values.*

story reflect the experience of many other Latino actors of
the time. Arriving in the sixties from Puerto Rico, he was not
at all self-conscious about being Puerto Rican. But by 1982 he
was already acutely aware of his "otherness" in Hollywood.
"There's a subtle kind of compartment I'm put in," he told
the *Los Angeles Times.* "Since I've proven I am a competent
actor, now they say, 'Oh, he's very good, very good, but he's
Puerto Rican.'" He went on to say that there were "still people out there—casting people, directors, producers—who see
me as a stereotype" (Clarke Taylor, "Raul Julia Does Battle
with Stereotyping," *Los Angeles Times,* July 20, 1982).

It became one of Julia's goals to break these stereotypes.
He turned down the typical Hispanic roles he was offered,
later noting, "Why do I want to play myself, unless it's a
great, meaty role—and how many of those are there?" He

acknowledged that opportunities for most Latinos were equally grim on stage, screen, and television. Although there were more Hispanics working in this period as compared with twenty years ago, he observed, they were playing mainly Hispanics. About his own ability to have demonstrated his versatility and dramatic talent, he said he had just been lucky enough "to meet producers and directors who have seen beyond the stereotype." He held the media partly responsible for the stereotyping: "People with a low view of Puerto Ricans are influenced by media horror stories. . . . I didn't come to New York to be a stereotype. I came to be an actor." What was needed, he felt, was to transform people's way of looking at Hispanics, which extended beyond show business into politics and attitudes toward Latin America. Although he realized that it was possible, and could be profitable, to milk stereotypes or typecasting, he rejected this approach: "There are actors who play one personality forever and they're happy doing it. But that isn't what I want. I would get bored. You can make a lot of money, but to me that's a fringe benefit" (Hodenfield 1980, 189).

As his career progressed, Julia came to be recognized as a highly talented and versatile actor. As John Frankenheimer, who directed his last movie, said of him after his death, "He was a magnificent actor and totally dedicated to his work. He was kind, intelligent, funny, loyal, brilliant and so very, very talented" (Galloway 1994, 83). However, even at the peak of his career, in the early 1990s, he tended to play lead roles in smaller-budgeted, Latino-themed films but only supporting roles in big-budget, star vehicles.

Hector Elizondo (1936–) also began his serious film career during the seventies. Born on 107th Street in Manhattan, his mother was from Puerto Rico and his father was a Spanish Basque who had been born at sea. His parents married in Puerto Rico, and they came to live in New York, where Hector and his sister were born. At an early age, Elizondo appeared with W. C. Handy on local radio and television; he was also a gifted baseball player and was scouted by the San Francisco

Hector Elizondo, successful in many fields, moves freely between starring roles on Broadway, on television, and in feature films.

Giants' and the Pittsburgh Pirates' farm teams. He attended public high school and went on to the City College of New York in 1954, intending to become a history teacher. By 1957 he had married, fathered a son, and divorced, and by the early sixties he had turned to a career in acting.

Elizondo has had a wide variety of experiences and is also an accomplished musician and singer. He has been a Conga player with a Latin band, a classical guitarist and singer, a weightlifting coach, a ballet dancer, and the manager of a bodybuilding gym. By the time he began serious work in film, he had been acting on stage and had already received an Obie for his leading role in *Steambath* (1969). Although he had some minor film credits between 1963 and 1969, he moved more seriously into film in 1970 and played a wide variety of parts and ethnicities—Mexican bandit, middle-class family man, football coach, Greek coffee-shop owner, and nonethnic hotel manager. He considers himself an actor, not a Latin actor, saying, "I'll be damned if they call me a Latin actor. Nobody calls Sinatra an Italian singer. I'm an actor period" (cited in Hadley-Garcia 1993, 215). Elizondo has appeared in more than eighty screen and TV movies, directed (*a.k.a. Pablo,* a Latino-themed TV show), and is a four-time Emmy nominee. He has been a cast member in numerous successful television series, including *Chicago Hope,* for which he won an Emmy award for his portrayal of Dr. Phillip Watters. He has been successful in many fields, and he continues to move freely back and forth between starring roles on Broadway, television, and in feature films. He has received many awards and accolades for his work and is an avid supporter of numerous charitable organizations.

Fighting Back and Creating New Images

During this period, two trends emerged that would become stronger in the eighties and nineties. One was the more insistent protesting of negative depictions on the part of Latino communities throughout the country, which yielded some successes: Mexican Americans succeeded in eliminating several demeaning characters from mass-culture, including such icons as Jose Jimenez, Chiquita Banana, and the Frito Bandito. When the president of Frito-Lay asked Ricardo Montalban what the problem was with the "cute little fellow we call Frito Bandito," Montalban replied, "Why didn't you make him the Frito Amigo, giving the chips away, sharing them with everyone because he loves them so? No. You make him a *bandit,* stealing the chips. Because that's the only way to think of a Mexican—as a bandit" (Montalban 1980, 152).

In his autobiography, Ricardo Montalban discusses the group he helped to found, Nosotros, whose purpose was to improve the image and employment of Latino actors. Although he was not a militant, he felt strongly that the image of Mexico and Mexicans had been damaged for many years by their portrayal in Hollywood film. "I felt that my native country had been betrayed by Hollywood," he says. "I realized that the filmmakers had not purposely aimed to be damaging;

they were simply adding color to their movies. A bank teller doing his daily job is not colorful. . . . But a man sleeping under a cactus tree or a bandit with a big mustache and a big hat and bandoleers across his chest—they are colorful." He has also maintained that if Hollywood, or Madison Avenue, were going to create such a character, the Mexican bandit should be presented not as a caricature but as a human being: "Give him a heartbeat, find out what kind of person he is" (ibid., 148, 153). Hollywood had perpetuated these images, he observes, out of ignorance about the harm they were doing.

Cautioned by another actor against becoming involved with a group like Nosotros, he nevertheless felt it was necessary to open a few doors, and so he agreed to do what he could to establish a dialogue with filmmakers. Montalban explained that the group asked no favors, simply that actors of Spanish-speaking origin be considered for acting opportunities. Spanish-surnamed actors seeking work at the time were commonly told by the casting director that there were no parts for Mexicans in the picture. Although Enrique Delgado, for example, a highly competent Puerto Rican actor from New York, did not have an accent, he could not get inside the studio door until he changed his name to Henry Darrow, after which he got a leading role in a television series *(High Chaparral)*. Nosotros was simply asking employers not to reject a prospect simply because of his name (ibid., 152).

Because of his involvement with the group, however, Montalban became the victim of a backlash. For four years he did not make a movie; television roles became scarce, and he was offered only Mexican roles rather than the variety of roles he had grown accustomed to. His statements on behalf of Nosotros were misquoted in the press. For example, his remark, "All I ask is that we are allowed to compete . . . not only for the part of the Mexican bandit but for any part we are capable of performing," was quoted in the press the next day as, "We are tired of Anglos playing us." Montalban's request for a clarification on the misquote was reported as, "We ran into Ricardo Montalban, president of Nosotros, on a set at Universal and he said, 'Why should Greeks and Italians play Mexicans?'" Montalban was sure that all Greek and Italian actors would now hate him for years and that producers and directors would say, What is this guy's problem, why does he stir up so much trouble? (ibid., 154).

Montalban did not regret his involvement, despite the price he paid, saying philosophically,

> I have no regrets. You choose a route, you go with it, and you pay the consequences. It was perhaps inevitable that I would be misjudged, just as I was misjudged as a boy because I spoke the Castilian of my parents. I was born in Mexico, and I loved my country with my very being, but that did not mean I could not love Spain, which had given me my parents. And so it is now. When I love the United States, does that mean that I must love Mexico less? I don't think so. We develop many loves during our journey through life—love of parents, of brothers and sisters, of teachers and sweethearts. We don't need to sacrifice one for another. (Ibid., 154–55)

Although many of the protests against specific films— *Fort Apache,* for example—went unheeded by the relevant Hollywood powers that be, they were not without consequence. Others heard them in Hollywood, and, perhaps more important, they were heard within the many communities in which they occurred. This contributed to greater consciousness and indirectly to the development of new, alternative films and more organized media activities in later periods. These protests heightened the awareness that the activism around Puerto Rican and Latino politics rarely made an appearance in Hollywood films, and when it did, it was often disparaged and ridiculed. These protests also involved competent Latinos at all levels, from professional lawyers, doctors, and writers to a wide range of community people without professional credentials.

The protests did not suggest that there were no drug dealers, prostitutes, pimps, and gunmen in Latino communities; the complaint was that these seem to be the only Latino characters portrayed in Hollywood movies. Even in *Fort Apache*, the Puerto Rican nurse (a rare characterization at the time) turned out to be a heroin addict. Missing from these films were the Latino characters that mirrored the majority of Latinos—whether involved in activist politics or not. Absent were the poor nonaddicts, those who did not abuse children or rape vulnerable women, the single moms who had no relationship to gangs or gang members, and the working families who were not dependent on welfare. In other words, missing were those who predominated in barrios throughout the country. Also absent were the traditional working- and middle-class families and professionals who had for generations had a strong presence in the Latino communities as lawyers, teachers, secretaries, students, and those involved in religious activities.

The "Others" Begin to Tell Their Stories

This era saw the emergence of alternative films by young independent filmmakers (often Latino). *Yo Soy Joaquin* (1969), directed by Luis Valdez and written by Corky Gonzales, and *Yo Soy Chicano* (1972), directed by Jesús Salvador Treviño, began to explore what it meant to be Chicano in the United States. Treviño would write and direct a follow-up film in the same vein, entitled *Roots of Blood* (1979) (released in Spanish as *Raíces de Sangre*). A documentary on a famous Puerto Rican poetess, entitled *Julia de Burgos* (1978), was produced by Sandino Films, a cooperative in Puerto Rico. Other independent films addressed the conditions and struggles of Latinos in inner-city neighborhoods: *The Devil Is a Condition* (1972), directed by Carlos de Jesus, told of Latinos' and African Americans' battle to improve housing conditions throughout New York City. Interestingly, this film was made possible through German funding and facilities (Jiménez 1997, 192). De Jesus also directed *The Picnic* (1976), a celebration and sharing of cultural values between Puerto Rican inmates and their families in a New Jersey prison. *In the Heart of Loisaida* (1979), directed by Bienvenida Matías and Marci Reaven, was another documentary about early housing takeovers by Latino tenants in New York City's Lower East Side.

Pablo Figueroa made *Cristina Pagan* (1976), a short narrative about a young mother who delves into spiritualism in an effort to accept the death of her child. Made with minimal funding, Figueroa's film demonstrated that Puerto Ricans in low-income areas could be both poor and working class as well as honest, clean, spiritual, loving, and concerned about their families—a seemingly simple and unremarkable set of characteristics but in its time, with respect to Latinos, a highly unusual representation. He also made *Dolores* (1988), an early and influential film about domestic violence. The political situation in Puerto Rico was addressed in *Paradise Invaded* (1977), made by a group of filmmakers in Puerto Rico, and *El Pueblo Se Levanta* (The People Rise Up) (1971), an early documentary about the Young Lords, was produced by Newsreel Films.

An interesting but little-known film, *Isabel la Negra* (1979) (released in English as *A Life of Sin*) was based on a classic literary work. One of the first films to address issues of race, it featured various well-known Latino actors, including Raul Julia, Jose Ferrer, Henry Darrow, and Miriam Colon. The bicultural-bilingual situation of newcomers to New York was addressed in *Los Dos Mundos de Angelita* (1982) (released in English as *The Two Worlds of Angelita*). Based on Wendy Kesselman's book, the film was directed by Jayne Morrison, and like many of the alternative films noted here it had an all-Latino cast and many Puerto Rican and Latino crew members. A slightly more established Robert M. Young would make *Alambrista* (1977) (released in English as *The Illegal*), a film about a young man's arduous and disappointing journey from Mexico to the United States "to make some money." The film provided a rare and unsensationalized look at the plight of illegal immigrants, and it won the Golden Camera prize at Cannes in 1977. It was unique for its time in that English was spoken only when its protagonist encountered English-speaking characters.

Young's *Alambrista* is also the film in which Edward James Olmos (1946–) made his major acting debut, playing a

Edward James Olmos is shown here as El Pachuco, a one-man Greek chorus, in *Zoot Suit* (1982).

wino looking for night work. Born in East Los Angeles, Olmos first wanted to be a professional baseball player, but at the age of thirteen he fell in love with rock music. At fifteen he was singing with bands on Sunset Strip in Hollywood. While he pursued his music career he began taking acting classes, did bit parts on television, acted in off-Broadway plays, and ran a furniture-moving business to pay the bills. A talented and powerful dramatic actor, he was signed by Luis Valdez for the starring role in the play *Zoot Suit* in 1978, for which he received a Tony nomination. In 1982 he played the same El Pachuco role (part alter ego, part Greek chorus) in the film version of this retelling of the Sleepy Lagoon murder case and the zoot-suit riots. Probably the most well known Chicano actor today, he too is recognized for his commitment to a variety of social causes.

During this early period Olmos acted in some of the best alternative Latino-themed films being produced. In addition to those noted above, he appeared in two made-for-television movies, *Seguín* and *The Ballad of Gregorio Cortez*, both of which aired on the PBS network in 1982. Olmos spent two years marketing and distributing *The Ballad of Gregorio Cortez* to theaters around the county, going so far as to run the film in a Los Angeles theater free of charge, to encourage attendance. He also coproduced and starred in *Stand and Deliver* (1988), for which he gained forty pounds—and endured two hours of makeup—to portray a balding math instructor. He received an Oscar nomination for this role.

Olmos first came to national attention in 1984 when he began to play the taciturn but morally steadfast Lieutenant Castillo in television's *Miami Vice*. About his few lines, he has said that he was the highest paid—per word—actor in the history of television. In contrast to the other highly praised roles he had previously played, his role as the taciturn detective revealed to a larger audience the intensity and depth of his acting. He received an Emmy and a Golden Globe for his performance in this role, and he was shown on the cover of *Time* magazine in an issue devoted to the "surging new spirit of Hispanic culture" (*Time*, July 11, 1988). Olmos went on to play major roles in a variety of well-received movies, and he produced, directed, and starred in an antigang dramatic film, *American Me* (1992). He continues to make notable TV guest appearances, and his latest projects have included a Smithsonian-sponsored photographic exhibit, a book by Little, Brown of this same exhibit, a concert at the Kennedy Center entitled "Americanos," and a starring role in *American Family*, the first dramatic series on PBS about a Mexican American family in Los Angeles. Both Olmos and these projects have received much critical acclaim.

Most of the films made by Latino filmmakers were, in the main, independent (often documentary) films, distributed through educational channels, although a few had showings in other venues, such as public television. There were also some commercially made films, however. León Ichaso directed *El Súper* (1979), a movie about Cuban exiles living in New York City who confront economic and generational struggles. A series of films—*Our Latin Thing (Nuestra Cosa)* (1971), *Salsa* (1973), and *Fania All-Stars: Live in Africa* (1974)—was made by the Fania All-Stars, a group of well-known salsa musicians. These films had minimal plot lines and mainly highlighted the music, bands, and personalities in the Latin music world at the time. But they were commercially successful and played a critical role in spreading New York's Latin sound throughout Latin America and the world. These films were the first to document the origins of salsa music as an expression of Puerto Rican and Latino social identity in the states.

Despite the paucity of Latino characters and actors during this period and the generally dismal representation of Latino communities during this era, the 1970s saw the beginnings of alternative filmmaking approaches that would blossom in the eighties. This introduction of new images was influenced by the social movements of the late sixties and seventies, the general questioning of mores and values of the time, and the growth of the Latino population, many of whom were coming of age and reacting to what they saw as inaccurate and offensive reflections in media. The existence of broader social programs at the time may also have created opportunities for development. What is clear is that independent filmmakers and writers (many of them Latinos) began to retell Latino histories in a way that challenged the stereotypic depictions found in earlier films. The awareness of the growth of a Hispanic market would subsequently fuel this development, as many realized that the hardworking, moviegoing Latinos wildly outnumbered the negative Latino characters portrayed in so many Hollywood films. As Cheech Marin put it, "We can't all be in gangs, right?" (quoted West and Crowdus 1988, 36). Hollywood's interest in some of these ventures would grow, non-Latino interest in Latinos would expand, and in the next era we would see many more Latino newcomers entering the acting world and having major success.

The Postmodern Era

The period from 1980 to the present is considered the postmodern period here because it is in the process of becoming something distinct from the preceding era, but it is not yet clear just what that is. For Latinos in film, the postmodern period is actually two periods: The first closely parallels the 1980s, and in it are seen a medley of contrasting images, continuations of the past and also strong new thrusts in films. In the second period, the 1990s, there was a profusion of Latino stars, films, and characters. Political and demographic changes mirror these periods.

Politics and Demographics

In 1981 the former actor Ronald Reagan began two terms (1981–89) as a conservative Republican president. His administration changed the way social and economic policy was conducted. Reagonomics, with its emphasis on the free market, fewer taxes, more military spending, and less regulation of businesses, dominated policy thinking. This facilitated business expansion, but it also led to greater concentration of wealth at the top, which Reagan economists argued would trickle down. A new social contract was hammered out that would eventually alter significantly the way social services were delivered. There would be greater emphasis on personal (as opposed to social) responsibility, and funding for social programs would be shifted to the states. The social-service safety net that had been in place for fifty years would begin to be dismantled. These changes would lead to greater gaps in relative wealth.

President George Bush (1989–93) finished out the decade and continued to move these policies forward into the early 1990s. In 1993 William Jefferson Clinton, a Democrat, was elected for two terms (1993–2001). In the early years of his administration he attempted to reverse the Republican policies, but somewhat in response to widespread Republican victory in the first midterm elections he switched to a centrist course that completed several of the earlier Republican initiatives and led many to question what the principal differences were between the two major parties.

In the first two years of the twenty-first century, the United States witnessed the unraveling of the Clinton White House as the president's sexual relationship with a White House intern, Monica Lewinsky, was denied, and then admitted to, by the president. Other allegations of White House impropriety were raised by Kenneth Starr and others, including the granting of special favors to large contributors, and Clinton finished his term struggling mightily (and ultimately successfully) against impeachment and criminal charges. In the 2000 election, George W. Bush, the son of the earlier President Bush, ran against Clinton's vice president, Al Gore, who won the popular vote but ultimately lost in the Electoral College.

In George W. Bush's first year in office, a coordinated terrorist attack on September 11 caused the collapse of the two World Trade Center towers in New York City and extensive damage to the Pentagon. Thousands died. Stunned, the country came suddenly to a standstill: All planes in the air were forced to land, all traffic in and out of Manhattan was stopped, and all television and radio networks focused on the unfolding tragedy. Life would be changed forever. The country entered a stage of high alert, and an Office of Homeland Security was established. The search for Osama bin Laden dominated the headlines before being shoved aside by talk of a preemptive strike against Iraq. The United Nations sent inspectors to Iraq to determine whether biological and nuclear weapons were being made there; no evidence of this was found. In the midst of all this, North Korea announced it had developed nuclear capabilities, and in 2003 Congress approved the resolution authorizing the invasion of Iraq, despite worldwide opposition and an absence of evidence of "weapons of mass destruction."

In 1980 the U.S. census for the first time counted all Hispanics in the country. In previous censuses, the counts of Mexicans, Puerto Ricans, and other Latinos had been based on samples. When the 1980 figures were released, everyone in the data-gathering community seemed surprised at how much the Hispanic population in the United States had grown. But it was not until the 1990 census that the general population took note of the burgeoning Latino population—an increase in size of more than 50 percent since the previous census count. In the same ten-year period the non-Latino white population had increased by only 6 percent. It began to dawn on many that the United States was becoming more Latino. Figures from the more extensive 2000 census confirmed this finding. By the start of 2003, the Bureau of the Census announced that Latinos had officially surpassed African Americans in number. Moreover, it was obvious to many that this trend would continue. As the twenty-first century began, one of every eight Americans was Latino, and within a few decades, it was estimated, that ratio would rise to one in five. Latinos under the age of eighteen already constituted one-fifth of that age cohort. The future was clear:

Latinos were younger than other groups, had more children on the average, and were immigrating in record numbers.

Officially, the U.S. Latino population encompassed 37 million people and constituted almost 13 percent of the total U.S. population in the year 2001. This was greater than the population of Spain or Canada. Moreover, these figures did not include the 3.8 million Latinos who resided in Puerto Rico when the last census was taken. Nor did they include, or estimate, the number of Latinos who were living in the United States but for one reason or another had not been counted in these figures.

However, the face of America was changing more generally; *Time* magazine had earlier noted the "browning of America" (Henry 1990, 28). By 1990 one of every four Americans was of non-European descent. This was a dramatic change from the composition of the U.S. population at the start of the century, when one of every eight U.S. residents had non-European ancestors. Immigration to the country was also starkly different. In 1900 almost 85 percent of the immigrant population had come from Europe and 2 percent from Latin America and Asia combined. At the end of the century, the picture was reversed: 15 percent from Europe and 77 percent from Latin America and Asia combined, most of this latter group having come from Latin America.

Immigration

The increase in Latino immigration was accompanied by significant changes in legislation. The 1965 Immigration Act, which had eliminated the quotas placed on migration from southern and eastern Europe in the 1920s, resulted in an increase in the migration of Asians and Latin Americans but not of Europeans. In the 1980s the United States enjoyed a booming economy; but it was clear that globalization was introducing intense competitive pressures. Employment in the United States, particularly in the low-skilled job sector, was endangered in this new economy. Many businesses and jobs were going overseas to offshore low-wage sectors. Other jobs were being eliminated as a result of computerization, automation, credentialism, and competition from abroad. In rust-belt areas throughout the country, increasingly more blue-collar workers were available than blue-collar jobs. Some jobs were being taken by new immigrants willing to work for lower wages and in nonunionized settings.

In 1986 the United States passed the Immigration Reform and Control Act, which established sanctions against employers who hired undocumented workers. Subsequent legislation (the 1990 and 1996 Immigration Acts) set caps on immigration, altered the basis for legal immigration so as to favor employer-sponsored immigrants (who tended to be those with higher skill levels), and increased deportations of those with a criminal past. California, a state with large numbers of Latino immigrants, passed Proposition 187 in 1994; the voter initiative sought to deny to undocumented immigrants a range of public benefits, including children's access to education and health care. Although the proposition was never implemented, it made clear the desire of many to end what was widely viewed as an invasion of illegal immigrants.

A Medley of Contrasting Images

How were these changing demographics reflected on the silver screen? Most of the previous patterns continued, but there were some important departures. More Latino-themed films, characters, and stars appeared than had in the past, though Latinos were few and far between in big-budget films. Even when films were set in cities that had substantial numbers of Latinos, there were few, if any, Latinos. Judging from these films, one would think that the major migration and increase of Latinos had never occurred. Occasionally, there was a background character, who generally conformed to a stock, stick-figure stereotype. The blockbuster film *Ghost* (1990) provides one example. Set in New York City, which at the time was 25 percent Latino, the film did incorporate some Latinos who spoke briefly: the repellent villain and a confused spiritualist seeker.

In films set in California, which at the time was one-third Latino, there were occasional Latino characters—inevitably a waiter, bellhop, or valet, as in *Beverly Hills Cop* (1984), or a criminal, as in *Beverly Hills Cop II* (1987), or the promiscuous Mexican maid in *Down and Out in Beverly Hills* (1986). In many big-budget films there were no Latinos. Even in the all-American favorite *Forrest Gump* (1994), which purported to portray the changing history of the United States through the life of the main character, Forrest encounters not a single Latino in all his exploits and travels. Of particular note, he finds none in Vietnam, where Latinos won more medals than any other group and accounted for many of the dead. *Pretty Woman* (1990) had two Latino characters: an unredeemable, drug-addicted prostitute and her pimp, drug-dealer friend. In *Terminator 2* (1991), there was a minor Latino character who, true to the bandito stereotype, smuggled weapons and drank tequila. In general, during the 1980s and the early 1990s, though there were some Asians and African Americans in major non-Latino-themed films (for example, *Rambo: First Blood Part 2* [1985]), Latinos were few, and when they were visible, they appeared in marginal roles or in menial and negative positions.

More Hollywood films had major Latino characters or themes during the 1980s, relative to the previous era, but the association of Latinos with crime continued. Moreover, as was true for films in general during this period, in many of the films the intensity of the violence increased—witness *Scarface* (1983), *Carlito's Way* (1993), *American Me, Mi Vida Loca* (1994), and *El Mariachi* (1992). In many of the films, Latino characters had thick accents or spoke "street" English. However, at the time these films were being made, the majority of Latinos in this country had been born in the United States, and not all of them spoke "street" English—certainly not all of the time. The established tradition of the spitfire endured, in *The Perez Family* (1995), but in some cases the generally simple and one-dimensional spitfire characters became more marginal, dependent, and vulgar.

It was also in this era, however, that the alternative film-making initiated in the 1970s came into its own, particularly that by Latino filmmakers. This contributed to the increase in the number of human-interest films, some of which were commercially successful, for example, *La Bamba* (1987), *Born in East L.A.*, and *Stand and Deliver*. Others, such as *House of the Spirits* (1993), *The Perez Family*, and *A Walk in the Clouds*, were less profitable but demonstrated a continuing interest in "Latin" themes. Films set in the United States that utilized more Latinos in their casts included *The Milagro Beanfield War* (1988), *Salsa* (1988), *I Like It Like That* (1994), and *My Family, Mi Familia* (1995). During the 1980s, the engrossing political situations in Central and South America also provided material for a few major films on Latin America: *The Kiss of the Spider Woman*, *Salvador* (1986), *Latino* (1985), *Missing* (1982), *Under Fire* (1983), and *Romero*. During the 1990s, the number of films set in urban areas increased, and by the end of this decade the situation of Latinos in film would improve, with greater numbers of Latino stars, films, and characters. Thanks, in part, to the release of the 2000 census figures, the world (in particular, the business world) became convinced of the existence of a Hispanic market.

DEPARTURES FROM TRADITIONAL
HOLLYWOOD FILMS

Latinos of Mexican origin, being the largest and earliest Latino group with the longest history of images in film, expanded the counterdialogue that had begun in the earlier era. Their films focused on cultural difference and political demands for equality and justice rather than on "political accommodation and assimilation," as had earlier Latino films (Noriega 1997, 98). They would also begin to present Mexican and Mexican American history from a radically different perspective. Other Latino filmmakers with similar perspectives would also come forth during this era for similar reasons. These filmmakers would begin to resurrect, reconstruct, and reclaim history. They would foreground the views of those who had formerly been excluded or marginalized *(El Norte* [1983] and *Stand and Deliver)*. They would contextualize Latino history and images *(The Ballad of Gregorio Cortez* and *Seguín)*. They would pay greater attention to the representation of Latino characters *(The Milagro Beanfield War)*. More Latinos would be part of casts and crews *(My Family, Mi Familia)*. Their films would focus on heretofore generally neglected areas—dance, music, and other cultural dimensions and nonurban settings *(A Walk in the Clouds)*. These departures from traditional Hollywood stories were significant, for they began to show different images of Latinos and thereby inspired audiences to question the traditional images projected in Hollywood films.

THE FILMMAKERS

Luis Valdez (1940–) was the first Chicano to write and direct a major studio-backed feature film. The film, *Zoot Suit,* was set against the backdrop of World War II America, with big-band sounds, patriotic flag-waving, jitterbugging, swing dancing, and servicemen in uniforms. *Zoot Suit* was a musical based on Los Angeles's Sleepy Lagoon murder mystery, in which several Chicanos were railroaded into life sentences on a faked murder charge. The 1942 trial garnered national attention. There were riots in Los Angeles in which zoot-suited Latinos were beaten or murdered by local ruffians and soldiers on leave from the war. According to some observers, the violence occurred with the tacit neutrality, and in some cases the active participation, of the local police. A defense committee, which included many well-known actors such as Orson Welles, Rita Hayworth, and Anthony Quinn, gave greater exposure to the case.

However, it was Luis Valdez's play that brought the events to the attention of filmland. Only mildly successful at the box office, the film nevertheless garnered a Golden Globe nomination for best musical picture. It was also cost-effective for Universal Films, having been shot (in the theater where it was performed) in eleven days for only $2.5 million. In 1987 Valdez also wrote and directed for Columbia Pictures—*La Bamba*, one of the biggest box-office successes of that year. The film's title song went to the top of the charts and is today considered a classic. Born in 1940 to migrant farmworkers, Valdez was a long-time activist. He founded El Teatro Campesino (Farmworkers Theatre) during the grape strike of 1965 to dramatize the cause of farmworkers and urban Chicanos. The works of this theater have won national and international recognition. Valdez continues to write and direct, recently directing movies for television, including *The Cisco Kid* (1994).

Another filmmaker who presented a different view of historical events is Jesús Salvador Treviño (1946–), a Chicano filmmaker who began making documentaries for Los Angeles public television before directing his first feature film, *Raíces de Sangre*, in 1979. His *Seguín*, an *American Playhouse* presentation, addressed the history of Texas. It was a historically accurate film that revealed the historical and social context of the times as few other films in the United States had done. It also incorporated Mexican views on the Alamo. Treviño is currently a well-known director, who has directed episodes of various television series, including *Chicago Hope, ER*, and *NYPD Blue*. He was also supervising producer for the Showtime series *Resurrection Blvd.* (2000) and won an award for best directing in a daytime drama for his television film *Gangs* (1988). León Ichaso (1949–), who was born in Havana, Cuba, another award-winning independent filmmaker, directed *Crossover Dreams* (1985). The son of a well-known television and film director and writer in Cuba, he left Cuba at the age of fourteen and finished his education in the United States. He went on to make commercials, documentaries, and industrial films before focusing on more-commercial films and directing television episodes in series like *Miami Vice* (1984–89) and *The Equalizer* (1985–89). His last major film was *Piñero* (2001), starring Benjamin Bratt.

Also active during the 1980s was Jacobo Morales (1934–), an actor, director, and writer of feature films in Puerto Rico. Like the other filmmakers covered here, Morales focused on subjects not often addressed in Hollywood's Latino-themed films. Yet his films differ in that they are generally set in Puerto Rico. They involve human dramas, although some also take a critical and satiric look at politics in Puerto Rico. Starring in many Puerto Rican theatrical productions and soap operas, Morales directed his first feature film in 1979, *Dios Los Cría* (And God Created Them), and went on to make two others in the 1980s. One, *Lo Que Le Pasó a Santiago* (1989), was nominated for an Oscar as the year's best foreign-language film. He has continued acting, writing, and directing feature films in Spanish, and his films have been well received. His most recent film was *Angel* (2003).

Gregory Nava (1949–) is another dynamic and successful Chicano director. Born in San Diego, California, of Mexican and Basque heritage, he attended the University of California at Los Angeles and won prizes for his student films, including the award for the best feature in 1976 at the Chicago International Film Festival for his *Confessions of Aman*. In 1983 he directed *El Norte* and was nominated for an Academy Award for the original screenplay, cowritten with Anna Thomas. A film much in use within educational circles, it was one of the first films to address the plight of Guatemalan refugees who enter the United States illegally. He has gone on to make highly successful feature films, including *My Family, Mi Familia*, and *Selena* (1997), and he is currently the creator, writer, and executive producer of the critically acclaimed *American Family*, the first dramatic TV series on television that focuses on a Chicano family. He has also succeeded in other commercial ventures, such as *Why Do Fools Fall in Love* (1998).

Moctesuma Esparza (1949–), also from California and a sometimes collaborator with Nava, received his bachelor and master of fine arts degrees in film at the University of California at Los Angeles and also helped to found the Chicano Research Center there. In 1973 he won an Emmy for

Cinco Vidas, a documentary that was based on his master's the-
sis. He was also nominated for an Academy Award for his film
Agueda Martinez: Our People, Our Country (1977), a portrait of
an older woman from New Mexico. In 1982 he worked with
Robert Young and the National Council of La Raza to produce
The Ballad of Gregorio Cortez, a powerful film focusing on the
historical origins of a well-known border ballad that recounts
the largest manhunt in Texas history at the turn of the century. The film illustrates how the ballad kept alive the history
of the border when other written sources did not. It also
recounts the larger, generally untold story of oppression and
persecution and demonstrates the way simple linguistic mis-
understandings often lead to more injustice and tyranny.
Edward James Olmos starred in and coproduced this film.

This film also featured Rosana de Soto, who gives a mar-
velous performance as a Latina living on the borderland
within a western setting. In this role, she conveys all the conflicts and complexities involved in the more universal role of
"translator." Translators are on the hyphen; their minds
become the border area where language, thoughts, concepts,
histories, stories, and perspectives are exchanged between
and within one individual. Esparza was also a producer for
The Milagro Beanfield War, a successful film starring Ruben
Blades and Robert Redford. He continues, along with Nava,
to be one of the most active Latino producers in Hollywood
and to produce major films both on the large screen, such as
Selena, and on the small screen, for example, HBO's
Introducing Dorothy Dandridge (1999).

Latina filmmakers also began to surface in the eighties,
mainly as documentary filmmakers. Particularly noteworthy
were the Chicana Lourdes Portillo and the Puerto Rican Ana
María García, whose films are well known, particularly in academic settings. Both focus on political and cultural issues. As
Liz Kotz (1997, 200–13) notes, they and other Latina filmmakers bring to their films a realist aesthetic that includes the
traditional concerns of documentary filmmakers for accuracy
and authenticity but also addresses the situations of those

people who have been ignored or underrepresented in the dominant media, often the silenced political voices. Portillo and García also document their own reality, culture, and perceptions. In contrast to the works of males, they tend to integrate factual and fictional forms, often mixing documentary, biographical works, autobiography, and personal diary. This approach allows them to present the complex relationships between women's external and internal realities.

Portillo and García also articulate political agendas that exist outside of traditional power structures. For example, in *Las Madres de la Plaza de Mayo* (The Mothers of Plaza de Mayo) (1985), Portillo seeks to mobilize and sustain popular memory to overcome institutional silence and repression. Similarly, Ana María García, in her classic work *La Operación* (1982), is concerned with showing how the personal is determined by the political. The film focuses on the sterilization of women in Puerto Rico, and she traces the inseparability of private lives from the dynamics of international imperialism and hegemony.

Both of these filmmakers also show how political structures influence the discourse and behaviors of people at all levels. They implicitly ask in their films, What are the places that are assigned to particular discourses, and how does this affect the social worlds within which we all live? Many of these documentary films were made to inform and generate both local and international support for particular issues. Portillo's film, for example, spread the voice of the mothers of the *desaparecidos* to the rest of the world to increase awareness of the political situation in Argentina. Portillo's *La Ofrenda* (The Offering) (1989) and García's *Rockeros y Salseros* (For Rock or Salsa) (1992) address the loss or change of culture. Both confront the question of how to present accurate images to a mainstream audience without capitulating to stereotypes. Many of the films made by Latina filmmakers are bilingual, addressing both English- and Spanish-speaking audiences. They also speak to common themes of immigration, dislocation and displacement, exile, rupture, transnational migration, and bicultural identity.

In the next decade, all of these filmmakers would continue to make films, and new Latino filmmakers would appear, notably, Joseph B. Vasquez (1962–95) and Robert Rodriguez (1968–). Vasquez, who was born in New York City, focused in his films on urban areas of New York. He wrote and directed five feature films, the most well known of which was *Hangin' with the Homeboys* (1991). He died of AIDS in San Diego, California.

Robert Rodriguez is the boy wonder of low-budget filmmaking. The legend (disputed by some) is that he made his first film, *El Mariachi*, at the age of twenty-three, with seven thousand dollars, most of which he had earned by subjecting himself to experimental drug studies. He wrote, directed, photographed, edited, and recorded the film and then sold the distribution rights to Columbia Pictures. Although Rodriguez was raised in the United States, he made *El Mariachi* in Spanish. It was, in fact, the first American film released in Spanish by Columbia, and it has received numerous awards. Rodriguez has also written a book about the process of making the film. His sequel, *Desperado* (1995), introduced both Salma Hayek and Antonio Banderas to American audiences. Rodriguez attended the University of Texas at Austin, and with his wife, Elizabeth Avellan, he has written, directed, or produced (and sometimes a combination of the three) more than twelve highly successful movies—including the *Spy Kids* series (2001, 2002, 2003) and *Once upon a Time in Mexico* (2003), his sequel to *Desperado*. Born in San Antonio, Texas, he is the third of ten children. He has been the recipient of many awards for his work in film.

What is most remarkable about these filmmakers is the dialogue they inaugurated. For many, this dialogue began in opposition; yet it has resulted in opening up the American experience and adding to the history of American film. These filmmakers and their films are part of the ongoing redefinition and expansion of American culture. In the same way that U.S.-Latino writers and poets express their birthright through their writing, these filmmakers bring to the screen their own unique and individual visions of what it means to be a Latino in the United States. In the process, they (like most filmmakers) have had particular messages to convey. As Cheech Marin has said of the film he directed, *Born in East L.A.*, he wanted to make audiences laugh, but he also wanted them to reflect more seriously on the film's theme: the deportation of a third-generation Mexican American. One of his aims was to "make people realize that Latino culture is part of American culture, just as much as English or Irish or Italian culture." He wanted the American Latino public to claim and take pride in their birthright. For Marin, American and Latino cultures are inextricably bound; there is no history of one without the other. "Besides," he has joked, "if we took away all the influences of Latino culture in the U.S., none of the cities would have names" (quoted in West and Crowdus 1988, 35).

The individual and collective visions of these filmmakers in many ways counter past views, but they also have introduced new connections and new understandings of universality. As these films air around the world, they extend the story of America.

THE LEADING LATINO STARS OF THE 1980S
In the first part of this decade, during the 1980s and the early 1990s, male Latino actors and characters were in greater evidence than Latinas. Ruben Blades (1948–), a well-known salsa singer, began acting in films in the early eighties and had the lead in *Crossover Dreams*, which he also cowrote. The film depicts the difficulties a Latino musician experiences in attempting a "cross over" into Hollywood. Blades also had a strong role as a sheriff in *The Milagro Beanfield War*, one of the first commercial films that attempted to include complex Latino characters as well as a more realistic and historically balanced story line. Blades was born in Panama City, Panama, where he says he was exposed to American rock, calypso, and Latin music, which later influenced his own musical compositions.

According to one source, he graduated from Harvard Law School; according to another, he got his law degree at

Ruben Blades, a 1994 presidential candidate in his native Panama, continues to be successful both in film and music. He is shown here as the sheriff in *The Milagro Beanfield War* (1988).

the University of Panama. In either case, it was after receiving his law degree that he began performing with salsa bands in New York, particularly Willie Colon's band. He ran for president of Panama in 1994 and came in third, winning 20 percent of the vote. Although he lost his bid, the party he founded won enough seats to ensure its continuance. He has continued to play a variety of parts both in major films and on television, where most recently he played the role of Dr. Max Cabranes in the TV series *Gideon's Crossing*. He has also maintained his musical career, composing for films, such as *Empire* (2002) and *Q & A* (1990), and for his publicly released albums. A man of diverse and extraordinary talents, Blades has won three Grammies and an Ace award, has been nominated for two Emmys, and had a lead role in Paul Simon's Broadway musical, *The Capeman* (1998). He continues to be active in Hollywood films.

Andy Garcia (1956–), born in Havana, Cuba, also began his career during this time. Garcia's parents fled the Castro regime when he was five and came to Miami Beach, where he was raised. A popular student and a good basketball player in high school, Andy attended Florida International University for a while and learned his craft in regional theater. He first began on television as a gang member in the pilot that was to become the popular TV series *Hill Street Blues* (1981–87). He made his big-screen debut in *Blue Skies Again* (1983) and went on to garner increased attention in major Hollywood films—*The Mean Season* (1985), in which he played a police detective, and *8 Million Ways to Die* (1986), in which he played a cocaine kingpin. He persuaded Brian de Palma to cast him as the agent George Stone, against type, in *The Untouchables* (1987). This move is similar to that of other major Latino stars who have gone out of their way to avoid typecasting.

Garcia went on to play a variety of characters, often Latino professionals or officers of the law. He received an Oscar nomination for his role in *The Godfather: Part III* (1990). He had starring roles in a number of films, including *Internal Affairs* (1990) and *A Show of Force* (1990), and by 1995 he was listed in the *Hollywood Reporter* as the top Latino star. As he continues to act in major films, he has also turned his hand to directing, producing, and songwriting. A conga and Latin music enthusiast, in 1993 he directed (and acted in) *Cachao . . . Como Su Ritmo No Hay Dos* (Cachao . . . Like His Rhythm There

Andy Garcia, listed in the *Hollywood Reporter* as the top Latino star in 1995, continues to have starring roles in major films but has also turned his hand to directing, producing, and song writing. He is shown here circa 1990.

Is No Other), a documentary about the legendary Cuban composer and performer, Israel "Cachao" Lopez. He also produced, for television, *For Love or Country* (2000), the story of the renowned Cuban trumpet player Arturo Sandoval. Garcia also played a singer and composer in *The Disappearance of Garcia Lorca* (1997). He is currently directing a new work, entitled *The Lost City*, and is busily employed in a number of other productions, all scheduled to be released in 2004.

Antonio Banderas (1960–) also entered Hollywood film during this era. Born José Antonio Domínguez Banderas in Málaga, Spain, he had wanted to play soccer professionally but broke his foot at the age of fourteen, saw *Hair*, and decided instead to pursue acting. He studied at the School of Dramatic Art, in Málaga, and then moved to Madrid in 1981. His father was a policeman, his mother a schoolteacher. Before coming to Hollywood he was a well-known, classically trained actor, and he had been an ensemble member of the prestigious National Theatre of Spain between 1981 and 1986. In 1982 he made the first of five films with the writer-director Pedro Almodóvar, one of which, *Women on the Verge of a Nervous Breakdown* (1988), was nominated for an Oscar. He has said that after this film was released, "there was a sudden interest from Hollywood. I was offered *The Mambo Kings* and Warner Bros. took the risk of hiring a guy who couldn't speak English" (cited in "Making a Name" 1995, 7).

He learned his lines for *Mambo Kings* (1992) phonetically. He would go on to have other important supporting roles, in *House of the Spirits* and *Philadelphia* (1993). Banderas had his first starring role in Robert Rodriguez's *Desperado*. His heartthrob image was enhanced in a number of major movies, *House of the Spirits*, *Philadelphia*, and *Assassins* (1995), in particular, and by his being listed as one of the fifty most beautiful people in the world in *People* magazine and one of the hundred sexiest stars in film history (number 24) by *Empire* magazine in 1995 ("The 50 Most Beautiful People in the World" 1996, 61; "The 100 Sexiest Stars in Film History" 1995). He seemed to find this image amusing but was perhaps resigned to its per-

Antonio Banderas, seen by some as the Latin lover supreme, has an extensive background in serious theater and has moved into comedy and directing.

petual, immutable existence. Asked in 1995 what kinds of roles were available to him in Hollywood, he replied, "In terms of casting, they try to put me in a cage or a box to determine what the hell I am—you know, Antonio Banderas, the Latin Lover. [Laughs.] I'll probably be seen as that Latin Lover type forever. Even if I get greasy and fat and lose my hair, they'll cast me and say, 'Yes, but he was a Latin Lover!' It's funny there's always that thing" ("Making a Name" 1995, 7).

His comments are understandable: At that point he had already done forty-three movies, he had been working in the acting profession for twenty years (since the age of fourteen), and he had always looked to change from movie to movie. Despite his heartthrob image, he is today known as one of the leading international actors of his generation and has received Golden Globe nominations for best actor in *Evita* (1996) and *The Mask of Zorro* (1998). Banderas made his directorial debut with *Crazy in Alabama* (1999), which starred his wife, Melanie Griffith, and in the summer of 2003 he began his Broadway career by starring in the well-received play, *Nine.* He continues to have an extremely active, successful, and well-remunerated career in film.

Jimmy Smits (1955–) was a household name during this period, having come to national attention for his extended television roles, first as the sensitive but tough Latino attorney, Victor Sifuentes, on *L.A. Law* (1986–91) and then as *NYPD Blue*'s sexy leading man, Detective Bobby Simone (1994–98). He received Emmy nominations for every year he was in each series. Born in 1955 in Brooklyn, New York, his mother was Puerto Rican and his father was from Suriname. He spent most of his youth in Brooklyn, where he was both a football star on a city-championship team and the star of his high school drama club. At Brooklyn College, he majored in theater, and in 1982 he received a master's degree in fine arts from Cornell University. Smits won accolades for his performance in *My Family, Mi Familia* and as the fiery revolutionary in *The Old Gringo* (1989). He has proved he can handle comedy as well, as his role in *Switch* (1991) demonstrates.

Jimmy Smits first came to national attention through his extended roles on TV's *L.A. Law* (1986–91) and *NYPD Blue* (1994–98), for which he received Emmy nominations in each of these years. He has also demonstrated his skill in films and his commitment to social causes. Smits is a founding member of the National Hispanic Foundation for the Arts, an organization dedicated to assisting young actors. He is shown here in *Vital Signs* (1990).

He continues to star in movies, most recently *Price of Glory* (2000), two films in the *Star Wars* series (2002 and forthcoming [2005]), and the Spanish-language film *Angel*. He is a founding member of the National Hispanic Foundation for the Arts, an organization dedicated to assisting young actors to earn their graduate degrees and to advancing the presence and quality of Latinos in media and entertainment

THE LEADING LATINA STARS OF THE 1980S
Although Latino actors seemed to predominate during the eighties, several Latinas were also well known. Maria Conchita Alonso (1957–) was born in Cuba but raised in Caracas, Venezuela, where she was a beauty contest winner, a popular soap-opera actress, and a singer. Emigrating to the United States in 1982, she made her film debut in 1984 in *Moscow on the Hudson* and has appeared in numerous films and television series since then.

Hailing from Maringá, Paraná, Brazil, was Sonia Braga (1950–). Like her Brazilian predecessor, Carmen Miranda, Braga was already well known in Brazil before she came to Hollywood. She had also gained international attention for her work in *Doña Flor and Her Two Husbands* (1978) before appearing in her first English-language film, *Kiss of the Spider Woman*. Like Banderas, she did not speak English well at this time: "I would say a line," she later recalled, "and wonder what it meant" (cited in Reyes and Rubie 2000, 430). Initially tagged "the Brazilian Bombshell," she made numerous films and television movies, including Robert Redford's *The Milagro Beanfield War, Moon over Parador* (1988), and *Roosters* (1993). But in her more recent performances she has moved away from this early image; she has had recurring roles in *Sex and the City* (as a lesbian lover) and in PBS's *An American Family*, in which she played the beloved mother. Braga is a cofounder (with Jimmy Smits and Esai Morales) of the National Hispanic Foundation for the Arts.

According to the *Hollywood Reporter*, the most bankable Latina star in 1995 was Rosie Perez (1964–). Like Jimmy

Tagged the "Brazilian Bombshell" in Hollywood, Sonia Braga was well known in Brazil and internationally before she appeared in her first English-language film, *Kiss of the Spider Woman* (1985). She has continued to work in U.S. film and television as well as abroad. Braga is a cofounder (with Jimmy Smits and Esai Morales) of the National Hispanic Foundation for the Arts. She is shown here in *Moon over Parador* (1988).

Smits, Rosie Perez was born and raised in Brooklyn. Her parents were Puerto Rican. She attended Grover Cleveland High School and then Los Angeles Community College, where she studied marine biology. Perez was twice "discovered" while dancing at a dance club—first by a *Soul Train* producer, who

Rosie Perez, shown here in *White Men Can't Jump* (1992), was listed in the *Hollywood Reporter* as 1995's most bankable Latina star.

invited her to dance on his show. This led to her involvement in choreography for musical stars, such as Diana Ross and Bobby Brown, and for the Fly Girls of TV's now-defunct *In Living Color* (1991–93)—for which she received an Emmy nomination. She was spotted dancing a second time by Spike Lee, who cast her as Tina, his Latina girlfriend and the mother of his child, in her first movie, *Do the Right Thing* (1989). Lee set the movie in Brooklyn, about six blocks from where Perez had grown up. Despite a complete lack of previous acting experience, Rosie Perez was a natural. She appeared in a number of movies, earning respect and visibility for her work in films such as *White Men Can't Jump* (1992) and *Untamed Heart* (1993) and receiving an Oscar nomination for her role in *Fearless* (1993).

Yet by 1994 she seemed to echo the sentiments expressed by Rita Moreno after her success in *West Side Story:* "The quantity of offers has increased," Rosie told a reporter, "but the quality is pretty awful" (quoted in Ulmer 1994). Rosie was tired of being asked to play more roles that required her to "[scream] at the top of my lungs" (Michael 1992). She demonstrated resourcefulness and a progressive bent in convincing the director of *White Men Can't Jump* to change the part, originally written for a WASP, Ivy League student, to a former disco queen from Brooklyn, which she would play. In her subsequent major films Perez also played women who were quite different from her first character, Tina. However, according to Rosie, people tended to see all her roles as the same person because the character was Hispanic. By 1999, when asked if she worried about being stereotyped as a "feisty, foul-mouthed, working-class Latina," Rosie replied, "All the time" (Peter Applebome, "Trying to Shake a Stereotype but Keep On Being Rosie Perez," *New York Times,* February 14, 1999).

Despite these concerns, she has pushed on and expanded into other areas. She was executive producer of TV's *Subway Stories: Tales from the Underground* (1997), coproduced and starred in the independent movie *The 24-Hour Woman* (1999), and was a voice in the animated film *The Road to El Dorado* (2000). She has also taken on a heavy schedule of benefit work on behalf of AIDS victims and prisoners and was recently arrested for protesting against the bombing of the island of Vieques, Puerto Rico. In 2002 she indicated that she would not play characters she felt deprecated her racially or culturally. Indeed, in her lead role in *The 24-Hour Woman* she played a successful television producer trying—like many other women of this era—to balance work, marriage, and motherhood.

The Seismic Shift: Latinas Shimmer, Latinos Bloom

Toward the end of the 1990s, Latina stars became hot again. Latinas who had had modest careers during the 1980s saw their careers accelerate. Like the men of this time, they came from a variety of backgrounds. However, most had been born or raised in the United States and had begun their careers in television, and they straddled both television and film throughout their careers. These included Angela Alvarado (Puerto Rican), Trini Alvarado (Puerto Rican and Spanish), Julie Carmen (New York), Elizabeth Peña (Cuban), Alma Martinez (Chicana), Zully Montero (Cuban), Madeline Stowe (Costa Rican and British), Lupe Ontiveros (Chicana), and Lisa Vidal (Puerto Rican). Others Latinas, such as Constance Marie (Chicana) and Lauren Velez (Puerto Rican), began their careers somewhat later in the nineties. Latino men who were already in film in the eighties—Edward James Olmos, John Leguizamo, Esai Morales, and Robert Beltran, among others—acquired a higher profile in the nineties, and others who began later—Benicio Del Toro, Benjamin Bratt, and Jon Seda—also became better known. Almost all continue to be active in film and television.

The nineties also saw the skyrocketing success of some Latinas who made American film debuts in the nineties: Jennifer Lopez, Salma Hayek, Penelope Cruz, and Cameron Diaz. Interestingly, after a long hiatus, Latinas who hailed from Latin America and Spain (Salma Hayek and Penelope Cruz) became major players in film toward the end of the century. Although they came from other countries, they were originally cast and marketed in much the same way as the U.S.-bred Latinas. Totally new stars also began to shine brightly in film and on television: Yancey Arias, Tatyana (Marisol) Ali, Bobby Cannavale, Delilah Cotto, Rosario Dawson, Jay Hernandez, Jacqueline Obradors, Gina Torres, Michelle Rodriguez, Tia Texada, Eva Mendes, and Wilmer Valderrama. Latino actors were more prominently featured in television, as well, and the characters they played had larger roles and suggested their Latino backgrounds more fully than in the past; these actors included Jessica Alba (TV's *Dark Angel*), Eddie Cibrian (TV's *Third Watch*), Shelly Morrison (TV's *Will and Grace*), Judy Reyes (TV's *Scrubs*), Jon Seda (TV's *UC: Undercover*), and Esai Morales (TV's *NYPD Blue*). Even the Latino ancestry of Martin Sheen (of TV's Emmy Award–win-

ning *The West Wing*) received attention off camera, as did that
of his two sons, Emilio Estevez and Charlie Sheen.

LATINIZATION

Accompanying this rise in the fortunes of Latino stars toward
the end of the nineties was a more generalized "Latinization"
that was sweeping the country. It could be heard in the hit
music that was being played—from Ricky Martin's ubiquitous "Livin' la Vida Loca" to songs that incorporated Spanish
words to songs that fused together Latino rhythms from the
Caribbean and Central and South America with more recognizably American styles, like rock, country, rap, pop, and
jazz. Moreover, there was an important international dimension. Salsa music had spread not just to different parts of the
United States and Latin America but also to Japan, Sweden,
and Africa. Subliminal Latinization was occurring, as well.
Without fully realizing it, Americans were hearing Latin
music backgrounds in commercials, TV programs, and films.
Spanish words were entering the mass vocabulary without
translation—like Arnold Schwarzenegger's "Hasta la vista,
baby" in *Terminator* or the Mexican Chihauhau's "Yo quiero
Taco Bell" in print ads and on television.

The market also drove this Latinization. McDonald's
introduced the classic Cuban sandwich, a "dulce de leche"
McFlurry, a Latin McOmelet, and last, but certainly not least,
a mango dipping sauce for Chicken McNuggets. Other
American commercial icons, like the Mars bar (made by
M&M), also introduced a "dulce de leche" flavor. True, many
of these products were calculated to cash in on the presence
of Latinos in certain areas, and they were often introduced
only in predominantly Latino markets. However, salsa was
outselling ketchup in the Midwest, nachos were beating hot
dogs at the movies, and salsa music was finding its way onto
hitherto unknown dance floors and into commercials all over
the country.

Latinization was not just a big-city phenomenon. Cinco
de Mayo was celebrated in rural Arkansas, and similar events

took place in other rural states where Latino populations had increased by more than 200 percent (Alabama, Georgia, Nevada, North Carolina, and Tennessee). In heartland towns, Spanish shops, restaurants, and schools sprang up within predominantly Spanish-speaking communities. Although 75 percent of Latinos were still concentrated in seven states (California, Texas, New York, Florida, Illinois, Arizona, and New Jersey), there were substantial concentrations in all states. As the president of the National Council of La Raza said, "Latinos were as likely to be found in Milwaukee, Wisconsin, as in San Antonio, Texas" (Raul Yzaguirre, National Council of La Raza press release, July 16, 2001). Automated teller machines all over the country were dispensing directions in Spanish, and when George W. Bush became president, the White House website added a section in Spanish. Space limitations prevent a detailed listing of the sports figures with Spanish-surnames (and sometimes Spanish accents) who appeared in the news, or the many politicians who were now speaking a little or a lot of Spanish in their public speeches or had visited countries in the Caribbean, Mexico, Central America, and South America as part of their campaigning or to curry favor from their constituents in the United States. In essence, from soccer to salsa—both the edible and danceable varieties—Latinization was sweeping the country (Woodward 2001).

It was not just Latinos who bought the records, videos, and albums that made megastars of Ricky Martin, Jennifer Lopez, Marc Antony, and Shakira. A "craze for all things Latino" influenced the development of Latino-oriented products, such as Mambo perfume (Eduardo Porter, "It's Not Easy to Bottle the Coolness and Heat of J.Lo's Decolletage," *Wall Street Journal*, August 9, 2001). Fashion lines also reflected this craze: Betsy Johnson's Muñequita ("little doll") collection, Christian Dior's accent on East Los Angeles gang dress, Cacherel's Spanish Harlem theme, and Valentino's flamenco look, with Panama hats, sexy layered lace, and over-the-top bullfighter themes sprinkled through-

Penelope Cruz, shown here in *Woman on Top* (2000), continues to receive praise for her starring roles in major U.S. films and abroad.

out his collections. Indeed, the shifts in fashion approximated a cultural zeitgeist.

The music world, more than any other sphere, reflected the Latinization. In addition to the megastars noted above, some, such as Carlos Santana, made major comebacks. Newcomers entered the field or came into their own: Christina Aguilera, Son by Four, Big Pun, and Julio Iglesias. Even Mariah Carey's Venezuelan African ancestry was now more foregrounded. Major mainstream magazines, which had largely ignored Latino talents, now placed them on their covers. Indeed, in the late 1990s it seemed that just about every major magazine and leading newspaper featured Latino megastars. At the traditionally cautious Radio City Music Hall, 50 percent of all bookings were Hispanic.

THE LEADING LATINA STARS OF THE 1990S

During this time Penelope Cruz (1974–), an import from Spain, rolled out picture after picture, in which she was often billed as the hot Latina. In the span of three years, she appeared in seven U.S. films, including *Woman on Top* (2000), *All the Pretty Horses* (2000), and *Blow* (2001). Penélope Cruz Sánchez was born in Madrid to a working-class family. Her mother was a hairdresser, her father a retailer. She studied classical dance for many years and at the age of fifteen started to take roles in Spanish TV and in music videos. She made her movie debut in 1991 in *El Laberinto Griego* (The Greek Labyrinth) and became a major star in Spain, where she is referred to as La Encantadora (the enchantress). But she came to Hollywood's attention when her third film, *Belle Époque* (1992), won an Academy Award. She also starred in the Academy Award–winning *All about My Mother* (1999) by Pedro Almodóvar. By the time of her American debut, in *The Hi-Lo Country* (1998), Cruz had already made twelve films.

Given the extent to which many Latina actors have been seen in the past as primarily ornamental or sexy, sultry beauties, Penelope Cruz's view on how the media has portrayed her is of particular interest. She has clearly been billed by the media as a Latina beauty, and she considers such comments complimentary. But she also feels they are somewhat irrelevant to her career, which she sees as built on something more than her looks. From her perspective, she has taken a lot of risks as an actress and has not been afraid to play extreme parts. Consequently, she does not see her career as having been delimited or defined by her physical beauty. In fact, she has said that her reputation as a beauty has made it difficult for her to establish a career as a serious actress: Few took her seriously once she became known as the pretty woman.

Cruz received a veritable avalanche of press coverage as the "Latin craze" swept the nation. Her romance with her costar Tom Cruise added to this media frenzy, and numerous puns were made on "cruising with Cruz and Cruise." In 2001 she graced the cover of *TV Guide* (October 20–26), the second-largest magazine in the country, with a readership of 14 million. Often not covered in media articles on her is her volunteer activity. She supports an organization in Calcutta that provides housing, education, and medical care for home-less girls and people with tuberculosis. Cruz donated the entire salary from her first U.S. film to Mother Teresa's organization.

Salma Hayek (1966–) was also born abroad, in Veracruz, Mexico. Her father was a Lebanese businessman, and her mother was a Mexican opera singer. Salma was sent to a Louisiana boarding school at the age of twelve, but after get-ting into trouble with the nuns for her pranks (setting the clocks back three hours, for example), she returned to Mexico and was eventually sent to live with an aunt in Houston, Texas, where she stayed until she was seventeen. She subsequently moved to Mexico City, where she studied international relations for a time as a university student but decided to drop out to pursue a career as an actress. (She had fallen in love with acting when as a child she went to the the-ater in her hometown.) She started out in local theater pro-ductions but eventually became a major star in a Mexican soap opera. However, in 1991, fearful of being typecast and anxious to make films, she decided to quit her hit show and left Mexico to pursue an acting career in Los Angeles.

After taking a year to study acting and English, Hayek went to endless castings and experienced numerous rejec-tions. She came to see what a small market there was for Latina actresses in Hollywood, where they were often rele-gated to playing menials, mistresses, and prostitutes. This was a tough time for this idolized star from Mexico, who found that her Mexican celebrity counted for little in the American film industry. By late 1992 Hayek had landed only bit parts. In 1993 she got a one-line supporting role in *Mi Vida Loca*, a film about Los Angeles gang girls. Appearing on the comedian Paul Rodriguez's Spanish-language talk show, she happened to be seen by director Robert Rodriguez, who cast her in his second film, *Desperado*, opposite Antonio Banderas—going against his studio's request that he cast a blond. She has also appeared in his subsequent films, *From Dusk till Dawn* (1996), *The Faculty* (1998), and *Once upon a Time in Mexico*.

Actress Salma Hayek is also the producer and founder of the
Ventanarosa Production Company.

Although Hayek has been a celebrity spokesperson for
Revlon products in the United States, like many other actresses
she has pleaded to be taken seriously and not simply regarded
as decoration. "I should be flattered," she has said, "when people say that I'm sexy or beautiful. I know that. It's amazing how
hard some women work so that they can be perceived as sexy.

They go through painful surgery, they go through so much. . . . But it would make me even happier if people could see beyond sexy because there is a lot more to me than that" ("Hot, Hot, Hot," *London Times*, August 7, 1999). Given the extent to which she has been cast in some films as the hot or sultry Latina, is she concerned that she will always be categorized? "Basically I'm not afraid of anything," Hayek remarks. "I rather think it's quite normal that they cast me according to my type. When they look for somebody with fire, (ding-dong) Salma Hayek comes to their mind. Whenever they put me in this category, I just try to make the roles more interesting. And since I now have a place at the negotiating table, I can try to get other roles for myself. But I don't take this tendency personally, that's just how this industry operates" (Lackner 2000).

Hayek has succeeded in seeking out different roles and in creating different films. She has made a number of independent films, including *Follow Me Home* (1996) and *Four Rooms* (1995), and she landed the lead role in *Fools Rush In* (1997). She also had a starring role in Barry Sonnenfeld's *Wild Wild West* (1999) opposite Will Smith and Kevin Kline. Alternating between commercial and independent movies— for example, *Chain of Fools* (2000) and *Timecode* (2000)—she also created her own production company, Ventanarosa, and has produced and acted in her own films: *In the Time of the Butterflies* (2001), for TV, and *Frida* (2002). Hayek made her directorial debut in the television movie *The Maldonado Miracle* (2003), of which she was also the senior executive producer, and she has other projects in production. She has worked again with Robert Rodriguez (in *Spy Kids 3D: Game Over* [2003] and *Once upon a Time in Mexico*) and continues to star in Mexican films that have been well received, including *El Coronel No Tiene Quien Le Escribe* (1999).

Asked about the new interest in Latino films, which has to some degree contributed to her production company's success, Hayek replies, "They finally understand in this film industry, which is entirely defined by money, how many Latinos live in the United States, 32 million potential customers, a minority that is growing rapidly and above all it's enthusiastic about movies. That's why, all of a sudden, we see Latinos on screen. Talent has only little to do with that" (Lackner 2000). Like her illustrious predecessor, Dolores Del Rio, she is proud of her Mexican heritage and anxious to display it in its best, but authentic, light. Having a strong role in defining her own films is one way to do this, but Hayek is also interested in creating artistically successful films. She seems to be well on her way to doing this: Her highly acclaimed film, *Frida*, won a Golden Globe for best original score and was nominated for seven Oscars.

The actress whose career best conveys the breadth and spirit of the current Latino craze is the Latina "supernova," Jennifer Lopez. In the summer and fall of 1999, the twenty-eight-year-old, Bronx-born J.Lo topped the pop music charts. *New York* magazine declared her to be "the world's hottest Latino actress," and she was seen to represent the dawning of a new era, "the face of the future of glamour and beauty" and "the future of entertainment" ("La Vida Lopez" 1999, 26–27). Her success worldwide led her manager to proclaim that "Jennifermania" had gone global (ibid., 27). In a startling gesture suggesting the degree of Latinization occurring, the magazine put Jennifer Lopez on the cover and retitled that issue *Nueva York*.

At the same time, other Latino megastars filled the radio airwaves, concert halls, television spots, magazines, newspapers, and films, and the summer-long national embrace of Latino culture announced by *New York* magazine was undeniable. In 2001 a similar wave of interest was felt in the film world as Lopez received kudos on the influential mass-market shows *Entertainment Tonight* and *Access Hollywood* and in the popular press for her music, her films, and her personal life. In the year 2002 she received more attention on these mass-media shows than any other single celebrity. Even the more cerebral *New York Times* devoted a full spread to the versatile J.Lo ("Homegirl, Working Woman, Empire Builder," *New York Times*, November 3, 2002). Having netted $200 million worldwide for three of her movies and sold more than 12 million albums, Lopez was deemed ready to "open" a movie, in accordance with Hollywood calculus. It was also ordained that Latinas were "hot" and that Lopez had synergy—her music career and her movie career amplified each other.

Jennifer Lopez (1970–) began life as the second of three daughters in the Castle Hill section of the Bronx. Both her parents had come to New York, as children, from Puerto Rico. Her father was a computer technician, and her mother taught kindergarten in the Holy Family School, which Jennifer also attended. At the age of five, she began taking singing and dancing lessons. In 1986 she graduated from Preston High School in the Bronx, where she was an excellent athlete and participated in track and softball; she also took dance lessons outside of school. She attended Baruch College for a semester but left to immerse herself in dance classes.

As is often the case with people who decide to pursue what is generally a high-risk career, her interests conflicted with those of her mother, who was concerned about her choice to pursue a show business career. So at the age of eighteen she left her parents' house and moved out on her own. For the next few years, Lopez worked in Manhattan offices during the day and took dance and acting jobs when she could, taking a small role in *My Little Girl* in 1986. She beat out two thousand other aspirants in a dance competition, impressing choreographer Rosie Perez enough to be hired as a "fly girl" on the Fox series *In Living Color*. Lopez also had a stint as a dancer for Janet Jackson. She appeared in her first TV movie in 1993, in CBS's *Nurses on the Line: The Crash of Flight 7*, and had parts in a few short-lived series: *Second Chances* (1993–94) and *Hotel Malibu* (1994), on CBS, and Fox's *South Central* (1994). She also cohosted a CBS special that recapped the best moments in the Tournament of Roses parade.

Lopez's career moved fairly swiftly once she began making feature films. In 1995 she had her first supporting role, in *My Family, Mi Familia*, and her first leading role, in *Money Train*. The next year she played a fifth-grade teacher in

Jennifer Lopez is shown here early in her career, in *Second Chances* (1993).

Francis Ford Coppola's *Jack* (1996), with Robin Williams, and was chosen to play the lead in *Selena*. After the success of this film and the acclaim she garnered for her performance in it, Lopez's career took off. She made two films in 1997, *Blood and Wine* (1996) (with Jack Nicholson) and Oliver Stone's *U-Turn* (1997) (with Sean Penn and Nick Nolte). It was in the latter movie that Lopez first played a non-Latina character. She told the director, Oliver Stone, "Whatever you do, don't make the character Latin because you're thinking of me to play it." She wanted to be—as she said—"*the* Latina actress" but she also wanted to "go beyond all that" (Rebello 1998, 93).

Two other films followed in 1998, *Antz* and the highly touted *Out of Sight*, with George Clooney—the "It" boy at the time, who had just left his highly successful TV series, *ER*. In this latter film, Lopez played Karen Sisco, a tough, intelligent federal marshal, still sexy but with some down-to-earth charm and humor. It was in this year that she made clear her strategy for success. She indicated that she had to do her share of commercial movies if she wanted to gain power and respect in Hollywood. She also said it was important to make independent movies because it made people realize that her "acting chops are [still] there" and made them aware that she was selective in the roles she took (ibid.).

Lopez followed up these films with the release of her debut solo album, *On the 6* (1999), which went triple-times-triple platinum. (The "6" of the title is the subway line she took from her home in the Bronx to her auditions in Manhattan.) It was also at the end of 1999 that she and her boyfriend, Sean "Puffy" Combs, were taken into custody as a result of a shooting that occurred at a Times Square nightclub while both were present. Lopez was never charged; Combs was indicted for illegal handgun possession and bribery but was acquitted of all charges in March 2001. She followed up her first album with another, *J.Lo* (2001), which went triple platinum. It also hit the top of the charts at the same time that her newly released movie, *The Wedding*

Planner (2001), was number one at the box office, making her the only performer in history ever to have the top record and the top film at the same time. She was also the first artist to have a remix-album number-one hit on the Billboard charts; this was *J to Tha L-O!: The Remixes* (2002). Her next album, *This Is Me . . . Then* (2002), outsold its predecessors within a week of its release.

Her name as it appears on each of these records reflects, to some extent, changes in her own career. In her first album she was Jennifer Lopez; in her second and third, she was J.Lo—a nickname she says her fans came up with and one that emphasizes her connection to the hip-hop community. In her latest album, seeking to establish her connection with a broader cross section of America, she is Jenny. Her film roles in 2002—*Maid in Manhattan* and *Enough*—suggest a similar move toward becoming someone familiar, someone viewers can easily identify with. As she reminds her audience in her album's hit song, "Don't be fooled by the rocks that I got, I'm just, I'm just Jenny from the block." She has been twice nominated for Grammies.

Lopez made no movies in 1999, but in 2000 she played a psychologist in a science-fiction thriller, *The Cell* (2000). In the following year, she switched to romantic comedy in *The Wedding Planner*, playing Mary Fiore, a workaholic wedding planner who manages to keep everything under perfect control—until she falls for the groom. Lopez followed this film, a major success at the box office, with two others: a romantic thriller, *Angel Eyes* (2001), in which she plays Sharon Pogue, a policewoman, and *Enough*, in which she appears as a battered wife who fights back. This last movie was released on Memorial Day weekend, a clear indication that she had become a bankable star capable of holding her own against two potential blockbusters, *Star Wars 2* and *Spider Man*, released at the same time. She played a Latina in *Maid in Manhattan*, another box-office success, True to her reputation as a hard worker, she has completed additional films scheduled for release in 2003 and 2004 and is working on others.

Jennifer Lopez is the only performer in history to have had the top-rated movie *(The Wedding Planner)* and the top-rated music album *(J.Lo)* in the same week (of 2001). She is shown here in *Angel Eyes* (2001).

While building her film and music career, Lopez also did her first concert (in 2001), a USO TV special for the troops in Germany (in 2002), numerous music videos, and photo shoots; she developed a line of clothing and a new perfume line, opened a restaurant in Pasadena called Madres, and started her own production company. In addition to this prolific entrepreneurial activity, she is one of the highest-paid performers in Hollywood. She has been described variously as an unstoppable twenty-first-century screen queen, the hardest-working multitasker in Hollywood, and a woman out to conquer the world everywhere at once. In essence, the image Jennifer Lopez projects to the media is that of a sexy, sweet, young Puerto Rican girl from the Bronx with the heart of a mogul. She has earned a reputation for being a hard-working self-inventor with a powerful ambition and a drama queen or diva. The latter description she considers unfair. Her careful attention to detail, steely determination, and laser-beam focus are the primary reasons cited for her success. In addition to her charm and likability, she is also seen to have a savvy awareness of her own limitations, to which she readily and openly admits in interviews.

J.Lo became a hot property, the "It" girl of the day, in part because her public image has garnered as much attention as her film and music accomplishments. Her personal life consistently makes the headlines. Since the breakup of a long-term relationship with a Latino from the Bronx, she has had four high-profile relationships, two of which have been short-term marriages, and in 2003 she was on her way to a third marriage to Ben Affleck, the actor voted the "sexiest man alive" (Miller 2002, 73–82). The media have begun to call her "Jen," particularly when she is in the company of her new fiancé.

Latinization and the times have helped Lopez rise to the top. For all her inborn talent and hard work, it is doubtful she could have been as successful in 1985; the world was not ready then. But there are other reasons for her success. She has great appeal to a variety of audiences. She appeals to the Latino and Latin American audiences and to the hip-hop set because of her music and Bronx image (the Bronx being the home of hip-hop). Her style and image project a biculturality and a multiracial growing-up experience that is increasingly the situation for many Americans. As she has said, "I'm as American as I am Latin. I don't remember growing up around just one kind of person. I grew up around a mix of people" (Friedman 2000, 92). Whereas an earlier generation sought to escape urban areas for suburbs that were imagined to be more homogenous, Lopez celebrates the diversity of the city and her upbringing in it, crediting this for her success, especially in music. Ironically, it is the children of those who fled to the suburbs fifteen and thirty years ago who are the main buyers of hip-hop records, grunge clothes, and other products of urban youth culture.

Another part of her appeal has to do with her body and with how she displays it. She appeals to the fashion conscious because of her fashion style, which is "provocatively sexy yet elegant" (Leslie Kaufman and Abby Ellin, "The J.Lo Line Hits a Snag on Its Run for the Top," 2002, *New York Times*, June 16, 2002)—a combination of "ghetto fabulousness" and "middle-class respectability" (Lynette Holloway, "Keeping J.Lo in Spotlight Has Risks as Well as Rewards," *New York Times*, December 9, 2002). She is not afraid to show her curves: "A dress should not look like it's on a hanger," she has said (Rebello 1998). She was inspired to celebrate her curves as a result of her lead role in *Selena:* "As a Latin woman in the United States, you're taught that you should be skinnier. . . . But Selena went out there and wore tight things and showed her butt and all of sudden, young girls were like, 'You know what? I'm beautiful.' She embraced her Latin-ness and showed the world the beauty in diversity" (Potter 1996, 16).

Some credit Lopez with shifting the perennial American focus from breasts to butts. Still others see the objectification of her butt as having everything to do with white America's gaze on ethnic bodies. In many U.S. communities—Latino, African American, some immigrant communities—and in other countries, well-endowed butts have always been in style. To move closer to being America's sweetheart, she has also "worked" (various theories on how, from surgery to exercise) to diminish the size of her rear end. Whatever the case (or size) may be, she clearly appeals to both men and women and has been listed numerous times in male magazines as the sexiest woman in the world.

Finally, part of her universal appeal is the image she projects as someone who, despite material wealth and success, has never stopped being "Jenny from the block." As Diane Sawyer said in her one-hour *Primetime* interview with Lopez on

November 13, 2002, she has the kind of drive that can propel a girl out of the Bronx and toward the stars. Yet she's never stopped being that girl. She is still the Bronx bombshell.

All of which makes people from the Bronx (and similar urban areas) feel very good, for a change. Her success cries out, Look what can come out of our communities, look at who lives in these areas that in the past were viewed as the last place you would want to say you are from. Her image and her movie, *Maid in Manhattan,* reinforce the message that opportunities still exist in the United States, that you can make it if you try, that you need not give up your identity or your pride in who you are. Jennifer Lopez seems to say, If I can make it, so can you. This side of her appeals to those who feel their backgrounds and identities put them outside the norm—and most everyone differs from the norm in some way. Like other Cinderella-type movies, it projects the possibility that people at the bottom of the social ladder (the Latina character Lopez plays, a single mom, and her multiracial support group of maids) could scale the gaps in relative wealth so evident during this time. Lopez also seems to be open, genuine, and well integrated. "I'm a first generation American," she says; "I'm all those things, and I think people accept me because it's organic" (Harris 2002, 148). As one of her early hit songs said, "I'm real." This message resonates in Hollywood's world of images.

Cameron Diaz (1973–) is not often thought of as a Latina star, despite her Spanish-surname. Nor does she emphasize her Spanish surname or ancestry. Her father is Cuban American, and her mother's heritage is German, English, and Native American. Cameron was born in California and graduated from high school in Long Beach, where she also was a half-time dancer at football games. She left home at the age of sixteen and traveled for five years around the globe. At twenty-one, she returned to California and was working as a model when her agent suggested she audition for a small part in Jim Carey's film, *The Mask* (1994). Without any acting experience, Diaz read for the part, impressed the director,

Cameron Diaz's father is Cuban American and her mother is German, English, and Native American. She is listed in *Guinness World Records, 2004* as the world's highest-paid actress.

and got the lead. She went on to make a series of low-budget films, including *Feeling Minnesota* (1996) and *She's the One* (1996), before returning to mainstream films—*My Best Friend's Wedding* (1997), her hit comedy *There's Something about Mary* (1998), and the *Charlie's Angels* films (2000, 2003, and forthcoming [2004]).

As measured by her paycheck, Diaz's career has sky-rocketed. In 2003, according to the Guinness book of world records, she was the world's highest-paid actress (*Guinness World Records* 2003, 169). She has also earned great respect as an actress, particularly in her most recent movie, *Gangs of New York* (2002). A blue-eyed natural blonde, she has been high on the numerous lists of the fifty most-beautiful or sexiest stars. That she has achieved this level of success with a Spanish surname yet without the epithets "Latina lovely" or "Latin spitfire" tacked on and without the traditional "Latin look" is an indication of just how different these times are for Latina stars in Hollywood. To some extent, Diaz brings to mind the earlier "blond Latin," Anita Page. But Anita changed her name from Pomares to Page—albeit quite openly—when she began her career in the late twenties.

RISING LATINA STARS

At the dawn of the twenty-first century, it appeared that the United States had entered an era in which Latinas were again taking center stage in many films. It also seemed to be an era in which obscuring one's Latin-ness seemed foolish—just as it had been in the mid-twenties and the early thirties. The new century's Latina stars seemed to be more physically varied than they had been in the recent past. Newcomers continued to reflect and expand on this variability. They were also more openly, sometimes nonchalantly, Latina. These Latinas were not being asked simply whether they were Latinas; instead, they faced a host of other questions: Do you speak Spanish? Do you identify as Latina? What kind of Latina are you—Puerto Rican? Cuban? Dominican? U.S.-born? Two Latina stars who have been particularly prominent as Latinas are Michelle Rodriguez, and Rosario Dawson.

Michelle Rodriguez (1978–) was born in Bexar County, Texas, where she lived until she was eight years old. Her family then moved to the Dominican Republic for two years and later to Puerto Rico. At the age of eleven, her family settled in Jersey City, New Jersey, where she was raised. She is of Puerto Rican and Dominican descent. Her parents divorced early, and her father is deceased. Described as a rebellious high school dropout, she had just gotten laid off from her job at Toys "R" Us when she spotted an ad for an audition.

Michelle Rodriguez is shown here in her first film role, in *Girlfight* (2000).

Having worked only as an extra in films, and never having boxed, she was selected from among 350 other hopefuls for the lead role as a female boxer in *Girlfight* (2000). The movie received the Grand Jury Prize for best dramatic film at the Sundance Festival and propelled Rodriguez into stardom.

Although she has been busily working in subsequent films, it is her character in *Girlfight* that resonates with so many women of all ages. Her character is the product of a neglectful home and is angry about it. She drifts more or less nowhere until chance sends her to a boxing gym, where she begins to train, and she eventually fights her way out of an oppressive economic and domestic situation. The strength of her performance has inspired comparisons with Marlon Brando. *Vogue* magazine describes the new starlet as "a new kind of Latina star; no longer consigned to the secondary roles but the charismatic center of attention. Ethnic and proud of it, but—and this is important—no longer making a big deal of her ethnicity" (Kerr 2000, 228).

Rosario Dawson (1979–) is another powerful actress who has been making a major impact in her films. Born in New York City, she is a mixture of Cuban, Native American,

Rosario Dawson was discovered sitting on a tenement stoop. She has appeared in a variety of film genres and has garnered much critical acclaim.

African American, Puerto Rican, and Irish American descent. Proud of her racial-ethnic background, she reportedly rejected an early prototype of a doll that was made in conjunction with her role in *Josie and the Pussycats* (2001) and asked that it be made darker skinned and with thicker hair. She was discovered in true fairy-tale fashion. In the summer of 1994, Dawson was a teenager, sitting on the stoop of a tenement building in downtown Manhattan, when the writer-director Larry Clark spotted her. He was looking for "fresh, authentic-looking talent" for his documentary-style film. She made her film debut in Clark's *Kids* (1995), and she has been busily engaged ever since, having already made twenty-one films, five of which were released in 2002, including *The 25th Hour, The Adventures of Pluto Nash,* and *Men in Black II.* She has appeared in a variety of film genres, from science-fiction popcorn flicks to socially conscious films and romantic and cartoon pictures. In each of her films, she has garnered enthusiastic reviews for her riveting portrayals.

THE LEADING LATINO STARS OF THE 1990S

New Latinos graced the silver screen during this period as well, in a variety of roles. Benjamin Bratt (1963–) was born and raised in San Francisco, the middle child of five. A self-described high school jock who balked at acting until prodded by his father, he worked his way through the University of California at Santa Barbara and the master's program at San Francisco's American Conservatory Theatre. His mother, who is of Peruvian Quechua descent, came to the United States at the age of fourteen with her grandmother, who worked as a domestic for an American family. When her grandmother passed away, the family legally adopted Bratt's mother. Bratt's father was an American of German and English descent. On his growing up, Bratt has said, "there was a great social pressure to homogenize and forget your culture and become American, so I think on some level my mom gave into that and we didn't grow up speaking Spanish. What we didn't escape was a kind of cultural DNA. We grew up with a strong sense of family." His mother was politically active regarding indigenous issues; she took her five children to be part of the Alcatraz prison takeover in 1970. Consequently, at a young age he became keenly aware of the indigenous aspect of his culture. He visited Peru for the first time when he was sixteen and has said that the beauty of the people there made him feel completely full (Lemon 2000, 122).

Bratt began to act on television in 1988 and made his first feature film, *One Good Cop,* in 1991. He acted in a number of movies, including *Follow Me Home,* written, produced, and directed by his brother, Peter Bratt. However, it was his role

Benjamin Bratt's mother is of Peruvian Quechua descent, and his father an American of German and English heritage. He is shown here as Detective Rey Curtis in NBC's *Law and Order* series.

as the conservative, well-mannered Detective Rey Curtis, from 1995 to 1999, on NBC's *Law and Order* series that brought him widespread recognition. In 1990 he had worked with Dick Wolf, the show's executive producer and creator, on the short-lived NBC series *Nasty Boys*. When Chris Noth left *Law and Order*, Wolf worked with Bratt to create the Curtis character. Bratt saw the character as bicultural and reflective not just of himself (with regard to cultural makeup) but of a huge number of people in the United States. Bratt made the leap to big-screen stardom with starring roles in *The Next Best Thing* (2000) and *Miss Congeniality* (2000). The actor's highly publicized four-year romance with America's

Benicio Del Toro won an Academy Award for best supporting actor for his role in *Traffic* (2000).

sweetheart, Julia Roberts, ended in 2001, and he married the talented Latina actress, Talisa Soto, with whom he has two children. Bratt continues a busy schedule of film work and has expanded beyond the cop parts he played often and early in his career into more demanding character roles, especially in *Traffic* (2000) *and Piñero.*

Benicio Del Toro (1967–) is another Latino who achieved major stardom during this time. Del Toro was born in Puerto Rico to two lawyer parents. After the death of his mother, when he was nine years old, his father moved the family to a farm in Mercersburg, Pennsylvania, where "I had to wake up at 4:30 A.M. on weekends to work on the farm" ("Unusual Suspect" 2000, 24). He was sent to boarding school, Mercersburg

Academy in Pennsylvania, at the age of thirteen, where he became a basketball player and an artist with an interest in acting. He went to the University of California at San Diego, intending to study business; however, he switched to a drama major, subsequently dropped out, and began studying method acting in Los Angeles and New York.

During the late 1980s he made a few TV appearances and made his film debut in *Big Top Pee-wee* (1988). He went on to make numerous films, including the James Bond film *License to Kill* (1989) and a series of independent films. He made a big splash in 1995 in *Swimming with Sharks* and in the Oscar-winning *The Usual Suspects*, for which he received an Independent Spirit Award for best supporting actor, and in 1996 he appeared in *The Fan*. He came to be seen as "weird," however, when, for his leading role with Johnny Depp in *Fear and Loathing in Las Vegas* (1998), he gained forty pounds and, to put himself more fully into the role (as method actors do), repeatedly burned himself with cigarettes for a scene. He was disappointed at the critics' reaction to his portrayal and at how his total immersion in the role had been received—and perhaps misunderstood.

Del Toro did not make a movie in the next two years, but in 2000 he returned to the screen and has been riding high on the waves of success ever since. He won an Academy Award for best supporting actor, a Screen Actor's Guild Award for best actor, and other awards for his role in *Traffic*. Since winning these awards, his work has been described as similar to that of Robert Mitchum, Marlon Brando, and Jimmy Dean; he himself has been described as the "Spanish Brad Pitt" and as a heartthrob; he was voted one of *People* magazine's fifty most beautiful people ("The 50 Most Beautiful People in the World" 2001, 86–87). Of his "Latin lover" image he has said, "That's the cross that Latin men have to bear. . . . It started with Valentino, and Ricky Martin and I have to carry the torch. But rumors are always better than the truth" ("Unusual Suspect" 2000, 24). He continues to make good films, although a wrist injury sustained while filming *The Hunted* (2003) sidelined him for a while.

The career of Esai Morales (1962–) has taken some interesting turns. He was born to Puerto Rican parents in Brooklyn, New York. His mother, who was a union organizer, left his father when Esai was two tears old and later remarried. As a teenager, Morales did not get along with his mother, in part because of a conflict over his wanting to pursue acting as a career. He subsequently had a falling out with his stepfather, as well. When his mother went to Puerto Rico for a visit, Esai asked a school counselor to have him placed in a group home. He became a voluntary ward of the state and spent three years in a home for boys during his teen years.

At the age of thirteen, Morales went to the New York High School of the Performing Arts. He began acting in the early 1980s and in 1983 starred in his first film, *Bad Boys*, opposite Sean Penn. By 1987 he had landed a part in *La Bamba* as Richie Valens's brother. Fearful, like many Latino actors, that he might be typecast in Latino roles, he often turned down "Latino" roles, feeling that if he did not play other kinds of personalities, people would not give him credit for being able to act. As he said in 1986, "They like to describe me as 'Latin actor Esai Morales.' I'm as American as anybody else. I was born in Brooklyn" ("The Choice of Esai Morales: An Actor, Not a Latin Actor," *New York Times*, July 4, 1986).

In 1992 Morales lamented the few opportunities he had to do anything besides what he called "the Hispanic three H's: to be humble, horny or hostile" (Patricia O'Haire, "He's Having a Wilde Time: Morales Feels a Bit Heady Playing Opposite Pacino in 'Salome,'" *New York Daily News*, June 3, 1992). During the nineties, he continued to make movies both on TV and on the big screen, including *The Burning Season* for television, *My Family, Mi Familia*, and *The Disappearance of Garcia Lorca*. Despite his success in these films, in 2001 he described himself as being on twin tracks in Hollywood: Within the Latino community he loomed large as an actor and a successful activist, whereas in the larger, predominantly white community he was surviving professionally as a bit player or a vaguely familiar guy from that East L.A. movie a

Esai Morales, a talented and gifted actor who has performed successfully in both film and television series since the 1980s, he has also
been involved professionally as the vice president of the Screen
Actors Guild. He is shown here in *Dog Watch* (1996).

long time ago. As he put it, "While part of society doesn't even
know if you're still in the biz, another part of society can't
believe they're breathing the same air you're breathing. . . .
I'm very aware of the relativity of it all and it informs me"
(Dana Calvo, "On Twin Tracks," *Los Angeles Times*, November
18, 2001). As of this writing, Morales appears to be in the middle of a career renaissance and is busily and happily employed
in excellent Latino roles. He is currently playing Lieutenant
Tony Rodriguez, the moral, dignified, and straight-talking
head of the unit in *NYPD Blue*, and a heroic single dad on PBS's
American Family series.

In addition, he has continued his active involvement with a number of professional organizations. He has served as vice president of the Screen Actors Guild's national board of directors and is a member of its current board. He continues his political activism on a variety of issues, from testifying at congressional hearings on the state of Latinos in Hollywood to benefit work on behalf of AIDS, foster care, wildlife preservation in Costa Rica, and antismoking campaigns. On the issue of Latinos in Hollywood, he says, "I yearn for the day not to have to talk about the Latino thing but until I see anything resembling a justifiable representation in television and the movies, I will talk about it" (Terry Keefe, "Esai Morales: Fighting the Good Fight in Hollywood," *Venice*, March 2002, 6, Morales clippings file).

Esai Morales has come a long way from the kid from Brooklyn who was declared a ward of the state because he could not get along with his parents. About that time, he has said, "The younger you are, the less you know that you don't know" (quoted ibid., 46). Some of his recent remarks also reveal the depth of knowledge he has acquired. Asked about the difference between the PBS audience and commercial network audiences, he has described the PBS audience as more sophisticated, more intelligent, whether they come from money or not. "It's not about money," he said; "it's about your desire to learn things" (quoted ibid.). On the repression of women by men, he says, "When men repress women, the person they most repress is the woman inside them" (Calvo, "On Twin Tracks").

His sense of what it means to be an American has also been honed and amplified. "I'm a big critic of our system," he has remarked, "because I love the nation that we're supposed to be" (Keefe, "Esai Morales," 46). Consequently, he sees his protests as part of being an American and as what our Constitution says we should do. He seems to be saying that we should always seek to make life better in America. To criticize our system, he adds, is not anti-American. On what it means to be an American, he says, "What is 'All-

American?' People think 'All-American' and right away they think 'blond hair, blue eyes.' And I think that's all fine and dandy, and that's been the status quo for years, but it's too narrow. Americans are robbing themselves of their true heritage, and it's a composite. No one's saying that Nordic features are now not-American, but at the end of the day, what is it to be an American? Is it really the color of your hair, eyes, skin, texture, whatever? It's a state of mind. An independent spirit" (quoted ibid.). This is how Esai Morales sees America. However, he also observes that the real people in America are not the ones you see on TV and in film.

Also entering films in a substantial way in the nineties was the comedian John Leguizamo (1964–). He was born in Bogota, Colombia; his father brought the family to New York when John was four years old, and they settled in Queens, New York. As an aspiring filmmaker John's father had studied in Rome, but his dream was cut short by financial pressures. In New York, he worked his way up from waiter to landlord, but it was a bumpy road. Although both of John Leguizamo's parents were working, he and his brother were sent back to Colombia twice when times got tough financially. He describes his parents as either working constantly or fighting constantly. His mother left his father when John was ten years old, taking her two children with her. His teenage clowning led to his being almost booted out of the public high school he attended in New York. He was advised to take acting lessons, which he did at the Strasberg Theater Institute.

He attended New York University long enough to appear in a student film that was seen by a casting director working with the television show, *Miami Vice*, and in 1984 Leguizamo made his first television appearance on that show. This was followed the next year by his first film appearance, in *Mixed Blood* (1985). He played a choice part in *Casualties of War* (1989), but, contrary to his expectations, after the film was released he got few offers, and those scripts that came his way called for him to play "token Hispanic roles—pimps, drug-dealers, and illegal aliens" (Smith 1991, 45–48). Soon after *Casualties of War*

John Leguizamo, comedian, actor, and writer for both stage and film, is shown here in *Freak* (1998).

came out he reflected on the absence of Latinos in the media as he was growing up: "When I was a kid, I never saw any Hispanics on television. And because you never see any thing, you start to wonder, God, maybe as a people we can't do it. . . . I want Latin people to leave with a sense of pride, saying that no matter how down we are, we can overcome anything" (quoted ibid., 48). Angry about the lack of roles, he began writing and performing his own material in an acting class he was taking. He was seen in one such class by Peter Askin, a director, who worked with him to produce his first one-man show, *Mambo Mouth* (1991). The show won Leguizamo an Obie, as well as other awards, and it aired on HBO.

Although he had spent most of the eighties playing comedy clubs in New York, in the more Latinizing nineties Leguizamo went on to write and perform more one-man shows that also aired on TV, including *Spic-O-Rama* (1993) and *Freak* (1998). He also wrote and starred in *House of Buggin'* (1995), a short-lived but Emmy Award–winning Latino comedy-variety show on Fox TV. In addition to acting and writing for others—*Carlito's Way, To Wong Foo, Thanks for Everything, Julie Newmar* (1995), *Summer of Sam* (1999), and *Moulin Rouge!* (2001), among others—he continued to create his own material. He wrote and starred in the film *The Pest* (1998) and established his own production company, which produces his films as well as others, including *Joe the King* (1999), *Nuyorican Dream* (1999), *King of the Jungle* (2001), and his made-for-TV *Sexaholix: A Love Story* (2002). His company has also been involved in the coproduction of *Piñero* and *Empire*.

RISING LATINO STARS

Finally, there is a long list of rapidly rising Latino stars: Jay Hernandez and Clifton Collins Jr. (also known as Clifton Gonzalez Gonzalez) (both of Mexican descent), Eduardo Verastegui (Mexican), Tony Plana (Cuban), Michael DeLorenzo (Puerto Rican and Italian), and Paul Rodriguez (born in Mexico, raised in California), who entered films after a successful career in live comedy and television. Receiving quite a bit of attention is Jon Seda (1970–), who was born in New York City of Puerto Rican parents and grew up in Clifton, New Jersey. He got his start boxing at several gyms in New Jersey and achieved a 21-1 record. His first major film role was in 1994, in *I Like It Like That*, but he has been acting in films since 1992 and in television since 1993. He had another major role in *Selena*, joined the cast of the television series *Homicide: Life on the Street* from 1997 to 1999 as Detective Paul Falsone, and has continued to make films on the big screen and on TV, including *Undisputed* (2002) and *UC: Undercover* (2001).

This volume presents a short review of a long history. It traces the long and illustrious (albeit often forgotten) line of Latino stars through the history of Hollywood. This review has also highlighted some major changes over time. For example, the early racial dividing line is now a bit more blurred, and perhaps the future will begin to see an even broader representation of "Latin looks." New Latina character types also made an appearance in this most recent period—the "buddy or counselor Latina," the "kick-ass Latina" (as in *Girlfight*), and, toward the end of the century, the "makin' it Latina." Some humor has also returned. Latinas and Latinos are again playing central characters, and there are more Latino-themed films of increasingly fine quality.

Nevertheless, there are still long-standing unresolved issues. The spitfire character has continued throughout this period. Although bolder and more explicit sexuality is in keeping with this era, sexuality still seems generally to be at a higher pitch for Latinos and Latinas than for other men and women in the same films. There always seems to be something hot, sensual, and sexual about "Latins." Consequently, many Latino characters are still exoticized and eroticized. In addition, despite promising changes in the depiction of Latinas, their appeal still seems to be more about bodies than brains, accomplishments, successes, or depth. Despite the increase in the number of actors, and in portrayals in central and starring roles, many observers are still left wondering: Where are the Latinas who are intelligent, accomplished, and powerful in areas other than sex?

It is similarly disturbing that even as the Latino population increased substantially, and as the stars of particular actors rose higher and higher, Latinos continued to be the most underrepresented ethnic group in films and on prime-time television. According to data from the Screen Actors

Guild, in 2000 Latinos received only 4.9 percent of the roles cast; yet they constituted 12.5 percent of the population that year. Moreover, these figures refer only to the quantity of roles, not their quality. The Children Now group has found a slight increase in Latino characters on prime-time television, up from the perennial 2–3 percent of all characters over the past five decades to 4 percent in the 2001–02 season. However, this increase occurred in secondary and nonrecurring roles, not in primary recurring characters. Consequently, in the opening credits Latino characters still represented just 2 percent of all permanent characters. Latinos are also more likely than whites to be cast in supporting roles rather than as leads. Other groups are also absent from television relative to their share of the population—Native Americans and Asian–Pacific Islanders—but given the relative numbers and growth of the Latino population, the Latino situation seems harder to understand.

It is not just racial-ethnic groups that are underrepresented in television but also women, people over the age of forty, and low-income workers. This situation is not for lack of talented actors or writers—as the stories of this volume demonstrate. Nor is it impossible to alter this situation, for the number of African American characters has gone from relative invisibility on television to overrepresentation—although the characterizations often leave much to be desired.

The history of Latinos in film is intricate. Leading "Latin" actors and characters have alternated over time between fairly integrated positions in early film to more marginalized roles and characterizations. These alternating cycles have occurred at least twice in the past century, with the era preceding this one having scarce employment and sinister (or crime-related) characterizations of Latinos in film. Now, with the dawn of a new century, we are beginning to see a more prominent Latino presence in film, leading many to wonder if history is repeating itself.

At the beginning of the twentieth century, there were sets of parallel phenomena. Similar to today, Latins were "in." There was also a comparable pendulum shift in the economy. Then, it was a shift from the good times of the Roaring Twenties and the Jazz Age to the Great Depression of 1929. Today, it is the shift from the economic boom times of the 1980s and early 1990s to the dot-com bust of the late 1990s, with corporate scandals and extraordinary and conspicuous concentrations of wealth pervading both the early and most recent period. As is the case today, there was also considerable immigration of Mexicans then. Like today, there was early concern about the numbers of "foreigners" entering the United States, so much so that legislation was passed to restrict immigration (the 1920 and 1924 Immigration Acts) and subsequent moves to send "undesirables" back to where they had come from, resulting in, among other things, the deportation of Mexicans and Mexican Americans. (See Chapter 1 of this volume.) In addition, there was evidence of extreme poverty and segregation among Latinos then, as there is today. On the other hand, there was then a certain "Latin allure," similar to today's public fascination with Latino stars. Finally, both periods have seen a more prominent Latino presence in film and more films with Latin themes.

The important question, of course, is whether this new "Latin craze" will fade from America's memory and public consciousness—as it did in the early era—or whether it signals a new era, a less segmented, more diverse America that acknowledges its present and past history of hybridization. As *Vogue* magazine noted in 2000, "In the end it may not be Latinos who are changing so much as it is the rest of America waking up, with new curiosity, to who it has been all along" (Kerr 2000, 270).

Selected Readings

Acosta-Belen, Edna, Margarita Benítez, J. E. Cruz, Yvonne González-
Rodríguez, C. E. Rodríguez, C. E. Santiago, Azara Santiago-Rivera, and B.
R. Sjostrom. 2000. *"Adiós, Borinquen querida": The Puerto Rican Diaspora*.
Albany: State University of New York Press, Center for Latino, Latin
American, and Caribbean Studies. Published in Spanish as *"Adiós,
Borinquen querida": La diáspora puertorriqueña: Su historia y sus aportaciones*.
Albert, Katherine. 1930. "Who Is Hollywood's Social Leader?" *Photoplay*,
December.
"All the Stars Dine Here." 1932. *Photoplay*, December.
Alvarado, Don. Clippings File. Billy Rose Theatre Collection. New York Public
Library for the Performing Arts.
Arnaz, Desi. 1976. *A Book*. New York: William Morrow.
Bernardi, Daniel, ed. 1996. *The Birth of Whiteness: Race and the Emergence of U.S.
Cinema*. New Brunswick: Rutgers University Press.
———. 2001. *Classic Hollywood, Classic Whiteness*. Minneapolis: University of
Minnesota Press.
Biberman, Herbert. 1965. *Salt of the Earth*. Boston: Beacon.
Bodeen, Dewitt. 1976. *From Hollywood: The Careers of 15 Great American Stars*.
South Brunswick, N.J.: A. S. Barnes.
Byrne, Bridget. 1981. "Eye View: Facing Up to Beauty." *Women's Wear Daily*,
November 2.
Carr, Larry. 1979. *More Fabulous Faces: Dolores Del Rio, Bette Davis, Katharine
Hepburn, Carole Lombard, and Myrna Loy*. Garden City, N.Y.: Doubleday.
Children Now. 1998. *A Different World: Children's Perceptions of Race and Class in
the Media*. Oakland, Calif.

———. 2002. *Fall Colors: 2001–2002.* Oakland, Calif.

Cortés, Carlos E. 2000. *The Children Are Watching: How the Media Teach about Diversity.* New York: Teachers College Press.

"Dating Anita." 1930. *Photoplay*, February.

Dávila, Arlene. 2001. *Latinos Inc.: The Marketing and Making of a People.* Berkeley: University of California Press.

De Cordoba, Pedro. Clippings File. Billy Rose Theatre Collection. New York Public Library for the Performing Arts.

de la Torre, Adela, and Beatríz M. Pesquera, eds. 1993. *Building with Our Hands: New Directions in Chicana Studies.* Berkeley: University of California Press.

Delpar, Helen. 1992. *The Enormous Vogue of Things Mexican.* Tuscaloosa: University of Alabama Press.

"Doug's Office Boy Makes Good." 1929. *Photoplay*, January.

Doyle, Billy H. 1995. *The Ultimate Directory of the Silent Screen Performers: A Necrology of Births and Deaths and Essays on 50 Lost Players.* Edited by Anthony Slide. Metuchen, N.J.: Scarecrow.

Ellenberger, Allan R. 1999. *Ramon Novarro: A Biography of the Silent Film Idol, 1899–1968.* Jefferson, N.C.: McFarland.

"The 50 Most Beautiful People in the World, 1996." 1996. *People*, May 6.

"The 50 Most Beautiful People in the World, 2001." 2001. *People*, May 14.

Foley, Neil. 1997. *The White Scourge: Mexicans, Blacks, and Poor Whites in Texas Cotton Culture.* Berkeley: University of California Press.

Fregoso, Rosa Linda. 1993. *The Bronze Screen: Chicana and Chicano Film Culture.* Minneapolis: University of Minnesota Press.

"Fresh from the Camera." 1930. *Photoplay*, September.

Friedman, Lester D., ed. 1991. *Unspeakable Images: Ethnicity and the American Cinema.* Champaign: University of Illinois Press.

Friedman, Linda. 2000. "Feeling So Good." *Teen People*, May.

Frolo, Etta. 1975. "Eye View: Mexico's Fabled Beauty." *Women's Wear Daily*, January 6.

Fuller, Kathryn H. 1996. *At the Picture Show: Small-Town Audiences and the Creation of Movie Fan Culture.* Washington, D.C.: Smithsonian Institution Press.

Galloway, Stephen. 1994. "Raul Julia Dies at 54; Versatile Film, Stage Star." *Hollywood Reporter*, October 31.

Garcia, Matt. 2001. *A World of Its Own: Race, Labor, and Citrus in the Making of Greater Los Angeles, 1900–1970.* Chapel Hill: University of North Carolina Press.

Garcia Berumen, Frank Javier. 1995. *The Chicano/Hispanic Image in American Film.* New York: Vantage.

Gerbner, George. 1998. "Women and Minorities on Television: A Cultural Indicators Project Report." Los Angeles, Calif.: Screen Actors Guild (December).

"Get Out Your Maps!" 1922. *Photoplay*, January.

Gómez-Sicre, José. 1967. "Dolores Del Rio." *Américas*, vol. 19, no. 11: 8–17.

Gonzalez, Myrtle. Clippings File. Biography Files. Margaret Herrick Library of the Academy of Motion Picture Arts and Sciences. Beverly Hills, California.

"Great Lovers of the Screens." 1924. *Photoplay*, June.

Guinness World Records, 2004. 2003. Edited by Claire Folkard. England: Guinness World Records, Ltd.

Hadley-Garcia, George. 1993. *Hispanic Hollywood: The Latins in Motion Pictures.* New York: Carol Publishing Group.

Harris, Carter. 2002. "The J.Lo Effect." *Elle*, June.
Henry, William A., III. 1990. "Beyond the Melting Pot." *Time*, April 9.
Margaret Herrick Library of the Academy of Motion Picture Arts and Sciences. Beverly Hills, California.
Hershfield, Joanne. 2000. *The Invention of Dolores del Río*. Minneapolis: University of Minnesota Press.
Hodenfield, Jan. 1980. "An Actor Whose Time Has Come." *GQ*, October.
"Hollywood's New Lover." 1932. *Photoplay*, May.
Jacobson, Matthew. 1998. *Whiteness of a Different Color: European Immigrants and the Alchemy of Race*. Cambridge: Harvard University Press.
Jarvie, Ian C. 1991. "Stars and Ethnicity: Hollywood and the United States, 1932–1951." In *Unspeakable Images: Ethnicity and the American Cinema*, edited by Lester D. Friedman. Champaign: University of Illinois Press.
Jiménez, Lillian. 1997. "From the Margin to the Center: Puerto Rican Cinema in the United States." In *Latin Looks: Images of Latinas and Latinos in the U.S. Media*, edited by Clara E. Rodríguez. Boulder, Colo.: Westview.
Kanellos, Nicolás. 1998. *Thirty Million Strong: Reclaiming the Hispanic Image in American Culture*. Golden, Colo.: Fulcrum.
Keller, Gary D. 1994. *Hispanics and United States Film: An Overview and Handbook*. Tempe, Ariz. Bilingual Review/Press.
———. 1997. *Biographical Handbook of Hispanics and United States Film*. Tempe, Ariz.: Bilingual Press/Editorial Bilingüe.
———, ed. 1985. *Chicano Cinema: Research, Reviews, and Resources*. Binghamton, N.Y.: Bilingual Review/Press.
Kerr, Sarah. 2000. "Latina Power." *Vogue*, August.
Kotz, Liz. 1997. "Unofficial Stories: Documentaries by Latinas and Latin American Women." In *Latin Looks: Images of Latinas and Latinos in the U.S. Media*, edited by Clara E. Rodríguez. Boulder, Colo.: Westview.
"La Vida Lopez." 1999. *New York*, September 6.
Lackner, Dorothee. 2000. "Salma Hayek: Interview by Dorothee Lackner." Vivamagazine.com, September. Available at hayekheaven.tripod.com/article_vista.html (October 2, 2003).
Lemming, Barbara. 1985. *Orson Welles: A Biography*. New York: Viking.
Lemon, Brendan. 2000. "Benjamin Bratt by Brendan Lemon: Even Mamas and Llamas Love the Guy———Not to Mention Pretty Women." *Interview*, May.
Lewis, Marvin A. 1987. "The Puerto Rican in Popular U.S. Literature: A Culturalist Perspective." In *Images and Identities: The Puerto Rican in Two World Contexts*, edited by Asela Rodríguez de Laguna. New Brunswick, N.J.: Transaction Publishers.
Robinson Locke Collection. Billy Rose Theatre Collection. New York Public Library for the Performing Arts.
López, Ana M. 1991. "Are All Latins from Manhattan? Hollywood, Ethnography, and Cultural Colonialism." In *Unspeakable Images: Ethnicity and the American Cinema*, edited by Lester D. Friedman. Champaign: University of Illinois Press.
———. 1998. "From Hollywood and Back: Delores Del Rio, a Trans(National) Star." *Studies in Latin American Popular Culture*, vol. 17 (Spring): 5–32.
"Making a Name: Spanish-Born Antonio Banderas Is Unknown No More." 1995. *Boxoffice*, August.
Maltin, Leonard. 1994. *Leonard Maltin's Movie Encyclopedia*. New York: Signet Books.
Martínez, Al. 1974. *Rising Voices*. New York: New American Library.

Massey, Douglas S. 1995. "The New Immigration and the Meaning of Ethnicity in the United States." *Population and Development Review*, vol. 21, no. 3: 631–53.

Michael, Renee. 1992. "They Change the Roles for Rosie Perez." *Long Beach [Calif.] Press-Telegram*, Lifestyle section, April 6.

Michelena, Beatriz. Clippings File. Robinson Locke Collection, series 2. Billy Rose Theatre Collection. New York Public Library for the Performing Arts.

Miller, Samantha. 2002. "The Sexiest Man Alive." *People*, December 2.

Montalban, Ricardo. 1980. *Reflections: A Life in Two Worlds*. Garden City, N.Y.: Doubleday.

Montejano, David. 1987. *Anglos and Mexicans in the Making of Texas, 1836–1986*. Austin: University of Texas Press.

Morales, Esai. Clippings File. Biography Files. Margaret Herrick Library of the Academy of Motion Picture Arts and Sciences. Beverly Hills, California.

"The Most Beautiful Home in Hollywood." 1924. *Photoplay*, March.

Motion Picture News Studio Directory. 1917. Vol. 2, no. 1 (April 12). Margaret Herrick Library of the Academy of Motion Picture Arts and Sciences. Beverly Hills, California.

Noriega, Chon. 1997. "Citizen Chicano: The Trials and Titillations of Ethnicity in the American Cinema, 1935–1962." In *Latin Looks: Images of Latinas and Latinos in the U.S. Media*, edited by Clara E. Rodríguez. Boulder, Colo.: Westview.

———. 2000. *Shot in America: Television, the State, and the Rise of Chicano Cinema*. Minneapolis: University of Minnesota Press.

———, ed. 1992. *Chicanos and Film: Essays on Chicano Representation and Resistance*. New York: Garland.

Noriega, Chon A., and Ana M. López. 1996. *The Ethnic Eye: Latino Media Arts*. Minneapolis: University of Minnesota Press.

O'Connor, Chris. 1981. "Dolores Del Rio Forever Beautiful." *Modern Maturity*, February–March.

Olmos, Edward James, Lea Ybarra, and Manuel Monterrey. 1999. *Americanos: Latino Life in the United States*. Boston: Little, Brown.

"The 100 Sexiest Stars in Film History." 1995. *Empire*, August.

O'Neil, Brian. 1998. "Yankee Invasion of Mexico, or Mexican Invasion of Hollywood? Hollywood's Renewed Spanish-Language Production of 1938–1939." *Studies in Latin American Popular Culture*, vol. 17 (Spring): 79–104.

———. 2000. "So Far from God, So Close to Hollywood: Dolores Del Rio and Lupe Velez in Hollywood, 1925–1944." In *Strange Pilgrimages: Travel, Exile, and National Identity in Latin America, 1800–1990*, edited by Ingrid E. Fey and Karen Racine. Wilmington, Del.: Scholarly Resources.

———. 2001. "The Demands of Authenticity: Addison Durland and Hollywood's Latin Images during World War II." In *Classic Hollywood, Classic Whiteness*, edited by Daniel Bernardi. Minneapolis: University of Minnesota Press.

Parish, James Robert. 1974. *The RKO Gals*. Carlstadt, N.J.: Rainbow Books.

Parsons, Harriet. 1931. "Let's Get Familiar." *Photoplay*, January.

Perez, Richie. 1997. "From Assimilation to Annihilation: Puerto Rican Images in U. S. Films." In *Latin Looks: Images of Latinas and Latinos in the U.S. Media*, edited by Clara E. Rodríguez. Boulder, Colo.: Westview.

Players Collection. Billy Rose Theatre Collection. New York Public Library for the Performing Arts.

Potter, Max. 1996. "Stoltz, Cube, and Lopez Wrapped Up in 'Anaconda.'" *Movieline*, October.

Quinn, Anthony. 1972. *The Original Sin: A Self-Portrait*. Boston: Little, Brown.

Quinn, Anthony, with Daniel Paisner. 1995. *One Man Tango*. New York: HarperCollins.

Ramírez Berg, Charles. 2002. *Latino Images in Film: Stereotypes, Subversion, Resistance*. Austin: University of Texas Press.

Rebello, Stephen. 1998. "The Wow." *Movieline*, February.

Reyes, Luis, and Peter Rubie. 1994. *Hispanics in Hollywood: An Encyclopedia of Film and Television*. New York: Garland.

———. 2000. *Hispanics in Hollywood: A Celebration of 100 Years in Film and Television*. Hollywood, Calif.: Lone Eagle.

Richard, Alfred Charles, Jr. 1993. *Censorship and Hollywood's Hispanic Image, 1936–1955*. Westport, Conn.: Greenwood.

Ríos-Bustamante, Antonio. 1992. "Latino Participation in the Hollywood Film Industry, 1911–1945." In *Chicanos and Film: Essays on Chicano Representation and Resistance*, edited by Chon A. Noriega. New York: Garland.

Rodríguez, Clara E.. 1991. *Puerto Ricans: Born in the USA*. Boulder, Colo.: Westview.

———, ed. 1997. *Latin Looks: Images of Latinas and Latinos in the U.S. Media*. Boulder, Colo.: Westview.

Rodríguez, Roberto. 1991. "The Columbus 1492–1992 Quincentennial Debate." Pt. 2, "How Columbus' Voyages Changed the World." *Black Issues in Higher Education*, vol. 8, no. 16: 18–25.

Rodríquez-Estrada, Alicia I. 1997. "Dolores Del Rio and Lupe Velez: Images On and Off the Screen, 1925–1944." In *Writing the Range: Race, Class, and Culture in the Women's West*, edited by Elizabeth Jameson and Susan Armitage. Norman: University of Oklahoma Press.

Ruiz, Vicki L. 1993. "'Star Struck': Acculturation, Adolescence, and the Mexican American Woman, 1920–1950." In *Building with Our Hands: New Directions in Chicana Studies*, edited by Adela de la Torre and Beatríz M. Pesquera. Berkeley: University of California Press.

Sánchez Korrol, Virginia. 1994. *From Colonia to Community: The History of Puerto Ricans in New York City*. Latinos in American Society and Culture 5. Berkeley: University of California Press.

Sandoval Sánchez, Alberto. 1997. "West Side Story: A Puerto Rican Reading of America." In *Latin Looks: Images of Latinas and Latinos in the U.S. Media*, edited by Clara E. Rodríguez. Boulder, Colo.: Westview.

Schrecker, Ellen. 1998. *Many Are the Crimes: McCarthyism in America*. Boston: Little, Brown.

"Shirley MacLaine Stars in 'Possession of Joey Delaney.'" 1972. *Hollywood Reporter*, May 17.

Shohat, Ella, and Robert Stam. 1994. *Unthinking Eurocentrism: Multiculturalism and the Media*. New York: Routledge.

Smith, Chris. 1991. "John Leguizamo's Spicy Slice of Latino Life." *New York*, June 10.

Suntree, Susan. 1993. *Rita Moreno*. New York: Chelsea House.

Thomas, Victoria. 1998. *Hollywood's Latin Lovers: Latino, Italian, and French Men Who Make the Screen Smolder*. Santa Monica, Calif.: Angel City Press, distributed by St. Martin's Press, New York.

Torres, Raquel. Clippings File. Billy Rose Theatre Collection. New York Public Library for the Performing Arts.

Ulmer, James. 1994. "In Transit: Rosie Perez May Take 'A Break from It All.'" *Hollywood Reporter*, September 20.

"Unusual Suspect." 2000. *Us Weekly*, September 18.

Valdivia, Angharad N. 2000. *A Latina in the Land of Hollywood and Other Essays on Media Culture.* Tucson: University of Arizona Press.

Valentino, Rudolf. 1923. Letter to the editor. *Photoplay*, January.

Vera, Hernán, and Andrew M. Gordon. 2003. *Screen Saviors: Hollywood Fictions of Whiteness.* Lanham, Md.: Rowman and Littlefield.

Welch, Raquel. Clippings File. Biography Files. Margaret Herrick Library of the Academy of Motion Picture Arts and Sciences. Beverly Hills, California.

West, Dennis, and Gary Crowdus. 1988. "Cheech Cleans Up His Act: An Interview with Richard 'Cheech' Marin." *Cineaste*, vol. 16, no. 3: 34–35.

"What Rich Stars Do with Their Money." 1923. *Photoplay*, February.

"Who Has the Best Figure in Hollywood?" 1931. *Photoplay*, March.

Wilson, Clint C., II, and Félix Gutiérrez. 1995. *Race, Multiculturalism, and the Media.* 2d ed. Thousand Oaks, Calif.: Sage.

Wilson, Harry D. 1931. "Long Hair or Short?" *Photoplay*, October.

Woll, Allen L. 1980. *The Latin Image in American Film.* Rev. ed. Los Angeles: University of California at Los Angeles, Latin American Center Publications.

Woll, Allen L., and Randall M. Miller. 1987. *Ethnic and Racial Images in American Film and Television: Historical Essays and Bibliography.* New York: Garland.

Woodward, Calvin. 2001. "Hispanic Influence Gaining in the U.S." Associated Press, September 5.

York, Cal. 1926. "Fighting for the Crown." *Photoplay*, November.

Index

CPSIA information can be obtained at www.ICGtesting.com
Printed in the USA
BVOW022350150112

280478BV00001B/5/P